SURFACE

AND

SYMBOL

ALL ART IS AT ONCE SURFACE AND SYMBOL—*Oscar Wilde*

# SURFACE

## AND

ROBERT MARTIN ADAMS

## SYMBOL

THE CONSISTENCY OF JAMES JOYCE'S *Ulysses*

NEW YORK / OXFORD UNIVERSITY PRESS / 1962

FOR ARIADNE,

WHO HELD THE THREAD

AND WAITED FOR ME TO COME OUT

# Contents

*Preface*

This book began as a co-operative project with the students of English 486, in the College of Arts and Sciences, Cornell University, during the spring of 1958; my first thanks are due to the several undergraduates who had the gumption to raise their hands and say "I don't think so"—with reasons.

On a more material plane, it is a pleasure to thank the J. S. Guggenheim Foundation for a grant which made it possible for me to visit Ireland in the spring of 1960 (and to worry about the book all summer). The Cornell Faculty Research Council and the Cornell English Department's Grant-in-Aid Fund have also supported my work generously.

I have met with unvarying courtesy and responsiveness from the staff of the Cornell University Library, particularly Miss Josephine Tharpe, Mr. W. R. Wilkinson, and the attendants of the Rare Book Room. I am also grateful to the staff of the National Library of Ireland in Kildare Street, particularly Mr. Patrick Henchy; and to the staff of the University of Buffalo Library. Mr. Edward Keene of Dublin has been most effective in pursuing municipal details on my behalf. Miss Nancy-Jean McLaughlin retyped the entire manuscript when it was in peril of choking on its own tentacles. When I needed a fresh eye, my colleague Walter Slatoff and Robert Scholes of the University of Virginia kindly lent theirs. Professor Richard Ellmann and

Mr. Matthew Hodgart generously guided me toward various timely surgeries, both corrective and preventive. A list of those who answered queries or looked into dusty records on my behalf would be immoderately long.

For permission to quote as yet unpublished Joyce manuscripts and one unpublished letter (that on p. 21), I am indebted to the James Joyce Estate and the Society of Authors. The Bodley Head, Ltd., holders of English copyright on *Ulysses*, and Random House, Inc., holders of the American copyright, have kindly granted permission to quote from the book. Permission to quote from a poem by Dr. Oliver Gogarty was granted by Devin-Adair, the American, and Constable Co. Ltd., the English holders of copyright.

The following crude and abbreviated conversion-table may be useful in transposing Random House references into the approximate pagination of other popular editions. (I have taken

| R.H. | Odyssey (plus) | Bodley Head (minus) | Shakespeare (1st ed.) (minus) |
|---|---|---|---|
| 5 | 0 | 4 | 2 |
| 50 | 4 | 4 | 2 |
| 100 | 5 | 6 | 3 |
| 150 | 5 | 9 | 5 |
| 200 | 9 | 9 | 6 |
| 250 | 12 | 9 | 7 |
| 300 | 16 | 10 | 8 |
| 350 | 21 | 10 | 10 |
| 400 | 27 | 11 | 13 |
| 450 | 26 | 13 | 16 |
| 500 | 22 | 15 | 20 |
| 550 | 17 | 17 | 25 |
| 600 | 8 | 22 | 28 |
| 650 | 13 | 23 | 31 |
| 700 | 18 | 24 | 33 |
| 750 | 22 | 25 | 35 |

the basic concept from the more elaborate table in the front-matter to Miles Hanley's invaluable *Word-Index to Ulysses*.) The equivalent of the page number in the extreme left-hand column is found by adding or subtracting the numbers in the right-hand columns.

Throughout, I have made my references according to the paging of the Random House edition, but I have regularly corrected my citations to the best text, that of the Odyssey Press, though I recognize that it too is often faulty. All page references in the text, not otherwise identified, are to the Random-House-Modern-Library edition of *Ulysses*.

I have also used the Modern Library edition of *A Portrait of the Artist as a Young Man*, and the Viking (Compass Books) editions of *Dubliners* and *Finnegans Wake*. For ready reference, I have made use of short titles as follows:

James Joyce, *Critical Writings*, ed. Ellsworth Mason and Richard Ellmann (London, 1959)     *Critical Writings*

James Joyce, *Stephen Hero*, ed. T. Spencer, J. J. Slocum, and H. Cahoon (New York, 1955)     *Stephen Hero*

J. J. Slocum and H. Cahoon, *A Bibliography of James Joyce* (New Haven, 1953)     Slocum & Cahoon

Richard Ellmann, *James Joyce* (New York, 1959)     *JJ*

*Letters of James Joyce*, ed. Stuart Gilbert (New York, 1957)     *Letters*

*Cornell University,*     R. M. ADAMS
*Ithaca, N.Y.*

# *Preliminary*

The interpretation of *Ulysses* has been proceeding apace for forty years now. Though all generalizations about prose fiction are rash, I do not suppose many novels have been questioned so deeply, so persistently, on so impressive a range of topics. The peculiar circumstance here is simply that *Ulysses* is a novel. Every age has its sacred, usually difficult texts, to which, for its own purposes, it applies its own brand of hermeneutics. If we try to interpret a novel as earlier ages tried to interpret Holy Writ, this is no sign that our task is any easier—or, for that matter, much different. Interpretation is always a matter of delicate adjustment between the things we want to know, on the one hand, and the things the book under interpretation is fitted to declare to us, on the other. Hermeneutics, a middle-man's art (and so compromised *ab ovo*), tends to be most difficult when its prerogatives and obligations are least rigorously defined. One reason why the interpretive quarrel is worth pursuing, even so, is that the dispute itself exacts our utmost resource of civilized comportment, of tenacity and restraint. Perhaps this is a better reason for criticism than the illusion that someday all the issues will be settled.

At our very first view of it, Joyce's novel proposes a disparity. Its title is *Ulysses*, yet it describes the events of a single day in Dublin, June 16, 1904. What is the relation of one element to

the other? Some critics say the Dublin story is a mere mocking
parody of the Homeric epic; others say the Greek epic offers
structural support for, and significant insight into, the Dublin
materials. At issue here is no less a question than whether
*Ulysses* is primarily epic or mock-epic in its feeling. This is but
one of many tangled problems which the book poses to a
thoughtful viewer. Some readers have been left with the impression that Joyce in *Ulysses* is bitterly hostile to the Roman Catholic Church, others that he is essentially orthodox, still others
that he describes a world without God, but protests bitterly
against it. Either he repudiates and satirizes the Irish nationalist
movement, or he accepts and supports it. His protagonist Bloom
is either contemptible or noble; he either overcomes the suitors
in the highest spirit of Christian heroism, or he abjectly submits
to them; he either discovers his spiritual son, or fails to recognize him; the book illustrates either a passionate, sensual accept-
ance of life, or a derisive, cynical rejection of it. All these and
a hundred other antimonies in the novel have been expounded,
explored, and explicated to triumphant conclusions of a dozen
different sorts. My concern in this book is not to review or aug-
ment, far less supersede, these interpretive studies, to many of
which I am obviously, and gratefully, indebted. It is, rather, to
do something toward clarifying the consistency, that is, the
texture, of the novel on which so much discussion has centered
for so long. I have undertaken to look afresh into *Ulysses* in the
hope that, by identifying some of the raw materials which went
into the making of it, I may be able to define some of the ways
in which it was put together.

Information about the consistency of *Ulysses* has an indirect
bearing on what the novel does and can mean, above all if we
suppose that "meaning" resides in the total structure of a work
of fiction. But an interest in process differs, at least in emphasis,
from an interest in import. So far as the meaning of *Ulysses* is

concerned (and this is no doubt our ultimate question about the book), the present investigation is preliminary. It seeks to define some of the conditions of a discussion, rather than to influence the discussion one way or another—to discover what the object was made with as a first step toward deciding how it should be looked at and (perhaps) what it should be measured with. I propose to make clear certain grounds of critical assurance, not to alter its specific objects.

To illustrate the sort of thing that I have made my primary concern, the scale of the discussion must be radically reduced, almost to the proverbial nutshell. On p. 234, in the midst of a list of bicycle riders who are portrayed careering through College Green, occurs the name of J. A. Jackson. To at least one alert student of *Ulysses*, this name has seemed to conceal a reference to the author himself, James Augustine, son of Jack Joyce. One wonders why Joyce, who carefully signed his name to the title page of the novel, and signed it extravagantly between the lines throughout, needed to work it into an enigma in a bicycle race. But perhaps he did; he was fond of enigmas. Let us suppose he did. But if we suppose "Jackson" has covert meaning on p. 234, mere economy of assumption will invite us to give it the same meaning on p. 662, where it occurs again. The second Jackson is George A. Jackson, who is said to have produced, in 1892, the scenery for a pantomime called *Sinbad the Sailor*. Are we to suppose that Joyce has inserted here a covert reference to his dead brother Georgie? It is queer to have George Alfred Joyce, who died at fourteen, producing scenery for a pantomime which took place when he was just five; but it is not much queerer than having James Joyce embroiled in the Trinity College bicycle races. Is the consistency of the novel such that we can suppose ourselves entitled to read "Jackson" with a covert meaning in one passage and not in the other? Must we find specific warrant for an enigmatic reading of either passage, or both? Must we find an excuse for sticking to a mere literal reading? How much rationale will either passage support?

But let us return to the original passage, which describes some bicycle racers. The races in which they took part were not invented by James Joyce. They were part of a public event; they occurred on the afternoon of June 16, 1904, in the presence of spectators. Among these spectators were newspaper reporters, who wrote descriptions of the races and published the results in Dublin's daily newspapers. At the time, they did not know that eighteen years later a novel would be published by James Augustine Joyce, son of John Stanislaus Joyce, which would mention the bicycle races; hence they may be cleared of the suspicion of doctoring their stories in order to produce anagrams of Joyce's name. They agree that in the half-mile handicap race, first event on the day's card, the winner was J. A. Jackson. In second place was W. E. Wylie, in third place A. Munro, and in fourth place W. H. T. Gahan. With minor changes, Joyce evidently copied the newspaper reports as he found them. Perhaps he copied J. A. Jackson's name because it made enigmatic allusion to his own, and the others just because they were there. Or perhaps he copied all of them just because they were there. Without asking him, I do not suppose we can know for sure which procedure he followed; and if we asked him, we should no doubt be committing a literary heresy of some sort, perhaps breaking a law. Still, it may be that simple economy of assumption will lead us to a conclusion about this passage.

As a matter of fact, if we look at another part of the novel which also describes the bicycle races, we can tell which newspaper provided the author of *Ulysses* with his material. On p. 250, Joyce describes the quarter-mile flat handicap, and includes the name of J. B. Jeffs among the racers. The *Daily Express* and the *Irish Times* omitted this starter altogether, and the *Evening Herald* printed his name unmistakably as "Jones."

The *Freeman's Journal* gave another racer's name as "Comyns," whereas Joyce and all the other papers gave it as W. C. Huggard. Lastly, the *Irish Independent* tried to print the fifth-place finisher's name properly, as J. B. Jones, but their type was dirty, and the result looks remarkably like "Jeffs." Joyce evidently copied it in that form, and followed through to give the other racers in exactly the order, and under the names, assigned to them by the *Independent*.

This little episode of the bicycle races represents in miniature one use of an investigation into the consistency of *Ulysses*. It serves to separate the surfaces from the symbols—the things which were put into the novel because they are social history, local color, or literal municipal detail, from the things which represent abstract concepts of special import to the patterning of the novel. This is not a clear-cut separation; we may assume that Joyce's frequent purpose, like Ibsen's, was to present both a solid surface and a luminous symbol at the same time. But in a book as large and complicated as *Ulysses*, it would be inevitable, even if it were not desirable, that one of these purposes should sometimes prevail perceptibly over the other. When we know what part of the book is mainly literal Dublin detail, we can give more, or at least different, weight to what is palpably symbolic. When we know what basic materials Joyce started with, we may be able to estimate his artistic intent from the changes he imposed on them, the selection he made among them, his omissions. In the specific instance, when we find the name J. A. Jackson in the *Irish Independent* as part of a story about the bicycle races which Joyce copied in its entirety, we need fewer symbolic uses for the name because it is better accounted for as a fact. If the only symbolic use we can find for him is as a rebus of J. A. Joyce, we may decide that J. A. Jackson is best taken as a very simple fact indeed. No doubt ordinary common sense could have told us he was a nuisance as a rebus,

whether we knew of his provenance as a fact or not; but it helps
to know. From an accumulation of such observations, it is possible we may be moved toward a general judgment of Joyce's
mind, the degree of abstractness or particularity, consistency or
casualness, at which it generally worked; we may learn something of its accuracy, the purposes of its inaccuracy, the temper
of its feeling, its customary definitions of relevance. We may
be able to guess then, with better likelihood of success, at the
most economical and rewarding ways of reading the novel. Finally (though this is a less solemn consideration), I confess to
thinking that matters of literary origin and procedure (the
model of a character or episode, the twist given to a phrase of
known origin) are agreeable to know about for their own sake.
The maze of Dedalus was properly appreciated only by those
who became its antagonists; it presupposes the attitude, if not
the abilities, of Theseus.

Partly as a matter of deliberate choice, partly by accident, the
present book has been encouraged to grow up around a series of
widely separated centers in *Ulysses*. Picking up what looked like
a loose thread, I tried to run it down. A word, an incident, a
name, an idea, a tune, a character, a building, a municipal office,
an insinuation, an omission, an anachronism, a disparity—any
and all of these things served to set me looking, according to the
general principle of seeking the concrete and literal fact before
resorting to the abstract or symbolic one. In writing the book,
I have tried to let it grow in somewhat the same way. The order
I have imposed upon my facts, or elicited from them, is, at best,
provisional. Where the particular fact is important, it has
seemed best to let the broad patterns of evidence emerge on
their own; and where no patterns seemed to exist, that fact too
has been allowed to form part of my argument. On the other
hand, simple charity for the reader has led me to limit radically
the number of my illustrations. Where Joyce simply took the

materials for his novel from an available, public source—Mrs.
Maybrick (p. 729) from the daily papers, old Troy of the
D.M.P. (p. 287) from *Thom's Directory of Ireland* and/or personal acquaintance, and *Liliata rutilantium* from the Roman
Ritual Tit. V, Cap. 7—and where no serious questions of interpretation have arisen, I have not felt obliged to provide anno-
tation. Since my interest was primarily in the selections and
adaptations of fact which supply evidence of intellectual consistency, it would have served no purpose to bury the potentially
significant observation beneath piles of details which illustrate
only Joyce's genius for transcription. The guiding principle was
simply to include as little as possible which did not cast fresh
light on the meaning or making of a passage, while generalizing
as widely as possible.

In this discussion there is perforce a special position for the
negative fact. When one is presenting a positive argument for
a particular textual interpretation, one is naturally concerned
to set forth everything which makes for or against this view;
other materials need enter the picture only so far as they are
demonstrably relevant. But in a discussion of consistency, the
odd fact is on every count more important than the regular one.
What does *not* fit the pattern becomes, in fact, of central importance. Some faults and flaws of pattern are in the nature of
the things; others are in the eye of the beholder. Scarcely any
other argument offers such opportunities for making a fool of
oneself. Yet to grasp them may be a service, in the end, to
truth; if only one constitutes a handy target for one's colleagues
to shoot at. The role of St. Sebastian is not too distressing, so
long as one retains the privilege of shooting back now and then.

SURFACE

AND

SYMBOL

# 1

## The Problem

Joyce's handling of social fact in *Ulysses* can be illustrated in a preliminary yet specific way with some concrete details about familiar characters. Joyce copied a number of his characters, with minor modifications as his fictional interests dictated, from figures in real life.[1] Richard Best, W. K. Magee ("John Eglinton"), George Russell ("A.E."), and Thomas Lyster were all real figures in Dublin; all appear in *Ulysses*, playing recognizably the same roles and carrying out the same actions which occupied them in daily life. (Magee even retained, though dimly, a memory of things said in 1904 which were reproduced in the novel when it was published in 1922.) Best is given a catchword ("Don't you know") which he did not use in real life, probably to make him look silly and effeminate; but in general, Joyce's technique with these characters is simply to reproduce selected elements of everyday reality. On the other

1. The details of this paragraph are summarized from Ellmann, *JJ*.

hand, one real-life original is sometimes split into two fictional figures. Joyce himself provides most of the materials for Stephen but also contributes some characteristics to Bloom. Occasionally, two or more figures from real life are conflated to make a single figure in the fiction; Molly Bloom is a synthesis of a whole covey of females, domestic and Continental. Richie Goulding is one of Joyce's uncles, with his name changed from Willie Murray (he works for Collis & Ward, just as Willie Murray did, and lives in the same district of Dublin), but Red Murray is the other uncle, John, under his own nickname. Mick Hart and Matthew Kane are mentioned in the novel under their own names (p. 689), but also appear, rather more liberally, in the characters of Lenehan and Martin Cunningham. Dead in the first capacity, they are very much alive in the second. Though Joyce often borrowed his personages from reality, he sometimes took them from great distances and overlaid their original characters with a whole series of imaginative shadings. The man who is depicted in *Ulysses* as editor of the *Freeman's Journal,* who is named Myles Crawford in the novel and was Pat Mead in real life, got the job later but did not have it in 1904, when *Ulysses* is supposed to take place. The man who in real life bore the splendid name of Almidano Artifoni never set foot in Dublin; he was the Trieste head of the Berlitz Language School. He is represented in *Ulysses* as a teacher of music and sympathetic friend of young Stephen Dedalus. His name is imaginary, but his role in the novel is taken from life, for in 1904 James Joyce was in fact taking singing lessons in Dublin from Italian *maestri.* Some notion of the complications made available to Joyce by this mingling of fact and fiction may emerge from a look at the factual warrants for a character named Crofton.

Crofton is the "decent Orangeman" who first appears in "Ivy Day in the Committee Room"; Wilkins the Conservative having withdrawn, Crofton is now canvassing, not very enthusiastically, for Tierney the Nationalist in opposition to Colgan, whose party is not indicated. The only time the Royal Exchange Ward was represented by any man with a name resembling these was when John M. Cogan was selected Councillor against Andrew Beattie and John Brophy in 1904. On the other hand, the visit of Edward VII to Ireland, which occurred historically between July 21 and August 1, 1903, is described in the story as still in the future, so the election must be supposed to take place before that time. Stanislaus Joyce claimed (in *My Brother's Keeper*, p. 206) that he described the committee room and the people who frequented it in a letter to his brother which was written in the late fall or early winter of 1902. But, whatever election it was that Stanislaus described, it cannot have taken place on Ivy Day (October 6) in the Royal Exchange Ward, for no elections were going on in October 1902; they took place in January 1903, when James Cummins ran against James Cahill. Joyce inquired of his brother in specific detail whether a municipal election could take place in October, and must have been told that it could not. But this discouraging fact did not bother him, and the finished story combines the grim weather of January with a calendar date in early October. Thus, though Joyce seems to be describing a real election in a real Dublin ward, he has altered the year, the time of year, and the names of the candidates. In this election, and in the story as a whole, Crofton is shown in the role of a silent, stupid, and somewhat arrogant hanger-on. His other appearances in Joyce's fiction confirm this impression. In the story called "Grace," Mr. Kernan recalls with admiration how Crofton once created a ponderous and obvious phrase to express an appallingly conventional idea. And in the course of *Ulysses*, after wandering into Barney Kiernan's pub as a companion of Martin Cunningham, Crofton takes dull but solid part in the Citizen's *conversazione*. On this occasion particularly, a good deal of trifling information is given about the past career of Crofton the Orangeman, and from these materials we can not only reconstruct his career, but identify his original. His name was J. T. A. Crofton and he was listed in *Thom's Directory of Ireland* for 1888 as one of John S. Joyce's associates in the Dublin Rates Office. On p. 330 of *Ulysses* we learn that Crofton was "a pensioner out of the collector general's"; so that in a misplaced and oddly timed election, involving real issues and imaginary candidates, we now have, evidently, a wholly real character. But his presence in Dublin on Ivy Day 1902, as well as Bloomsday 1904, is due entirely to Joyce's imagination, for between 1899 and 1907, Crofton was not in Ireland at all. Where he actually was is harder to say, but we do know that he incautiously returned in 1907, and was promptly laid low by the Irish climate, expiring August 22, 1907, at the age of 69. The obituary article in the *Irish Times* reported that he had been out of the country for the past eight years. With the characteristic petty ambition of a Joycean drifter, he claimed to be a J.P. despite his long absence from the country; and, true to his religious principles, he was buried in the Protestant cemetery at Mount Jerome (*Irish Times*, Monday, August 26, 1907).

As a character in a novel, Crofton is of course the essence of triviality. He does little to advance, retard, or influence the action of *Ulysses*; he is never anything but a dull, unresponsive figure in either the novel or the short stories. Precisely because he is so undistinguished, it is curious that Joyce should have gone to his memory for that which his imagination, or his brother's observations, could so easily have supplied. Having no use for his father's old friend except as an epitome of stupidity, it is also surprising that Joyce did not at least disguise the man's name.

The mixture of fact and fancy which we observe in Crofton is the typical texture of the characters in *Ulysses*. Many of the "real" characters in the book appear under the thin disguises of borrowed names; even though they appear in their own like-nesses, they are generally made to perform imaginary or anach-ronistic actions. So far as these alterations represent simple transpositions of time, place, and person, intended to effect economies or achieve specific and clearly visible effects in the structure of the novel, they have only passing interest for this investigation. The Lord Lieutenant did not ride through Dublin on June 16, 1904, to open the Mirus Bazaar; he arrived in haste, without Lady Dudley, from a tour of the southern counties, on Tuesday, May 31. Lady Dudley did not accompany her husband for the sufficient reason that she was expecting a child, to arrive in August. Some of the people whom Joyce describes as accom-panying the Lord Lieutenant actually did so; others, whom he describes as present, were not; others accompanied him on an-other occasion, but not on the ride to the Mirus Bazaar; and still others, who were actually present, are not mentioned in *Ulysses*. Joyce himself was not living in the Martello Tower at Sandycove on June 16; he moved there sometime early in Sep-tember, and left September 19th.[2] Looking through the pages of the *Evening Telegraph* for June 16, Bloom is startled by a name which seems to be Boylan's (p. 631), but it is only "H. du Boyes, agent for typewriters or something like that." There was no such ad in the *Telegraph*, but H. Boyes, agent for Williams' Typewriter, is the last name before Boylan in *Thom's Directory*

2. Throughout August, his letters to Nora are dated from 60 Shelburne Road, i.e. Mrs. McKernan's. In a letter to Nora, dated from 103 North Strand Road (Uncle Willie's) on the night of September 19, 1904, he assures her that he slept very badly indeed on the previous night, waking no less than four times. Apparently he was not unwilling to have her think that wakefulness induced by Trench's nightmares and Gogarty's play-fulness with a gun was really the effect of a lover's insomnia. (Letter in the Cornell University Library.)

for 1904.[3] Alexander J. Dowie, the quack evangelist who decided
in 1900 to call himself "Elijah," was not in Dublin, or announced to appear there, on June 16, 1904. He had just arrived
in London (Saturday, June 11), and was having trouble finding
accommodations there. Just one week later he left Liverpool
for America aboard the *Lucania,* arriving in New York on the
morning of June 25th. Herr Karl Bleibtreu, the German faddist
who identified Shakespeare with the Earl of Rutland, did not
publish his book on the subject till 1907; he was in Berlin over
the summer of 1904, playing chess in the Café Kaiserhof, but
if I read correctly his letter to Joyce (in the Cornell Library,
dated 28 November, 1918), he had not yet created his theory
about Shakespeare, and so was most unlikely to have been consulted on the matter by Piper (an historical figure) in 1904.
Several songs are sung in *Ulysses* at a time when they had not
yet been written; for instance, "Has Anybody Here Seen Kelly?",
played by a barrel organ on p. 96, was first published in 1909.
A number of episodes are described as taking place in 1904,
before they actually did take place; for instance, Reuben J.
Dodd's son did not actually jump over the Liffey wall till 1911,[4]
and the Seddon murder case (mentioned on p. 578) did not
occur till 1912.

These few preliminary examples illustrate the freedom with
which Joyce handled some of his factual materials. Mostly these
minor alterations of the crude stuff of history are a result of
Joyce's deliberate effort to enrich and unify the background
of his book. Time is foreshortened and life freed of its custom-

3. The antiquity of this motif in Joyce's planning of the novel may be
judged from a brief entry in a notesheet listing materials for the novel:
"L.B. misreads B.B. in *E.T.*," *U. of Buffalo MSS,* "Notes for the Episodes,"
Circe (Slocum & Cahoon 5,b,i).
4. But note that in the *Telegraph* of June 16, 1904, and the *Independent*
of June 17, a man named Tierney was described as having pulled a boy out
of the Liffey at Sir John Rogerson's Quay.

ary clutter in any work of literary art; that is one reason why it is a work of literary art. Joyce certainly needs no defense for having done what every artist must do—that is, arranged and patterned his materials. Indeed, this is so much the norm for a writer of fiction that I have set aside most transpositions and adjustments of this kind, along with direct and unquestioned transcripts of social fact, as largely irrelevant to this study. The really interesting problem lies in the selections and adaptations of social fact which testify to Joyce's intent—or, more precisely, to the intent of his book.

Imaginative works like *Ulysses*, with hard, noncommittal shells and masses of semi-private references, invite us to read them unquestioningly. Mounted upon that "willing suspension of disbelief" which has been recommended to readers of Coleridge's poetry, we canter easily enough over all roughnesses and complexities of texture, all the subtleties, confusions, and doubts to which we are exposed when we look at the details as if they meant something. In the process, we are likely to miss the detailed contours of an elegant irony or a private Joycean joke, even the fullness of a structural pattern. The uneasy sense of missing something, of not quite getting the point, must be familiar to many people's experience of *Ulysses*—I am sure it is to mine. And so, challenged by the sense of loss, we dismount and proceed on foot—to the accompaniment of ominous advice from Oscar Wilde. He tells us, rather portentously, that those who look beneath the surface of a work of art do so at their peril; those who read the symbol do so at their peril.

So be it. Literary perils, though they may whiten the face of a resolute reader, rarely reduce him to complete panic. But the interpretive jeopardy is double; it menaces author as well as reader. There are certain passages of *Ulysses* which we can understand better than we did before when we see what basic factual materials Joyce started with and how he handled them.

There are a few passages which we cannot understand at all unless we go through this process. There are some others where our knowledge of the elements used to compose a scene makes its final embodiment appear forced and unnatural—or even confused. Every proper critic should, I daresay, intend to do his text every favor he can; but no man, entering into a field of investigation, is bound to find only what makes for a particular conclusion. Joyce once asked for an ideal reader, suffering from an ideal insomnia, who would give nothing less than a lifetime to reading the works of James Joyce. More unequivocally still, he has demanded that we go behind the façade of his books by his decision to conceal there all sorts of meanings (supplementary, or even exclusive) which are available only to an eye informed with outside information. He cannot very well have it both ways. If he invites us to look behind the façade by concealing significant meanings there (either really or apparently significant), he cannot very well complain if we uncover dust, sweepings, and untidy joinery as well. It is a nice literary problem how to extract as much profit as possible from one's reading without mutilating what is, after all, a work of art. As readers we wish to get as much pleasure from the novel as we can; but self-respect requires that this should not be done by blinding ourselves to flaws, failures, and inconsistencies. It is only through the vigilant, the militant, use of our critical faculties, that we can confer any real benefit on the authors whom we love.

But it is time to come to cases. I have selected, as introductory material, three passages of *Ulysses* where the possession of background information gives to one's reading a special measure of direction, outline, and point—as well as some other, less welcome, qualities.

Boyd?

As they pass out through the Castleyard gate, during the episode labeled "Wandering Rocks," Mr. John Power and Mr. Martin Cunningham are discussing possible ways of providing for Paddy Dignam's orphaned children.

—You could try our friend, Mr. Power suggested backward.
—Boyd? Martin Cunningham said shortly. Touch me not.

(p. 242)

After forty other persons named Boyd, *Thom's Directory* for 1904 lists among the inhabitants of Dublin and suburbs, the following: "Boyd, William A., Esq., general sec. City of Dublin Y.M.C.A., 43 Sackville Street, upper, 11 Brighton Square, Rathgar." A major point of the passage is evidently Martin Cunningham's mistrust of any Protestant assistance for Paddy Dignam's children. One could not possibly get this notion without knowing who or what Boyd was. Another, more available point is the cryptic, allusive manner of political intimates and insiders; "our friend" is a particularly vague and indefinite way of referring to someone who would not normally come to mind under the circumstances, but Martin Cunningham gets the reference at once. Lurking at some unmeasurable distance behind this dramatic effect may be the historic circumstance that Boyd lived just around the corner from the house in which Joyce himself was born. That might do something to make him "our friend." There seems to be no special significance to Martin Cunningham's sardonic adaptation of *Noli me tangere* (John xx:17); it may imply either financial closeness or a holier-than-thou attitude in Boyd, or a suspicious horror of him in the speaker. There is no further mention of William A. Boyd in *Ulysses*, and no means within the novel of connecting

him with either the Protestant churches or the Y.M.C.A. There
are several other fugitive Boyds, however, from whom he must
be disentangled. When Miss Kennedy refers to "that old fogey
in Boyd's" (p. 255), she is thinking of a clerk in the North
City branch of Boileau and Boyd's (late Boyd, Samuel), at 46
Mary Street. And the Bloomesque expression about "planking
down the needful and breaking Boyd's heart" (p. 611) is evidently a slang expression involving a reference to the Honorable
Walter J. Boyd, Judge in the Court of Bankruptcy. It is a
reference highly localized both in time and place. But then all
three of these references to "Boyd" are at the same time esoteric
and commonplace—commonplace to anyone within the circle
of turn-of-the-century Dublin, esoteric to anyone outside it. The
reader unequipped with outside information is in no position
to identify, distinguish, relate, or understand the three references to "Boyd" in the novel. This is not to say, by any means,
that these three references are inartistic; there is some reason
for wishing the reader of *Ulysses* to be aware of social complexities he cannot comprehend and social distances he cannot
traverse, or even measure. To be sure, there is a sharp limit on
how much deliberate mystification any novel or novel reader
can absorb, but in itself the device is legitimate. Here, however,
the purpose is not simply to baffle; had it been so, completely
meaningless names would do as well as or better than these
partially recognizable ones. Let us merely note for the present
a mixture of motives—an evident desire to record exact municipal details, an evident indifference as to whether they create
an exact impression in the mind of the general reader.

## Father Conmee and the Three Little Boys

Readers of *Ulysses* have not always been sure how they should interpret the figure of Father John Stephen Conmee, who appears in several episodes of the novel. Father Conmee, even before his appearance in *Ulysses,* existed vigorously on two levels of Joycean reality; he was an important figure in the life of Joyce and a significant character in the *Portrait of the Artist as a Young Man.* Under both constellations, his aspect was distinctly benign. After vindicating Stephen from the unjust charges of Father Dolan (in the *Portrait*) he was cheered by the boys as "the decentest rector that was ever in Clongowes" (*Portrait,* p. 64); and a memory of this verdict carries over into *Ulysses,* where it is remembered that "he was their rector: his reign was mild" (p. 221). Quite aside from the great case of the pandy-bat rescue, Joyce in real life had reasons for feeling warmly toward Father Conmee. Through Father Conmee's decision, he had been admitted to Clongowes at a specially early age, and at specially reduced rates; later, Father Conmee had rescued him, after two unhappy and humiliating years with the despised Christian Brothers, and gained him admittance, without fees, to Belvedere College. Directly or indirectly, the greater part of Joyce's early education was the work of Father John Conmee. Joyce testified to his gratitude on several occasions, and indignantly corrected Stuart Gilbert's condescending description of Father Conmee as a "very decent sort of chap." Rather, he chose to have him appear as a "bland and courtly humanist" (Ellmann, *JJ,* p. 28).

Within *Ulysses* this affectionate tone is, to some extent, maintained. Father Conmee is announced to preach on St. Peter Claver, famous for his missionary work among the African slaves in South America; Father Conmee takes the charitable view of salvation for non-Catholics; and the main errand he performs, in *Ulysses*, is an errand of mercy. As Superior of the Jesuit Order (an anachronism, for he did not become Superior till 1906), he is on his way out to Artane to discuss with Brother Swan (Reverend Br. William A. Swan, director of the O'Brien Institute for Destitute Children: *Thom's Directory*, 1904) the admission of one of the Dignam boys.

All this is admirable behavior, and Joyce's tone is properly admiring. Kevin Sullivan, in his book *Joyce Among the Jesuits*, goes so far as to say (pp. 16-17) that Father Conmee's journey through Dublin is warm, vital, and humane, standing thus in direct contrast to the cold, inhuman splendor of the Lord Lieutenant's procession. Father Conmee is Christian charity; the Lord Lieutenant is soulless bureaucracy.

Yet it is possible that Father Conmee is just a little too agreeable, on his journey through Dublin, to merit all this paralyzing seriousness. So many consecutive paragraphs begin with the words "Father Conmee" (no less than 22 in 5½ pages) that the construction comes to have an almost simpering, simple sound. Father Conmee is almost unnaturally courtly in his address to the wife of Mr. David Sheehy, M.P. (his inquiry after the boys who are attending Belvedere is anachronistic, since Richard, the older, was a contemporary of Joyce's, and Eugene, the youngest, had finished at Belvedere in 1899, just a year after Joyce himself); and as he smiles, he is aware of having cleaned his teeth with arecanut paste.[5] This is less the mind of a devoted priest than of a self-posed posturing mannikin, a well-pleased clerical pleaser.

Father Conmee is also courtly in his behavior to Mrs. Mc-

5. Joyce seems to have got Father Conmee's special dentifrice from ads for Cracroft's Area Nut Toothpaste, e.g. in the *Daily Express* for Friday, June 17, 1904, p. 1.

Guinness the pawnbroker (of 38 and 39 Gardiner Street, Upper: *Thom's Directory*, 1904).[6] As Father Conmee bows to Mrs. McGuinness, so, a few blocks away, Mr. Dennis J. Maginni bows to Lady Maxwell; and there is evidently ironic counterpoint in the courtly, meaningless gestures. A further point against Father Conmee is his charitable opinion of Father Bernard Vaughan. Joyce had parodied Father Vaughan in "Grace" under the name of Father Purdon—giving him, deliberately, the name of a street in the red-light district of Dublin; and he followed Father Vaughan's career with an almost excessive delight in its absurdities and vulgarities. To make Father Conmee an apologist, even an embarrassed apologist, for Father Bernard Vaughan, was for Joyce a way of demeaning him.

Finally, the three little boys whom Father Conmee encounters playing in Mountjoy Square have a buried significance which constitutes still another assault on Father Conmee's preternatural simple-mindedness. They go to Belvedere College, actually attended by Joyce, which is just around the corner; and their names are Jack Sohan, Ger. Gallaher, and Brunny Lynam. Now Jack Sohan is no doubt John Sohan, pawnbroker &c., of 38 Townsend Street (*Thom's Directory*, 1904); Brunny Lynam is given meaning a few pages later (p. 229), when Lenehan decides to "pop into Lynam's to see Sceptre's starting price";[7] and Ger. Gallaher is identified by Ellmann as a brother of Fred,

---

6. We will learn later, in "Wandering Rocks," that Mrs. McGuinness refused to lend money on books being offered to her in pawn by the starving Dedalus children. "Maginni" is of course an elegant variation on an original plebeian "McGuinness."

7. Gogarty gives the name another, and even worse, connotation with a reference to Richard Lynam, the "king of the kips," *As I Was Going Down Sackville Street*, p. 89. Note, however, that a Bernard M. Lynam was a member of Joyce's class entering University College, Dublin, in 1898. The relation among these scions of the house of Lynam is not clear.

who appears in both "A Little Cloud" and *Ulysses* as Ignatius Gallaher, the successful, insensitive journalist.[8] Joyce was familiar with the entire family (they had been his neighbors on North Richmond Street), knew perfectly well that in 1904 Ger. Gallaher was not of an age to attend Belvedere, and doubtless had reasons of his own for inserting this raffish young man into the company of a bookie and a pawnbroker, to be blessed benignly by Father Conmee. Whatever Joyce's reasons were, it is clear that there is a joke here, and the butt of it is Father Conmee.

Indeed, there is bound to be something more to the passage than meets the eye; for when Father Conmee blesses three little scoundrels and invites them to continue their play, the episode takes on a tone and a point which it previously lacked. The "key" to this passage provides not merely a supplementary meaning but the only one. There is of course no reason in nature why Father Conmee should not encounter ten, twenty, or a hundred nice little boys, as he walks across Dublin; but in a novel, even one is too many, unless he serves some purpose. Hence the positive achievement of understanding the scene by means of a key is really a negative one of keeping the passage from seeming completely pointless. The fact is that without an outside key, in the shape of information about three obscure Dublin characters, the passage is entirely devoid of meaning. Many *romans à clef* have a surface on which the reader can repose with a measure of satisfaction, whether he possesses the key or not. The key is an extra, sometimes a gratuitous, item of information. But Joyce's novel demands a kind of knowledge, at once

---

8. In a letter to his brother, dated around August 10, 1906, Joyce concludes a discussion of Gogarty's marriage by referring to the couple as Mr. and Mrs. Ignatius Gallaher (letter in the Cornell Library). But I do not think this implies that Ignatius Gallaher was modeled upon Gogarty, so much as that Joyce considered them equally brash, insensitive, and ambitious.

public and intimate, if the reader is not to be left groping un-
easily after a private joke which he senses but does not understand. The excess sweetness of tone in the Father Conmee
episode demands an object, a satiric point. We are driven to
look for this point outside the novel itself; and ultimately, in
municipal records and biographical byways, we find it—which
is gratifying, of course. But it suggests a general principle of
construction not very economical of the general reader's time,
and not very neat so far as the economy of forces within the
novel is concerned.

The author is evidently willing to count upon the labors of
the reader in unearthing his buried references, but he will not
give those labors direction, or make his patterns distinct enough
so that one can distinguish intention from accident. For instance, within this very passage, I have supposed that the encounter of Lady Maxwell with Professor Maginni (p. 217, lines
22-26) exists to parallel the encounter of Father Conmee and
Mrs. McGuinness—as one might say, the fake gentleman (Maginni) encounters a real lady, the real gentleman (Conmee) a
fake lady. Courtly Father Conmee looks at Mrs. McGuinness
and thinks "how like a lady"; we look at him, and think "how
like a dancing-master." But, unfortunately for the neatness of
the parallel, the lines have already met. Before encountering
Professor Maginni, we learn (p. 221), Lady Maxwell had been
to see Father Conmee, and had prevented him from reading
the proper passage in his breviary. There is nothing in this circumstance which lacks verisimilitude; but, like a random stroke
in an otherwise symmetrical design, it creates the possibility
that the design itself is random and accidental. Lady Maxwell
cannot be intended to mock the polite emptiness of genteel
manners if she is given a real social existence and the possibility
of significant spiritual problems. Her function in the novel falls
rather awkwardly between that of a social fact, having solidity,

complexity, and a claim on existence of its own—and that of a moral or social indicator, significant chiefly in relation to Father Conmee.

## Deasy

In the second section of *Ulysses*, designated "Nestor," Stephen Dedalus is seen teaching at the school where he is employed, and in conversation with its headmaster, "Mr. Deasy." A good many of the details incorporated in this section were derived by Joyce (with minor, prudential alterations, as noted) from specific social facts. The school, in which Joyce taught, was the Clifton School, which existed at Dalkey through 1904; and Mr. Deasy, the headmaster in the novel, was in real life named Francis Irwin. He is somewhat altered, however, from his real-life original. For one thing, the school had to be closed down shortly after Joyce left it because of Mr. Irwin's habitual intemperance; this failing is not even suggested in the novel. Again, Mr. Irwin was an elderly bachelor, who lived with his sister; Joyce has given him a wife, and made her, if not faithless, at least a source of anger and discomfort to Mr. Deasy. Finally, Mr. Deasy, in his capacity as a Nestorian "tamer of horses," has been given an interest in horse-racing and a concern with the foot-and-mouth disease which has been modulated eight years back in time, and transferred to the character Deasy from Joyce himself. The letter which Mr. Deasy entrusts to Stephen for delivery to the Dublin papers was in fact adapted from one written in 1911 by Henry Blackwood Price, and forwarded, through Joyce's instrumentality, to William Field, M.P. Mr. Field was, in 1904 as in 1911, president and chief spokesman of the Irish Cattle Traders and Stock Owners Association. (Joyce could have learned from the *Freeman's Journal* of June 14, 1904, p. 3, that

the Association held weekly meetings on Thursdays at its offices
in the City Arms Hotel.) All these details, along with the essence of Price's 1911 letter, Joyce reproduced in his novel.[9]

Now in all these respects Joyce was clearly tailoring his basic
social materials to fit the purposes of his fiction. He had enough
drunks in the novel already; there was no need (and at 10 o'clock
of a Thursday morning, no real opportunity) to show Mr. Deasy
as a toper. Joyce did need someone to enunciate the "faithless-
wife" theme, and to show it as a recurrent episode in Irish history; wise old Nestor served this purpose nicely. As for the foot-
and-mouth disease, Joyce like Stephen Dedalus felt it to be a
somewhat plebeian topic for a literary man to be associated
with; consequently he imputed to "Nestor" an interest and a
connection which were in fact his own. He wrote, in September
of 1912, a subeditorial on the topic, which appeared in the
*Freeman's Journal* (*Critical Writings,* pp. 238-241); he was careful, however, to keep his name from being connected with the
subject.

But Mr. Deasy himself invites our further interest. As he
appears in the novel, he is of course an Orangeman, a Protestant, and in his relations with Stephen a kindly but patronizing
old duffer. To fill in some of the details of his representation,
let us begin by noting that his last name, "Deasy," had particularly bitter overtones in Irish history. The so-called "Deasy
Act," passed in 1860, was an extremely brutal attempt to regu-
late the relations of Irish tenants and landlords in the interests
of the landlords. It provided, in essence, that any improvements
made on Irish properties which were not explicitly, and by written contract, assigned to the tenant, should belong to the landlord. In effect, it assigned to landlords 99 per cent of the im-

9. Mr. Ellmann in his splendid biography of Joyce has not only resurrected
the original letter on which Joyce drew, but has discussed the rather complex circumstances that brought it to his attention.

provements made by tenants, without any compensation for the tenants. Even for the Irish landlord class, it was too brutal and discriminatory an act ever to be put into effect; and it therefore remained a dead letter. But Joyce, in assigning the name "Deasy" to an Orangeman, was certainly playing on bitter memories.

Mr. Deasy is related, in the novel, to the Blackwood family; his cousin, Henry Blackwood Price, has written from Austria of the way foot-and-mouth disease is treated there. Though Mr. Deasy claims descent "on the spindle side" from rebels, on the other, the male side, he is descended from Sir John Blackwood, whose motto he quotes emphatically and approvingly, "Per vias rectas." It is indeed the motto of the Blackwood family, as *Burke's Irish Gentry* still attests; one might translate it either "By right roads" or "By straight roads." But though Mr. Deasy goes straight to the point, he is always wrong. For instance, he declares emphatically that Sir John Blackwood voted for the Union. "He voted for it and put on his topboots to ride to Dublin from the Ards of Down to do so" (p. 32). Now it is not difficult to find out that Sir John Blackwood was firmly opposed to the Union; one need only look up the title in Cokayne under the heading "Dufferin, Dufferin and Claneboye of Ballyleidy and Killyleagh and Dufferin and Ava." Sir John was offered a peerage if he would support the Union, but he pointed to the family motto "Per vias rectas," and declined. This story is told again, in a version which compounds even further Mr. Deasy's felonious mishandling of facts, by Sir Alfred Lyall, in *The Life of the Marquis of Dufferin and Ava*, London, 1905, I, 3. Sir John Blackwood was indeed firmly opposed to the Union, and declined the bribe of a peerage for supporting it; but he never rode to Dublin to vote for or against it, because he died in the act of putting on his topboots in order to go vote against it. And this second, more complex version of the story was perfectly well known to Joyce, in a context which associated it, curiously, with the foot-and-mouth disease. A letter to Stanislaus of August 7, 1912, reads as follows:

Price writes me a letter every day. He has a cure for the foot and mouth disease which is devastating Irish cattle. Styrian oxen suffer from it and are cured, but 2000 Irish beasts have been killed. He writes (like you) "Be energetic. Forget Leinster for Ulster. Remember that Sir John Blackwood died in the act of putting on his topboots in order to go to Dublin to vote against the Union. You will get your name up if you write this up." I cannot do so. I have written the whole thing to W. Field MP (pres. of Irish Cattle Traders Society) who of course never answered. I am writing to explain to Price. Do you think he is right or I? I wanted Field who is in the line to take it up not I myself. I think Price ought to look for a cure for the foot and mouth disease of Anna Blackwood Price.[10]

Not only is Mr. Deasy wrong three ways about Sir John Blackwood; all his notions of history are upside down. He makes reference to early Irish annals, for example, to show that women have always been responsible for the downfall of Ireland's leaders. "A faithless wife first brought the strangers to our shore here, MacMurrough's wife and her leman O'Rourke, Prince of Breffni." Once again, the actual story has been reversed. Dermot MacMurrough, King of Leinster, was the "leman"; he seduced Dervorgilla, the wife of Tiernan O'Rourke, lord of Breffni, and though he later sent her back to her husband, this was not exactly a compliment either. O'Rourke sought vengeance, and MacMurrough appealed for English aid, which first arrived in 1167. Mr. Deasy has assigned the lovely Dervorgilla to the wrong husband. We know that these errors were conscious on Joyce's part because none of them (neither those involving Der-

10. Letter in the Cornell University Library. Copyright 1962 by Harriet Weaver and F. Lionel Munro as administrators c.t.a. of the Estate of James Joyce.

vorgilla nor those involving Sir John Blackwood) occur in the *Little Review* version of *Ulysses*; they were introduced (clearly as part of the characterization of Deasy) in the process of preparing the novel for appearance in a volume.[11]

Finally, to cap the climax of his historical absurdities, Mr. Deasy is made to say that "the orange lodges agitated for repeal of the union twenty years before O'Connell did." This is simple madness. No doubt there was Protestant opposition to the Act of Union, but the Orange lodges were pro-Union and could not rationally have been anything else. They were founded "to support and defend her Majesty Queen Victoria, the Protestant religion, the laws of the country, the legislative union, and the succession to the throne." They were proud to proclaim that "Orangeism is now what it ever has been, an organization for the maintenance of British authority in Ireland," and they could not conceivably have retained this objective while agitating against the Union.

*Per vias rectas*, Mr. Deasy is bound to be wrong. He refers to Stephen as a "fenian," and talks about "the prelates of your communion," as if he were addressing a faithful Catholic and an earnest Irish republican.[12] He quotes Shakespeare to support

11. In notes made preparatory to the writing of *Exiles*, Joyce repeated the error regarding Dervorgilla, O'Rourke, and MacMurrough, a fact which raises the possibility that he himself was confused about the story. But it seems an important point for him to be ignorant of; and his correcting the *Little Review* text into error, at the same time he was introducing other deliberate errors into Mr. Deasy's speeches, can scarcely have been inadvertent.

12. He is as wrong about Stephen's politics as about his religion, of course; but note that Stephen deliberately sits down, as a gesture of disrespect, in front of a portrait of Edward VII, while the pictured horses "stood in homage, their meek heads poised in air" (p. 33); this may reverberate from the story, much bruited at the time (cf. p. 325), that on the occasion of Edward's visit, the prelates of Maynooth loyally decorated his room with pictures of his horses.

his contention that Stephen should concentrate on making money, and quotes a villain. Only on this point is he corrected, and in a most subdued tone:

—Iago, Stephen murmured.

He cries out positively that the tag about "the sun never setting on the British Empire" is not an English boast; "a French Celt said that." As usual, he is explicit, positive, clear, and wrong. Dictionaries of quotations give many sources for this common-place, which was applied to the Roman, Spanish, Portuguese, and Dutch Empires long before it came to be applied to the British. Conceivably French Celts have repeated it from time to time; but its origin has never been assigned to one of this interesting breed.

A final error, more difficult to track down, concerns a recurrent mirage of Irish nationalism. Mr. Deasy refers to "the Liverpool ring which jockeyed the Galway harbour scheme." The jockey metaphor makes this charge a little vague, but it seems to refer to the persistent failure of a series of efforts, over the last half of the nineteenth century, to develop Galway as a transatlantic port. A further reference to this scheme (which Joyce described at length in an article in the *Piccolo della Sera* of 5 September, 1912) is found in *Ulysses*, pp. 623-4. John Orrell Lever, mentioned in these pages, was a moving spirit in the enterprise; and the incident which crushed the whole plan occurred in 1860, when the *Indian Empire* entered Galway Harbor on the 14th of June, and struck on the Marguerite Rock. But there is no evidence at all that a "Liverpool ring" of any description "jockeyed" the scheme; and Joyce, though he often sounds in his writings for the *Piccolo* like a disciple of the Citizen himself, makes no reference to any such practices. As a matter of fact, English and Irish capital were equally involved

in the Galway Line; and the failure of the plan is attributed by
Frank C. Bowen (A *Century of Atlantic Travel*, Boston, 1930,
p. 105) to the fact that not one of the interested parties knew
the elements of the shipping business.

Now the modern Nestor, if he is at all to resemble his Homeric original, is bound to provide Stephen-Telemachus with a
good deal of useless information. As he appears in Homer's
poem Nestor is a garrulous, long-winded old gentleman, who
answers all the questions except that which Telemachus has
asked him. But at least the information he provides is substan-
tially correct, though irrelevant. Mr. Deasy's mistakes are gross
and deliberate; they suggest that, in addition to Nestor, he derives from Don Quixote and perhaps the Headless Horseman.
They fortify our perception that his anti-semitism is the last
refuge of a disordered mind—in effect, he *is* the nightmare of
history from which Stephen is trying to awake—and they enable
us to level a few shrewd guesses at the choked and disordered
symbolism which attends the final appearance of Mr. Garrett
Deasy in *Ulysses*. Through the nightmarish mists of Nighttown
he rises, a ghastly jockey riding the favorite and coming in dead
last in a weird parody of the Gold Cup. "Cock of the North,"
his mount, wears his own white gaiters; the name makes multiple reference to his Ulster origins, his sexual inadequacies,
and George, the fifth Lord Gordon, who commanded the Gordon Highlanders when they put down the 1798 rebellion in
County Wexford (a tune by this name is the regimental march).
He wears a green jacket with orange sleeves to show his divided
sympathies; he brandishes a hockey stick because that was the
school game, and he is bewildered about what sport he is engaged in. His face is probably nailscratched because he is hen-
pecked, and plastered with postage stamps because, like old
Major Tweedy who collected stamps, he is a soldier in confused

and meaningless wars. (The Gordon Highlanders once staffed Gibraltar where Major Tweedy served; and a stamp, like a soldier, is gaudily dressed, arbitrarily valued, and fulfills its function when cancelled with a blow.) Derided by the orange and green lodges alike, he is deluged in a torrent of mutton broth which "a yoke of buckets leopards all over him" (p. 559). The phrase seems to compress a reference to his wife (yoke-mate) who threw soup over the waiter at the Star and Garter in an effort to cause the leopard to change his spots; while the dancing coins of cut-up vegetable mock Mr. Deasy's ineffectual concern with money. Yet he still cries "per vias rectas" in the teeth of the circumstance that he is a humiliating last in the race of life.

So much for this depressing vision of a modern Nestor. But Mr. Deasy, after all, is only symptomatic. His presentation faces us with two sorts of difficulties. There is a factual background, taken for granted though never presented, and by no means within the range of common knowledge; one is supposed to see and calculate the range of Mr. Deasy's mental deviations, with this rather special information in mind. Then there is a symbolic presentation of the man, surrounded by freely associated trappings, in which one is free to see whatever significance one can. Here matters are perfectly open and unstructured; the sort of infantile ingenuity exercised above on the soldier-stamp parallel is as legitimate as any other interpretive approach. Naturally, under these circumstances, one never knows whether one has understood the passage fully or not. Grammatically, the odd point of the passage is the use of the noun "leopard" as a verb meaning "pour" or "spatter." Taken in connection with the various other unresolved dualisms of his existence, it may reinforce, through the double heritage of the leopard ("a pard, a panther, got in spousebreach," p. 47), the idea of Mr. Deasy's double-mindedness. But here we are evidently wandering among phantoms of our own construction, having little or nothing to do with the rather specific effects available to the reader of a work of fiction.

These three different episodes from *Ulysses* display in different ways Joyce's penchant for building his novel around a series of holes in the pattern of reader-information. With regard to "Boyd," there is no substitute for the basic knowledge of who Boyd was, and perhaps (to avoid secondary confusions) of who he was not. To know these facts is pure gain; not to know them is to be present, for a moment of the novel, at a conversation being conducted in Chippewa or Ashanti. The episode of Father Conmee and the three little boys depends, once more, for most of its tonality, on the reader's possessing outside information. In addition, it raises a broader question regarding the mode of the fiction. Is a character in *Ulysses* "explained" when he is fitted into a literary pattern, when he is derived from an historical original, or when his behavior is associated with emotional attitudes peculiar to James Joyce? Is one principle of "explanation" better than, contradictory to, or just as good as, the other? (By *explanation* I mean simply an accounting for the character's presence and behavior, an understanding of his function or his effect.) The episode of Mr. Deasy, finally, involves still more elaborate outside information, of a peculiarly private yet public nature. It raises the question, also, of Joyce's freely associated images; how far can one look for consistent meaning in them, and how much of what one finds or creates is really relevant to the novel? Evidently there is some limit beyond which the reader is not justified in imposing *his* private associative ingenuities on the novel; did the novelist impose any such limitation on himself?

# 2

## Animus and Anxiety

One of the more formidable ways in which a novelist confers importance on his characters or withdraws it from them, is by positioning them on his canvas. This is not simply a matter of foreground and background, of large-scale versus small-scale representation; it is also a question of relative brightness on the representational scale, and of the reader's readiness to receive an impact. The enigmatic little hunchback who reads Sir Walter Scott in the National Library occupies less than a page of *The Portrait*; but he draws together many disparate threads of the novel, he is given a distinctive manner, and he appears at a moment of important intellectual decision. He was a simple social fact in Joyce's Dublin, but in the novel his work is not simple at all. He appears in Stephen's fantasy as the child of an aristocratic, incestuous affair; as Stephen imagines the encounter, the girl's features are dark and indistinguishable, but her brother-husband has the hands of Davin, the innocent athlete. If it is

not altogether meaningless, that detail ties in with Stephen's
jealousy of Davin, whom a nameless peasant girl had invited
to share her bed; it relates to phrases of degenerate aristocracy
like "a Firbolg in the borrowed cloak of a Milesian" (*Portrait*,
p. 209) and Stephen's later desire, "before their squires begat
upon them," to breed from the daughters of Erin "a race less
ignoble than their own" (*Portrait*, p. 280). Joyce thus converts
the "captain," with his mock-military title, his midget stature,
his innocence, and his idiotic Scott-nostalgia, into a decisively
degenerate representation of modern Ireland.[1] Serving so many
purposes of such serious import, and rendered vivid by a selective
lighting which brings out only his monkey face and grotesque
imbecility against a lush romantic background, the "captain" is
a rich dot of fictional energy.[2]

In presenting this figure Joyce acted specifically to fortify (by
omission and emphasis and contrast and multiple thematic relatedness) what even perceptive contemporaries saw merely as
an odd, insignificant creature. He has succeeded in rooting the
"captain" so solidly in the specific fictional business of the novel,
that if he had not existed, we feel it would have been necessary
to invent him. Stephen's splendid program to improve single-
handedly the breed of the Irish nation may seem excessively,

1. What grounds Marvin Magalaner has for supposing the "captain" was,
or was supposed to be, a homosexual, like the personage in "An Encounter" (*Time of Apprenticeship*, pp. 105-8), I do not know. Mr. J. F. Byrne
assured me that the "captain" used to be a familiar figure around the
National Library.

2. He seems to recur in *Ulysses*, p. 205, in a momentary misgiving of
Stephen's that he may be already a father. The phrase "Shrunken, uncertain
hand" has no analogues in *Ulysses* and no exact analogue in the *Portrait*;
but it is a good deal closer, verbally and thematically, to p. 268 of the
*Portrait* than to anything in *Ulysses*. Whether Joyce's adventures with pros-
titutes involved the hope or fear of committing incest we may safely leave
to the psychoanalysts.

almost comically, disinterested; but his vision of the "captain" is unanswerable.

But not all the figures at the emotional nodes of *Ulysses* work out as well as the "captain" in the *Portrait*. Where they do not have dramatic or symbolic muscles to carry the weight assigned them by the structure, we may find specially interesting places to probe in search of latent animus and anxiety in the mind of Joyce.

## Father Malachi O'Flynn and
## Mr. Hugh C. Haines Love, M.A.

At the depth of the section known as "Circe" a black mass is celebrated under highly dramatic circumstances. Amid all the paraphernalia of apocalypse—screaming birds, a blackened sun, monstrous apparitions, spectral warfare, the resurrection of the dead—rises the field altar of Saint Barbara. She is appropriate here because she is, evidently, mythical in origin; because she protects against lightning, sudden death, and impenitence; and because she is the special patroness of firework-makers, artillerymen, architects, and grave-diggers—with all of whom Joyce, in this section, has an affinity. On her altar lies the naked woman who is a traditional figure of the black mass. This ghastly victim is the pregnant Mrs. Purefoy, flesh run idiotically rampant, and representative of Mother Ireland herself—fettered, teeming, and exhausted. Over this prostrate form two priests celebrate the traditional black, or backwards, mass. Their names are Father Malachi O'Flynn and the Reverend Mr. Hugh C. Haines Love, M.A. Father O'Flynn wears a petticoat (he is a transvestite priest) and a reversed chasuble; his two left feet are back to front.[3] Mr. Haines Love, M.A., wears, less contortedly, both cassock and mortarboard, to represent his connections with the church and university. Like Father O'Flynn's left feet, his head and collar are on back to front—one man looks forward and walks backward, the other looks backward and walks forward. Over the celebrant's head the Reverend Mr. Love holds an open umbrella, arch-symbol of the contraceptive device.

Father Malachi O'Flynn is clearly a composite of Malachi Mulligan (neither St. Malachi nor King Malachi fit in the context at all) and Father O'Flynn, the subject of Alfred Percival Graves' famous poem. Bloom has thought previously of its refrain, "Father O'Flynn would make hares of them all" (p. 168). Father O'Flynn is intended as a type of the Irish parish priest, shrewd in his simplicity, who manages to look out very well for his cloth and himself. In his mixture of unthinking levity and unthinking selfishness, he is a very proper match for Malachi Mulligan; lay and clergy, this precious pair represent everything in the Catholic tradition that Stephen hates and fears.

The other celebrant is a bit more complex, at first glance. One of his names is Haines, which is, of course, that of the Englishman visiting in the Tower with Mulligan and Dedalus (his real name was Samuel Chenevix Trench). Haines damns himself by the bland and exasperating calmness with which he admits that "we have treated you rather unfairly" and then passes the blame off upon an abstraction—history (p. 22). More Gaelic than the old milkwoman herself in a language he can afford to annex as a curiosity, he is inhumanly condescending after the best British manner. The green stone in his cigarette lighter is Ireland, a casual adornment. His archetype is Glad-

3. Christ is represented in the Book of Kells with two left feet; in the present passage, this connotation is as optional as that which would connect Mr. Haines Love's twisted head with the similar distortion of the Diviners and Sorcerers in Dante, *Inferno*, Canto XX.

stone the verbal liberal, whom James and Stanislaus agreed in describing as the great impostor (*Diary of Stanislaus Joyce,* pp. 126-7).

The Anglican cleric with whom Haines is paired is the Reverend Hugh C. Love, M.A. His last name immediately reflects that of Haines (*haine* means *hate* in French); and the first name "Hugh" in connection with "Love"—so hard a word for Bloom to define—reminds the alert reader of Boylan. But this is only, or perhaps not even, the beginning. We are given a good deal of pretty specific information about Mr. Love. He is from Rathcoffey, and presently has an address at St. Michael's, Sallins; he is writing a book on the Geraldines, on which he consults Ned Lambert (pp. 226-8). He salutes the Lord Lieutenant, aware that this is or once was a welcome source of ecclesiastical largesse (p. 249); and he is distraining for rent against Father Bob Cowley, the spoiled priest, who serves as accompanist for Simon Dedalus and Ben Dollard in the Ormond-bar concert.

Now all these impressively detailed circumstances fail to form a factual pattern, or indeed a pattern of any sort, about the Reverend Mr. Love. There is no book on the Geraldines by a man so named; nor are there even any articles. The people who wrote on the Geraldines around this period have no other points of contact whatever with our Mr. Love. Rathcoffey, not far from Clongowes Wood in County Kildare, is not the seat of a Protestant church, nor even of a post office; it is remarkable only for a ruined castle, former residence of the Wogan family. St. Michael's, Sallins, is the residence of an Anglican archdeacon. Both places are close to Maynooth, ancient seat of the Geraldines and of a religious college where Professor MacHugh (Hugh MacNeill) taught. No Hugh C. Love ever held office in the Church of Ireland.

But Stanislaus Joyce tells us (*My Brother's Keeper,* p. 75) that Love was a young clergyman who owned a house in Windsor Terrace, Fairview, and rented it to John S. Joyce; and, indeed, parts of this story are supported by outside facts. During the 1890's a certain Mary C. Love did purchase 28, 29, and 30 Windsor Avenue, Clontarf; as late as 1905 she had not sold them. Thus Hugh C. Love was either an owner of or (through close family connection) an agent for the property at 29 Windsor Avenue, from which Bob Cowley is said to have been evicted. The Joyces once lived at 29 Windsor Avenue.[4] Hence Joyce, in putting Hugh C. Love into *Ulysses* as a hard-hearted landlord, is evidently paying off an old family score. There is a slight displacement of roles; John S. Joyce, who in real life was the victim, becomes (as Simon Dedalus) in the fiction one of the consolers. There is also a four-year displacement in time; the Joyces were tenants of unhappy Mr. Love in 1900, not 1904. But at least we have a reason for Mr. Love's name and one of his actions in the novel.

Why, then, did Joyce make Mr. Love a Church of Ireland clergyman, to such overpowering effect that he misled even the retentive memory of Stanislaus Joyce? (Born at Belfast in 1872, Hugh Love was a civil servant in real life, a clerk in National Education.) Why did Joyce have him working on a history of the Geraldines, why the second address out at Rathcoffey? To these questions no unequivocal answers appear. Possibly the real-life Hugh C. Love did take some interest in Irish history; but if that is the only justification for his doing so in the novel, Joyce shows little sense of fictional economy. More probably, Joyce intended to suggest that the history of his country, like its language, was the diversion of well-mannered, well-spoken, but essentially cold and selfish usurpers. Perhaps the Rathcoffey connection and the Geraldine interest both derive from a grafting process, by which one or several other people were called

4. Note that 92 Windsewer Ave. is one of the addresses to which the letter, written by Shem and delivered by Shaun, is vainly carried. *FW*, p. 420.

upon to contribute characteristics to the Reverend Mr. Love. Perhaps Mr. Love's name, which is historically the name of John Joyce's landlord in the Bob Cowley context, becomes symbolic in the Rathcoffey-Sallins context, and commemorates a juvenile erotic experience. Speculation might run riot on these points. But we are already far outside the bounds of a reader of fiction; we are treating *Ulysses* as an enigma, not as a novel. This is very wrong. On the other hand, the fact that Mr. Love was a landlord who evicted the Joyce family shows that the novel is, in fact, a partial enigma already. The further we pursue our understanding of it, the more enigmatic we are likely to make it. If, for instance, we were to learn that the Wogan family which inhabited the castle at Rathcoffey traced its descent through a certain Cavalier Ughi of Florence to Ugus, a Roman patrician of the Augustan era,[5] we might be thought to have solved another aspect of the enigma. At least we should have made a connection between a particular Hugh and a family of Hughs—with Professor Hugh MacHugh not far off at Maynooth. But we should also have made the novel depend on some pretty esoteric bits of information, and the possession of that information does not noticeably enrich one's reading of the fiction. On the contrary, it distracts. The "solution" is more complicated than the problem.

Love, his father's hardhearted landlord, was for Joyce in the nature of an *objet* happily *trouvé*; but, like most *objets trouvés,* he had to be adapted to a work of art. It may be felt that in making him a young Protestant clergyman who for some reason owned a house in Clontarf but lived in the County Kildare and did research on Geraldines, Joyce was stretching his character pretty thin. In fact the novel does not make him seem bad enough to belong at the altar of St. Barbara with such odious creatures as Haines, Mulligan, and Father O'Flynn. Father Bob

5. See *Journ. Royal Soc. of Antiq. of Ireland,* XXI, 119.

Cowley, the alleged victim of Love, does not appeal to our warmest sympathies; even if he did, we should be more likely to direct our indignation against Reuben J. Dodd, who has set bailiffs upon him, rather than against the Reverend Mr. Love, who has merely distrained for rent. Landlords who expect their money can never be popular heroes; but it is not necessary to think Mr. Love an utter villain to understand his objections to Father Bob as a tenant. There is in fact a disparity between Mr. Love's generally mild and agreeable behavior in St. Mary's Abbey and Father Cowley's assertion that he is distraining for rent; it may be that this completely undramatized statement of fact carried so many bitter memories for Joyce that he felt it needed no dramatic emphasis in the novel. At all events, understanding the novelist's personal animus against Love, we understand, on at least one level, the prominent position he occupies in the "Circe" scene, a prominence which in fictional terms alone may seem excessive.

I speak of the Joyce family's real-estate relations with Hugh C. Love as "explaining" a certain feature of the novel; but it is a curious sort of explanation at best, which merely enables us to know that there is no proper fictional reason for some of the things that are said, thought, and done in *Ulysses*. Autobiography has evidently usurped over narrative; at least, by exerting a subsurface influence, it has allowed a disparity to be felt between two different parts of the novel. And by coming to the surface under pressure it has further encouraged us to look upon the novel as an infinitely extensible enigma, has set us off on wild-goose chases after Hugh-connections, St. Michael-connections, Geraldine-and-Sallins-connections, beyond number.

One last suggestion grows out of the passage; it either explains or complicates another phrase in Joyce, and in either event shows how much these two processes are akin. In reading over *Finnegans Wake* for Joyce, James Johnson Sweeney came to a passage (*FW*, p. 324) giving what Sweeney gradually realized to be the telephone number of Earwicker's pub in Chapelizod—"Clontarf one love one fear." Historically, the battle of Clontarf was fought in the year 1014, and "love" stands for zero in tennis (as the macaronic association-string fear-vier-fourfore leads us to a cry in golf); but in the biographical context, there is every reason why the period of the Joyces' residence in Clontarf should have been associated with "one love," the landlord, and one fear, eviction. The second battle of Clontarf was fought, it seems, in 1900. Whether this exasperates the reader or delights him, I do not think it inconsistent with the lines on which Joyce's mind operated in patterns of intricate detail.

## The Twenty-five Lovers of Molly Bloom

The reader of *Ulysses* approaches the end of the volume with a sense that Molly Bloom is a woman of abundant sexual vigor, and her husband is a man afflicted with grave sexual inhibitions and problems. But while the loss of Rudy and the background of sexual difficulty consequent thereon are not likely to be overlooked, one does not have the impression that Bloom and Molly have been for ten years at an absolute sexual impasse. One senses in a way that Bloom's interest in Molly's lovers, actual or potential, is curiously involved: he dodges elaborately out of Boylan's way in Kildare Street, but pushes a picture of Molly ostentatiously into Stephen's way at the cabman's shelter. He is proud of her attractions, and her ability to excite men; he is humiliated by imputations, variously expressed, that he is a "pishogue," a half-and-half, a sexual weakling. He is subservient to Molly, getting her breakfast in bed; yet he is a husband, a provider, a father, and does not squander the rent money in pubs. He is womanly, to the extent of experiencing something

like a menstrual cycle; he is also manly, if an excessive interest
in, and responsiveness to, feminine underwear is any evidence
of masculine sexuality. He is not only more sensitive than Boylan
("he understood or felt what a woman is," p. 767), he "has
more spunk in him" (p. 727), i.e. more semen but perhaps also
by implication more courage. He is sadistic in teaching girls
whom he picks up in the street to say dirty words they do not
understand (p. 364); he is masochistic in ways too enormous
to need recounting; he is a philanderer with Martha, and a
merry, playful, generous father with Milly. This is not a very
tidy picture, but it is comprehensible and apparently compre-
hensive; and it leaves Blazes Boylan in a position of central
importance within the novel's architecture; he is the coarse-
fibered lover who usurps over Poldy as Mulligan has usurped
over Stephen.

Thus it comes as a bit of a surprise to discover, on p. 716,
that Molly has had no fewer than twenty-four lovers before
Boylan. As she was not nubile till fifteen, and is now thirty-four,
she has thus averaged better than one per year, not, of course,
counting her husband, and discounting no time at all for two
pregnancies. If we suppose that she was faithful to Poldy for as
much as a year after their marriage, and relaxed her efforts during the last six months of her pregnancies, her average score
rises to a lover and a half per annum. One is not prepared for
so grandiose a performance; its epic quality is enhanced by the
circumstance that a good many of the names appear here for
the first (and in some instances for the only) time in the novel.
Appalled by the problem of adjusting to Molly's vigorous sexual career with this untidy collection of males, some students of
the novel have taken the safe course of denying that Joyce really
meant the list as a list of lovers at all. Some of them may be
lovers, as Mr. Ellmann concedes; but some are gynecologists

who have inspected Molly professionally, others are priests who
have heard confession from her, and still others are men who,
taken by her charms, have (let us say) lusted after her in their
hearts or flirted with her, without carrying matters any further.
Others, perhaps, are simply men in whom she has felt a passing
interest, listed without regard to whether they have displayed
an overt interest in her. Examples of these various types are Dr.
Francis Brady (gynecologist), Father Bernard Corrigan (priest),
Maggot O'Reilly (indifferent), and the gentleman at the Gaiety
Theatre (flirt). And when one has eliminated all these phan-
tom lovers, one is left with just two genuine ones—Boylan,
whose title to the role can scarcely be denied, and (says Ellmann) Bartell D'Arcy, who kissed her on the choir stairs after
she sang Gounod's *Ave Maria* (p. 730). As a matter of fact,
Bartell D'Arcy's claim is not proof against a really skeptical
scrutiny. A tenor may kiss a girl or even a married woman very
vigorously indeed on the choir stairs, and yet not effect formal
entry into her bed. There is no specific statement in the novel
that Bartell D'Arcy did effect such formal entry. Therefore a
really determined doubter might conclude that Boylan is the
only lover Molly ever had. . . .

But here we come up against the whole tenor (so to speak)
of the woman's thought and character, as well as the matter of
inherent probability. Molly is a gusty woman, plain-spoken and
in fact startlingly vulgar in her everyday inner thoughts (they
are not just the thoughts of Everywoman, any more than
Bloom's sexual feelings are the feelings of Everyman). She has
yielded to Boylan on his first invitation, just as, ten years ago,
on the night of the Glencree banquet, she played a merry frolic
in the company of the sponger Lenehan, and in the very presence of her husband, without any invitation at all. For ten years
now (as we learn on pp. 720-21) she has been deprived of all

sexual contact with her husband, except for his now and then kissing, unsatisfactorily, her bottom.[6] The notion that she would be content with one sexual contact in ten years is simply grotesque, and in fact she has not been preserving her "virtue" all this carefully.

So she must have had more lovers than Joyce explicitly tells us she had (one), but how many more? Shall we count Valentine Dillon, whom she remembers seeing at the Glencree banquet, but not, apparently, since? After a long and vigorous career in posts of prominence, he had died about two and a half months before, and was buried on April 2, 1904 (an account of the funeral appeared in the *Freeman's Journal* for Monday, April 4, 1904, p. 7); but Molly betrays no awareness of these facts, and no awareness of his existence since the night in 1894 when he ogled her at the Glencree banquet. Shall we include Simon Dedalus, whom she describes as "such a criticizer" (p. 753), with his quizzing-glass and his sarcastic tongue? Or "old frosty-face" (p. 732)[7] Professor Goodwin, superannuated, incompetent, and generally stone-drunk? If she has made herself available to any of these men (and if to one, why not to all?— we are given no grounds on which to discriminate), it was evidently on a crude, sensual footing, involving physical gratification and nothing else. The "bootblack at the General Post Office," the "Italian organ-grinder," and the "farmer at the Royal Dublin Society's Horse Show," certainly point in this

6. In early versions of the book, it is interesting to note, the sexual difficulties of the Blooms were much more explicitly indicated than in the final text. In an early notebook, Ned Lambert is made to say of Bloom, "I don't think our friend does the trick of the loop at all," and everyone in Barney Kiernan's is aware of, and discusses freely, the fact that the Blooms have recently been contemplating divorce. *U. of Buffalo MSS*, "Cyclops" (Slocum & Cahoon 5, c).

7. The epithet was originally John Joyce's, applied by him to Canon Keon, as a note of Joyce's recalls (Cornell University Library Bound MS 35).

direction. When we come to see Molly's inmost thoughts, we find that not only does she express this indifferent and undiscriminating attraction to men, she has erotic fantasies about sailors and gypsies (p. 762), bathing boys (p. 760), the statue of Narcissus (p. 761), and practically anything masculine on her horizon.

There is nothing inconceivable about the character of a hard-bitten nymphomaniac, except that it does not fit very well with the other things we know about Molly Bloom, her character as shrewd, prudent, limited *Weib*. As Joyce very acutely remarked about her in an early note, "Earth knows which side her bread is buttered" (*British Museum Additional MSS #49975*, "Penelope"). Not only does the image of Molly as nymphomaniac muddle the novel on the emotional and moral levels; it rips and tangles the texture of physical possibilities as well. For if we accept Dillon, Dedalus, and Goodwin as occupants of Molly's bed, what shall we do about the gentleman of fashion in the Gaiety Theatre? She does not recall, she does not *know* his name; and at the time when he stared upon her charms, she was in the full tide of her period (p. 754). The possibility of her having been able to arrange a sexual affair with him, on some more opportune occasion, still without knowing his name, is so bizarre as to be quite out of the question.

The list as given on p. 716 has some other odd qualities. It includes Harry Mulvey, the first of Molly's lovers (his counterpart in real life was Willy Mulvey, the first of Nora Barnacle's admirers); but it does not include Lieutenant Stanley Gardner (pp. 731 and 733) who seems to have been quite as vigorously embroiled with her as anybody. It includes John Henry Menton, whom she actively dislikes ("of all the big stupoes I ever met and thats called a solicitor," p. 724); it includes Ben Dollard whom she despises ("grinning all over his big Dolly face like a wellwhipped childs botty didn't he look a balmy ballocks sure

enough," p. 759). It includes Alderman John Hooper, who gave
the Blooms a stuffed owl as a wedding present (p. 692); having
previously been an Alderman in Cork, and being presently
the father of Paddy Hooper, already well established as a reporter for the *Freeman's Journal*, he would have been an elderly
man indeed at any time within Molly's lifetime. It includes also
Pisser Burke, a derelict; two of Bloom's former employers, Wisdom Hely and Joe Cuffe; and "Maggot O'Reilly" about whom
we know only that once in the remote past he went on a picnic
with the Blooms, Mrs. Breen, and Mrs. Joe Gallaher. A major
quality of the list is evidently its miscellaneous, heterogeneous
character. If we suppose that all these men have been in Molly
Bloom's literal bed, we have certainly a notion of her undiscriminating receptivity; we are also faced with an expanding
number of problems regarding her emotional make-up and the
practical details of her activities.

At any point, of course, we are free to solve these problems
by saying that some of these men slept with Molly and others
didn't, and one major point of the passage is that it doesn't
make much difference. Molly exists in an atmosphere of sexual
provocation, her sexual appetites are literally insatiable, and the
men who have exchanged amiable leers with her are, on at least
one level, the same as the men who have possessed her sexually.
Certainly from Molly's point of view, all men are the same. We
learn this, if nowhere else, from her limitlessly multivalent use
of the masculine pronouns "he" and "him."

I do not myself feel that the author's vaunted knowledge of
feminine psychology is much in evidence here. A medieval
monk, with somewhat different emphases, might have told us
much the same thing, that woman is an overwhelmingly sexual
animal, and that (with very minor and superficial discrimina-
tions) she looks upon men only as so many machines to satisfy

her sexual needs. Women have not hastened to recognize themselves in this mirror. Joyce's feeling in the matter, as we now know from Mr. Ellmann, was not that of a medieval monk, but of a man severely disappointed because his non-intellectual wife did not pay sufficient tribute to his intellectual accomplishments. In his failure to transcend this rather specific situation, he has sharply limited his image of the female sex, and blurred the social texture of his novel.

Joyce's eye was so cold and clear in most of its social perceptions that we are ill-prepared to find it feverish, confused, and remarkably undiscriminating in this one. The portrait of Molly Bloom was painted by a devouringly jealous man, who used the object of his jealousy as a model. The author's personal anxieties and animosities, while they ring her figure with a halo of powerful polar feelings, have militated strongly against his characterization.

They have limited his characterization, that is, on the personal level, so far as Molly is regarded as the portrait of a woman. But she is many other things in the book. Like Bloom, she was created more by a process of projection than by one of accretion; she represents Joyce's fantasies and fears, as well as the prosaic details of an Irish housewife. As Penelope, she is a weaver, and there is a sort of Gargantuan humor (even a half-buried pun) in making her into a weaver of suitors. As a weaver, she is a spider; and Joyce in thinking about her went so far as to remind himself that "female spider devours male after" (*British Museum Additional MSS #49975*, "Penelope"). But this does not limit, it enhances Joyce's delight in her as mindless, natural, Bergsonian *élan vital*. By contrast with the haunted Stephen and her inhibited husband, she exemplifies creativity, fertility, and the love of life, on very much the terms sketched by A.E. in his article on "Religion and Love," *Dana* (June

1904), pp. 45-9. She is nothing less than the earth, turning on its axis.[8]

But of course the symbolic view of Molly is something of an evasion; during the greater part of the novel, she exists for the reader as a person, not a symbol; and it is idle to deny that as a person she does not achieve resolution. This effect may in itself be deliberate. One of Joyce's most persistent qualities in his fiction is an impulse to tantalize. Early in the *Portrait*, the

8. E. R. Steinberg, "A Book with a Molly in It," *James Joyce Review*, II, 1-2, 55-61, and J. M. Morse, "Molly Bloom Revisited," *James Joyce Miscellany II* (Carbondale, Illinois, 1959), pp. 139-49, vigorously deny that Molly is the earth or a fertility symbol. They do not find her agreeable enough or fertile enough. It is true that she is vulgar, slatternly, disapproves of Mrs. Purefoy, and yet has not produced much of a brood herself. But in the representational scale Joyce is using, Molly need not, indeed must not, behave like a model housekeeper and multiply like a rabbit. "Fertility symbol" is a rather clumsy concept here. Molly, like the perceptive reader, is properly horrified at the vision of Mrs. Purefoy blindly breeding brats into squalor. But this does not align her with the Anti-Fertility forces. Molly is lazy and ignorant and vulgar in her habits—but then Bloom, though undeniably a sun-god, isn't exactly the Apollo Belvedere. A symbol, in other words, need not be a paradigm, much less a paragon; an advantage of the symbolic method is that it does not have to be. Venus herself, if memory serves, was neither chaste, fruitful, nor domestic to any degree of admiration. It is odd that precisely on this point of Molly's being the Earth—planetary, uninterrupted, and common as the dirt underfoot—Joyce has left most explicit evidence of his intentions. Aside from the well-known letter to Budgen (*Letters*, pp. 169-70), there is the identification reproduced by Mr. Litz from the British Museum note-sheets, "MB = spinning Earth" (*The Art of James Joyce*, p. 46), and that reproduced above, p. 39. "Penelope," as Joyce told Budgen, is the *clou* of the book; and it is so precisely because it drives into intimate conjunction an affirmation of pure spiritual joy and the smudged vulgarity of the everyday. Joyce's special gift was the discovery of "the remarkable in the commonplace" (Ellmann, *JJ*, p. 163); he exercised it to most surprising effect in his relationship with Nora Barnacle. That relationship, with its astounding depths, contradictions, and ambivalences, was in many ways a model for the one which Joyce imagined between Bloom and Molly. To use one element of the contradiction to argue against the existence of the other is precisely to miss the point of their conjunction.

boy named Athy asks Stephen a riddle (*Portrait*, p. 24). When he fails to guess it Athy tells him the answer and then adds that there is another way to ask it. Stephen wants to know what this is and so (for what it is worth) does the reader, but Athy won't tell, so nobody ever finds out. This is a richly significant gesture; it is not only repeated but magnified in the representation of Molly. One is particularly intrigued to see that Joyce, who everywhere else delights to stand above the reader and tantalize him, here assumes the role of victim as well.

## Treachery

The young men whom Joyce describes congregating about the Martello Tower in Sandymount, University College in Stephen's Green, and the National Library in Kildare Street, are a remarkably competitive and suspicious group of fellows. Stealthy, furtive, and fierce to cherish a grudge, they eye one another with the legendary ferocity of Dobu tribesmen. Their quarrels and jealousies are intricately complicated by the fact that most of them are, or aspire to be, phrase-makers; and a great deal of bickering goes on, not only over the usual young-man topics, money and girls, but also over priority rights to a particularly telling phrase. Collectors, obsequious or condescending, assail Stephen Dedalus at every turn, waiting for the next gem to fall from his lips. He himself continually quotes other members of his circle. There is social anxiety here, and an evident desire to shine; there is also a curious assumption that what goes on among these young men, lounging about the street-corners or studying in a second-rate university, is bound to be of interest to posterity. Who discovered whose talent is often a latent and sometimes an overt question, and the always-anxious problem

of who is to play precursor to whose redeemer seems to be
uppermost in many minds.

So far as we can judge from independent reports, Joyce has
reproduced the society of his youth pretty accurately on this
score. Some of the jealousy which he transfers to other people
was apparently felt in real life by his brother Stanislaus, who
bitterly resented hearing his brother use upon others a fine
phrase which Stanislaus had himself incautiously given away
(Ellmann, *JJ*, p. 139). But part of it also is drawn direct from
nature. After a short period of friendship with Joyce, Gogarty
did find him exasperatingly defiant and demanding. At the
same time, Joyce applied ruthless moral pressure on Gogarty,
who did not want to be known as a fellow who had rejected
starving genius in its hour of need. This fierce yet covert struggle
for moral advantage culminated in the ten days of Joyce's residence in the Martello Tower (September 9-19, 1904), and provides some background for understanding the complex tangle
of feelings which surrounds the presentation of Buck Mulligan
in *Ulysses*.

In the first place, a palpable and no doubt deliberate confusion exists within the novel on the subject of money relations
between the two young men. When Stephen declares that he
gets paid today, Mulligan is delighted. "The school kip?" he
says, "How much? Four quid? Lend us one" (p. 12). Stephen
says listlessly, all right, if he wants it, he can have the money;
creating thereby an impression of his own lofty indifference to
mere mercenary concerns and Mulligan's greed. In his condescension, we see, Mulligan will let Stephen wear his second-
hand shoes and trousers, but he will also put out a free Bohemian hand for Stephen's wages and spend them on drink. He
wants the key of the Tower, on which Stephen has paid the
rent (p. 24). Clearly, he is presented as a sponger on the material level, besides being a parasite on the intellectual plane. Thus

it comes as a bit of a surprise to learn (on p. 31) that Stephen owes Mulligan "nine pounds, three pairs of socks, one pair brogues, ties." Mulligan's request, "Lend us one," makes no sense at all in this context; when you lend money to your creditor, you are in effect repaying him. In point of historical fact, Mr. Ellmann has shown, it was Gogarty who paid the rent on the Martello Tower [9]—not that this bit of history should enter into the novel, except so far as it seems oddly uncharacteristic of Stephen to pay out twelve quid cash rent at a time when he owes nearly £17 in cash to various people, plus five weeks' board to Mrs. McKernan, in addition to assorted lunches and items of clothing. Indeed, the Stephen we encounter in *Ulysses* has not seen twelve unencumbered quid in a long time. After starving in Paris, he has for some months done nothing in Dublin. His teeth are decaying in his mouth, his clothes are borrowed, his family is in wretched want, and, bohemian as his tastes doubtless are, he is not the sort of person to squander twelve quid on the rent of an empty tower. In fact, he is allowed to

9. Gogarty says (*It Isn't This Time of Year At All*, p. 86) that Joyce "stumped up the rent from a prize of twenty pounds that he had won in some examination." But there is no record of Joyce's winning such a prize during the period when he was back from Paris, and it would have been curious behavior indeed to spend such a windfall on rent for the Tower. Though always imprudent about money, Joyce was never at this period imprudent on such a magnificent scale. Gogarty, never reliable in matters of detail, says further (p. 87) that he and Joyce lived for two years in the Tower. This is clearly impossible, since Joyce was only in Ireland for eighteen months all told, between the time he returned from Paris and the time he departed with Nora. Actually, there is no evidence to show that he spent, or could have spent, more than 10 days in the Tower as a resident. Gogarty, one would guess, was trying to make as much as possible of his association with Joyce. Joyce, on the other hand, may have had some interest in concealing from Nora and others the extent of a dependence on Gogarty which he felt to be humiliating. For whatever reasons, he apparently received mail and sent it as from his Aunt Josephine's (103 North Strand Road, Fairview), even while living at the Tower. He wrote to Nora only once (September 10) on Tower stationery.

think only once of the rent he has supposedly paid, and then rather baldly, as if making a mechanical point.

As an accounting statement, then, and also as a psychological document, the novel contains contrary indications; but I am not inclined to lay great stress on them. Joyce wanted to create the impression of Stephen's ill-treatment at the hands of a callous usurper. Mulligan should be given all the material advantages and none of the moral ones.[10] So the money he has loaned to Dedalus is slipped into an unemphatic corner of the book, while the gifts of humiliating second-hand clothing contrast, in the foreground, with Stephen's careless generosity in handling real money. For what it is worth, the real-life relations between

10. Solemn moral accountants have calculated that Mulligan commits, symbolically or actually, most of the deadly sins in the course of the morning of June 16. Joyce, according to this view, was making conscious use of a moral structure derived from St. Augustine, which would show Mulligan as No Good and Dedalus as All Right. Actually, the distinction between the two characters is much less mechanical and heavy-minded than this view implies. Dedalus is sensitive and Mulligan is not, but this sort of distinction doesn't show up at all on St. Augustine's scale of values. One might as well try to measure a quart of milk with a yardstick.

More broadly speaking, a writer of novels who wishes his reader to assume a point of view as special as that of St. Augustine is under some obligation to make this demand explicit and its applications clear. If we are going to tick off Mulligan for gluttony in eating his breakfast, sloth in not getting the milk, and so forth, we shall have to fill the novel with excuses to exculpate Stephen from the same, or similar, or worse failings. St. Augustine's moral machinery, admirable in a theologian, would have to contribute much more than it does to Joyce's fiction to be worth the heavy load of explanation that it imposes.

In the other direction, and with rather more force, it has been urged that Mulligan's failings toward Stephen are not very plain—that the words he is said to have spoken, however rough and thoughtless, do not constitute the sort of offense over which one breaks friendship. Joyce may have sensed this himself, and expressed it in a grotesquely subtle juxtaposition. On p. 9 Stephen looks at Bray Head, which in fact cannot be seen from the Tower, and then turns to talk about Mulligan's offense, which, one may be intended to gather, isn't visible to the naked eye, either.

the two men always involved the flow of money from Gogarty who had it to Joyce who didn't. As late as December 2, 1907, Gogarty was offering to pay Joyce's fare on a trip to Athens— no doubt this is the basis of the trip mentioned on p. 6 of *Ulysses*.

Money is manipulated, thus, to throw an unfavorable light on Mulligan; and if the different stories Joyce tells are not precisely consistent, one must take a pretty narrow view of truth to be worried by them. More interesting and complex are the views which Joyce takes, or allows us to take, of Mulligan's motivation. He offers at one point to make common cause with Stephen against Haines and some unnamed others, in the interests of Hellenizing the island (pp. 8-9); but a six-year-old could see that Stephen is not much of an ally in this project, and in fact Mulligan tells Haines so in the D.B.C. (p. 245). Further, Mulligan's program for Hellenizing the island and installing a new paganism along the verbal lines of Oscar Wilde does not accord very well with his wary gestures of superstitious or derisive respect toward the clergy (pp. 23-4). Bloom suggests at one point (p. 605) that Mulligan is out to pick Stephen's brains, but this idea does not accord with his frank mockery of Stephen's theories, or his attempt to leave Stephen in the lurch at Westland Row. Some of these paradoxes are doubtless deliberate. Bawdy in manner, Mulligan is conventional at heart, while Stephen inverts the antithesis. Hence, while Dedalus is coldly devoted to the inner discipline of his art, Mulligan is casual and opportunistic. But the Buck's disorder goes so deep that his character falls into no clear focus; we do not have much notion of what he is up to, he merely capers.

If Mulligan is mostly a manner, Vincent Lynch is only an action. He appears in *Ulysses* for the first time late in the book, simply in order to abandon Stephen in his hour of need. Why does he do so? Not visibly more cowardly or self-seeking than the average, not particularly trusted by Stephen, Lynch behaves in *Ulysses* almost automatically, as if carrying out a pre-established pattern. He has been parasitic on Stephen, at Burke's and in Nighttown; he sneaks off when Stephen is in trouble, and his cowardice is nicely underlined by Cissy Caffrey's plaintive, funny plea, "I'm faithful to the man that's treating me though I'm only a shilling whore" (p. 572). But as Lynch has not been in any evident sense a disciple, it is hard to envision him as a genuine Judas. Joyce's art is often unclimactic in this way; the little, ill-defined betrayal in Beaver Street can stand for many bigger and clearer betrayals, and the fact that it is performed without a demonstrated personal motivation shows how inevitable it is.[11] We may learn from Ellmann's biography (*JJ*, pp. 156-7, 288-90) what actions by Vincent Cosgrave qualified him for the role of Judas; *Ulysses* presents us only with a moral darkness, a moving and dramatic void.

I have suggested that the act of treachery was hard for Joyce to dramatize or motivate properly; one reason was that he generally saw himself as the predestined victim, and the whole incident as cosmically inevitable, and so more impressive if performed without personal motivation on the part of Judas. Stephen's Judas-drama is always enacted without benefit of the

---

11. The most distinct but illogical betrayer of Stephen Dedalus is Cranly in the *Portrait*. It is several times suggested (*Portrait*, pp. 273, 296) that he has supplanted Stephen in the favor of that shadowy young lady, E.C. This would be a betrayal indeed, for Cranly is not only a disciple, he has accepted and still maintains the role of precursor to Stephen's redeemer. But Stephen's suspicions of betrayal are pretty dimly founded, and there is no effort to explain what Cranly thinks he is up to in ostentatiously betraying with one hand the redeemer he creates with the other. That Joyce *did* think Byrne had betrayed him we learn from his letter to Nora (Ellmann, *JJ*, p. 177). It is all the more curious that he should be asking Byrne for intimate advice on personal matters a few days later (Ellmann, *JJ*, p. 181). Apparently, Joyce was completely puzzled by what he saw or imagined of Byrne's behavior in real life, and simply transferred his confusion and his speculations about it into the *Portrait*.

thirty pieces of silver. Either the reward is itself unclearly defined, or we do not see how the betrayal of Stephen Dedalus will lead Judas any closer to it. Joyce saw in the "betrayal" of Parnell, and the "betrayal" of Oscar Wilde, analogies of his own suffering, the same pure, disinterested malice of which he thought himself the predestined victim. It is hard not to sense a touch of paranoia here. Likely, Joyce's presentation of Judas is most effective where, as with Lynch, it is left darkest and most enigmatic.

# 3

## Piling, Scaffold, Adornment

The liberal use which Joyce made of "pilings"—figures drawn
from real life, upon whose more or less buried support he erected
the structure of his fiction—gives us good occasion to appreciate
the mingled subtlety and boldness with which he controlled his
materials. No general rules seem to cover the complex transformations which he now and then imposed on these materials;
sometimes we find him elaborately circumstantial about the
surroundings of an imaginary character; sometimes he presents
only those few elements of a real character which make it seem
not only imaginary, but actually caricatured. He divides, he
multiplies, he adds, he subtracts; he draws freely upon the resources of an encyclopedic memory, upon the memories of his
friends and relations, and upon a vast, undirected store of miscellaneous reading. The unevenness of his practice in matters
of fact is the more likely to throw a reader off balance because
he never explains, and because, in the matter of individualizing
details, he is remarkably sparing.

It may seem strange to describe Joyce, whose tissue of social fact is so richly woven, as a sparse author. But in the matter of individual characterization, and in *Ulysses* particularly, he writes a very bare prose indeed. There are a whole group of men who are scarcely distinguished from one another—the cronies of Simon Dedalus. Ned Lambert, John Power, John Wyse Nolan, Martin Cunningham, Tom Kernan, Paddy Leonard, J. G. Lidwell, Joe Hynes, Crofter the Orangeman, and C. P. McCoy are very much men of a piece. Tom Kernan is perhaps the most highly individualized of the lot; [1] we know some of his favorite expressions, and have an idea of his strutting, pompous manner. But the rest of Simon's cronies flow together with scarcely a distinguishing peculiarity of speech or appearance. Lidwell is a lawyer and Nolan a journalist, John Power and Martin Cunningham (whom we know pretty well from "Grace") have domestic difficulties somewhere in the middle distance, and McCoy is something close to a derelict, but really, if we were not told, we should not know who was speaking at any given point, and if we met a group of these men on the street, we should not be able to distinguish one from the others. This is not a reproach or complaint; the Dubliners whom Joyce is representing all wear the commonplace uniform of the age and talk the commonplace dialect of Dublin. They are not supposed to be striking individuals, and Joyce's abstention from exterior description leaves them almost completely uncharacterized. Upon this neutral background, the small, telling fact sometimes stands out as

1. The question has been debated whether Kernan's stream of consciousness is or is not radically different from Bloom's. There is no doubt that isolated passages may be cited to show that he is really duller and less imaginative than Poldy; but certainly it is not a very startling difference. One wonders why, if he is a complete dullard, he should be given, as a catch-phrase, the words which best describe *Ulysses* itself—a "retrospective arrangement." I concede that this is something of a problem, however clever or stupid we consider Kernan.

if etched in fire; Father Bob Cowley's first action, for example, is to stroke nervously the moustache which he would not have if he were a real priest (p. 240). Where so small an act can mean so much, the shadings which Joyce imposed or failed to impose on his borrowings from real life have a special interest, for every least flicker of action or description is potentially significant.

## Mrs. Sinico's Accident; Miss Lizzie Twigg, and other Figures of Fun

When he was writing *Dubliners*, Joyce was understandably cautious about using the actual names of specific people in contexts which might prove even remotely embarrassing to them. The technique of using real names in a work of fiction was unusual in itself, and the almost psychotic suspicions which it provoked in readers and publishers of *Dubliners* would have been enough to discourage a man less stubborn than Joyce from using it at all. Consequently, he took some pains to disguise the originals of his characters and the episodes on which his stories were modeled, wherever they took him outside the reach of his own family, or into the range of a possible libel suit. He did not conceal the originals of his characters, scenes, and episodes as carefully as he told George Roberts he had done; but he did conceal them. Thus we must penetrate a rather tangled hedge of transformations and transpositions in order to relate Mrs. Sinico's fatal accident (in "A Painful Case") to its real-life original. The *Freeman's Journal* for July 14, 1904, contained on p. 5 an account of a fatal accident at Sydney Parade Station, in which Mrs. Sarah Bishop, the station-master's wife, was knocked down by a slowly moving train of the Dublin and Kingstown Railway. Taken to St. Michael's Hospital in Kingstown, she died shortly after admission. In adapting this episode to "A Painful Case," Joyce modified some of the circumstances to sort with the facts of his story. Mrs. Bishop was eighty years old; Joyce's character had to be less, and he made her forty-three. The incident in real life took place at 3 o'clock in the afternoon, and there was no suggestion of intemperance on Mrs. Bishop's part; Joyce made it happen at 10 o'clock at night, when his heroine was wandering about under the influence of drink. Joyce's newspaper story condenses into one item both the accident and the autopsy, which in real life took place two days apart. Finally, Joyce has done something to alter the names of minor personalities in the case, though the originals still peep out a bit. For instance, he calls the engine-driver James Lennon; the news story calls him James Flynn; but the acting guard of the train, according to the paper, was Edward Lennon (*Freeman's Journal*, Saturday, July 16, 1904, p. 3). In fact, Joyce took from the *Freeman's Journal* nothing but the manner of Mrs. Sinico's death and a few of the attendant circumstances. Though drab and conventional, the newspaper story did not use the specific formula "a painful case"; and the human part of the story (Mr. Duffy's alienation from the world and the one person who could bring him into contact with it) is based upon an episode related to Joyce by his brother Stanislaus (*My Brother's Keeper*, pp. 159-60). Mrs. Sinico's name comes from that of a Trieste musician; Stanislaus thought that Mr. Duffy's name derived from a memory of a certain Pisser Duffy, with whom young Stanny had a fight in Drumcondra (*My Brother's Keeper*, p. 54), but it also makes sardonic allusion to a well-known Dublin publisher with strong ecclesiastical connections, James Duffy & Co.[2]

2. His brother's rather sour isolation from life evidently struck Joyce as analogous to clerical celibacy; and he would have got a special wry relish

Reduced to its elements, the indebtedness of "A Painful Case" to the *Freeman's Journal* is, thus, unimpressive. Whatever Joyce got from the newspaper, he combined with other elements, to the point where we can barely discern the basic relationship. Yet I do not think that without the cruel, remorseless rhythm of the Kingstown line's slow freight, the study could have been quite so memorable; and the train is the one thing (aside from its own drabness) which the news-story clearly contributed.

Writing *Dubliners* with the anticipation that it would be published in Dublin itself, Joyce naturally took some precautions to avoid obvious identifications. But *Ulysses*, written at great distances both of time and space from the city it describes, handles real persons, places, and incidents with a somewhat bolder touch. In the section known as "Lestrygonians," for example, Mr. Bloom reflects on one of the answers which he has received to an advertisement inserted in the *Irish Times*. His appeal for a "smart lady typist to aid gentleman in literary work" (p. 157) has already drawn forty-four responses, but the one he particularly recalls came from a poetical lady named "Lizzie Twigg." In explaining her qualifications, she had declared, "My literary efforts have had the good fortune to meet with the approval of the eminent poet A.E. (Mr Geo Russell)" (p. 158). Bloom is not much interested in the lady's accomplishments in the field of letters, indeed they are a good deal too extensive for what he has in mind, and he imagines her

---

out of an ecclesiastical name applied to a figure representing the ferociously anticlerical Stanislaus.

Pisser Burke, who finally wound up in possession of the unlovely nickname, was originally known as Stink Burke; in early versions, some of his functions as an observer around the City Arms Hotel were fulfilled by a character known as "Gaffney." *U. of Buffalo MSS*, "Cyclops."

as a rather repellent bluestocking: "No time to do her hair drinking sloppy tea with a book of poetry." Later he meets her in the street, or at least he sees a woman whom he supposes to be Lizzie Twigg, as she is walking along beside A.E. listening to him talk occultism. What Bloom notes chiefly is that her stockings are loose over her ankles (p. 163).

In reading this episode, one generally takes for granted that Lizzie Twigg is an imaginary personage. For one thing, her name has all the marks of being invented for the occasion; for another, Joyce would seem to be using outsize artillery on very small game indeed in employing his novel to mock a woman with the sensitivities of a poet on the score of her personal appearance and her names. This, however, he has done. Miss Lizzie Twigg was a real person, who published verses in the *United Irishman* for February 7, 1903, pp. 6 and 7, and in the issue for June 6, 1903, pp. 2 and 3. Under her Gaelic name of Elis ni Chraoibhin she published also a volume of *Songs and Poems*, which appeared in 1905. Like most young literary people in Dublin, she was a protégée of A.E.'s; Joyce himself, aspiring to this position, felt he had not been received according to his merits, and thus had some reason to show Stephen jeering at cults. In any event, Lizzie Twigg was not an exclusive or esoteric cultist, for, as her publishing in the *United Irishman* suggests, she was an ardent Irish Nationalist. Joyce himself found the bitter but vigorous patriotism of Griffith's paper attractive (though he had reservations about all chauvinism), and read it often in his Trieste retreat. None of these considerations, however, prevented him from scarifying Lizzie Twigg in his novel. In fact, she was not even a particularly bad poet, but he found her name irresistibly funny, and having determined that she would be a blue-stocking, made over her appearance to suit his purposes.

Her ridiculous name was for Joyce the only real thing about
Lizzie Twigg. No doubt he felt some jealous contempt for
feminine artists, as for the idea of female priests; his preference
was always for considering woman a sexual animal rather than
a rational or sensitive human being. In addition, he resented
A.E. and his bevy of literary acolytes with the special arrogance
of a lonely man. These preoccupations of his own he projected
freely into the figure of Lizzie Twigg; the qualities which she
had as a person in her own right he ruthlessly truncated. That
he needed to retain the name, unaltered and undisguised, and
had so little use for the person accidentally attached to it is a
striking feature of his compositional selectivity.[3]

Even more striking is Joyce's action in co-opting the name
of Grissel Steevens as that of a woman supposed to have given
birth to a pig-headed monster (p. 404). In fact, Grissel Steevens
herself was widely but unjustly reputed to have been born with
the features of a pig. She was the sister of Richard Steevens,
a physician who in the early eighteenth century left his estate
to found Steevens' Hospital in Dublin. Actually, the money
was left to Grissel with a proviso that after her death it be
applied to the hospital; but, instead of forcing the project to
wait during her life, she voluntarily surrendered her interest in
the money so that construction could begin in 1710. Heartened

3. Another notable instance of his indifference to personal feelings involves
Dr. George Salmon. He was a mathematician of genuine distinction and
liberal sentiments, who for many years till 1904 was Provost of Trinity
College. Dr. Salmon died on January 22, 1904, and was succeeded by a
lesser and less liberal figure of the Protestant Establishment, Anthony Traill.
Traill was a familiar administrative type, an ex-athlete with expanded
muscles and limited ideas; he would have been a more fitting object of
Joyce's satiric comment than Dr. Salmon. But his name was not such easy
fun. Joyce revived Dr. Salmon from the grave, and kept him alive in *Ulysses*,
so that Bloom could play little games with his no doubt eminently humorous
name.

by this good deed, she survived till 1746, when she died at the age of 93. Needless to say, she did not have the features of a pig. The fable grew up that, as her mother had been cursed by a disappointed beggar, Grissel was born deformed; it flourished on the mild circumstance that she often wore a shawl. As the myth became popular during her lifetime, she took rather pathetic steps to counteract it, by sitting at an open window and having her portrait painted. This picture still hangs in the hospital board-room, and though it shows the lady as heavy-set indeed, is not especially piggish. But the story has flourished since (the Irish have a way of dealing unkindly with their benefactors), and Joyce happily included both name and fable in his fiction, simply because he found them grisly.

There are a couple of occasions in *Ulysses* when characters resort to that happy hunting ground of the onomatophile, the obit column, and Joyce's handling of the details in these lists offers a couple of curiosities. Bloom's reading (on p. 90) of the *Freeman* obituaries for June 16 is wholly imaginary. The list he reads does not correspond in any way with the actual one. Joyce either invented his list or copied it from some other source. On the other hand, when the Citizen is protesting against all the English names in the *Irish Independent* (p. 293), he reads them off from the actual birth, death, and marriage columns of that paper's issue of June 16. Every name which he reads is recognizably in the day's paper, though he makes a good many errors of transcription ("Carr" for "Cann," "Playwood" for "Haywood," "Whitehall lane, London" for "Whitehorse lane, Thornton Heath, London," and the like) and some dozen omissions, mostly random.

One name, however, comes up for particular mention; it is "Cockburn, at the Moat house, Chepstow."

—I know that fellow, says Joe, from bitter experience (p. 293).

At least for the clean-minded reader, this sardonic interjection might be a reference to bad debts, personal animus, or the like; but, looking over the Citizen's shoulder at the *Irish Independent*, we see that "Cockburn" was historically Frances Mary, who died June 10, 1904, in the sixtieth year of her age. It is not a great addition to the reader's understanding of *Ulysses* that Joe is seen to be referring to a case of venereal infection; perhaps it says something about Joyce's haphazard sensibilities that he is willing to sacrifice so many of the amenities for a passing pun. We are confirmed in our view of this transaction when the French translation of *Ulysses* (which Joyce personally supervised), after giving all the other names of the list in their English originals, renders "Cockburn" as "Chaudelance."

Curious complications also arise around the original character and fictional representation of Jack Power, who first appears in the pages of *Dubliners* in the role of Mr. Kernan's guide and support. He is employed with the Dublin Municipal Police; he is handsome, fairly successful, and reported to be on his way up the social scale, as Mr. Kernan is on the way down. His father, we learn on page 160, was a G-man, i.e. a plain-clothesman attached to the G-division of the police force. He is of course distinct from the journalist whose name in the novel is John Wyse Nolan (he was Power in real life). I think we may identify Jack Power with Mr. John Power who inhabited 34 Rutland Street Upper until his death on 14 September, 1919, at the age of fifty-four. He was a D. M. P. pensioner, and a son of the late Pierce and Anastatia Power, of Fermor, Tramore; the identification is helped out by the fact that Pierce Power is found in the records of the Royal Irish Constabulary.

Now a rather circumstantial story is told about the Jack Power in *Ulysses* both by Bloom and by his wife, to the effect that he kept in Platonic splendor a barmaid from the Moira or Jury Hotel, to whom he was sometimes seen bringing a pound of rumpsteak (p. 92).[4] Clearly, this is not the sort of story which can be verified at the distance of half a century. More importantly, it has no narrative connection with anything else in *Ulysses*, no discernible symbolic import, and decorative effect in about the same measure as any three random lines from a gossip column. Lizzie Twigg at least contributed a funny name to the novel; Jack Power and his barmaid look like nothing more than a gratuitous bit of scandal.[5]

Most curious of all is the fact that both Joyce and his brother Stanislaus, disregarding the man who contributed his name to "Jack Power," identify the original figure as Tom Devin (letter to Alfred Bergan, May 23, 1937, in Ellmann, *JJ*, p. 718; *My Brother's Keeper*, p. 41). Devin was an old friend of the Joyce family, who appears in *Ulysses* under his own name and in company with his two daughters. Joyce's children were visiting with the Devins in Dublin when *Ulysses* was published (*Letters of James Joyce*, p. 191); and Joyce blandly identified him as the original of Jack Power at the moment when Devin had just died.

These curious circumstances present us with two somewhat uncomfortable alternatives. If Devin was the original of Jack Power, Joyce managed to remain on good terms with a man for fifteen years after publishing to the world an intimate, not to say disgraceful, detail of his private life. If John Power was the original figure in behavior as he was in name, the identification with Devin is in the nature of a smokescreen. I think I can guess which of these alternatives is more probable. But the main

---

4. A MS version of "Circe" (*U. of Buffalo MSS*, Slocum & Cahoon 5,b,xi) shows that Bloom's fantasies on breach of promise (p. 280) were originally intermingled with the story of Jack Power and his barmaid.
5. Had we ever seen the career of Mr. John Power as outwardly respectable, there might be some dramatic point to revealing it as inwardly corrupt. But Mr. Power's curious addiction to the Moira barmaid is as undramatic as a case of shingles. That is, it may, and doubtless does, have a certain symptomatic interest.

point is that Joyce could not refrain from hanging this queer story on the name of one of two identifiable men, despite the fact that it served no clear novelistic effect to do so. The only effect of a "curious" story like this, illustrating an unexplained oddity or quirk of human nature, is to make the reader think it must be true. "That's the way life is"—it inspires reflections not much loftier than this. Joyce seems to have needed, more than most novelists, this sense of actual fact underlying his episodes and characters; he gives us the odd, quirky detail to buttress our sense, and perhaps his own, of the actual.

Pilings are buried and disappear under a finished structure; scaffoldings sometimes remain, to clutter and embarrass a reader. But Joyce also used actual figures in his fiction as decorations, as appliqué. Above all, as he gained in confidence and felt himself more and more liberated from the confines of Dublin society, we find him inserting Dublin names freely into his text, without much concern as to whether they are respectable, or for that matter comprehensible in context. The story on p. 85 of Jack Fleming who gambled, embezzled, absconded, and now keeps a hotel in America (*facilis descensus Averni*) was a late addition in proof; so was the scandalous story of Walter Bapty (p. 276). On p. 94, the entire paragraph which begins, "Dead side of the street, this," and proceeds to list (out of *Thom's Directory*, 1904) the various shop-fronts was also a late addition; so was the editor's reference to "Jakes McCarthy" (p. 134); so was Bloom's memory of seeing Mrs. Miriam Dandrade "in the viceregal party when Stubbs the park ranger got me in with Whelan of the *Express*" (p. 158); and so was Mr. Dudley White, B.L., M.A., who stands in a curious quandary on p. 248. Most of these figures seem to be tossed into the book without much concern whether they are either scandalous or comprehensible to the reader; they represent an increasingly bold imposition of raw Dublin materials on the book. One would guess that they mark Joyce's increasing assurance that he is writing for a cosmopolitan audience which will be amused by local scandal and tolerant of, or intrigued by, a fictional surface roughened by random particulars which it does not understand.

## Matthew Kane and Paddy Dignam

Paddy Dignam, whose funeral Bloom attended on June 16, is an imaginary person, living, like Bloom, at an address (9 Newbridge Avenue, Sandymount) which, though real, was in actual fact vacant in 1904. Paddy Dignam's former employer, John Henry Menton, was a real person, with a real office at 27 Bachelor's Walk, where *Ulysses* locates it. The friends of Paddy Dignam include a number of real people, generally under fictional names—for instance, Martin Cunningham (Matthew F. Kane), Tom Kernan (R. J. Thornton), Simon Dedalus (John S. Joyce), Jack Power (John Power, D.M.P., and perhaps Tom Devin), and Ned Lambert (who despite a variety of enticing clues continues to elude identification). The family does its shopping at Tunney's, a real store at 8 Bridge Street, Ringsend, and at Mangan's, late Fehrenbach's, at 1 and 2 William Street. Among the neighborhood ladies condoling with Mrs. Dignam, Joyce mentions Mrs. Stoer, Mrs. Quigley, and Mrs. MacDowell (p. 247). The latter is no doubt Gerty's mother, whoever she was (there were a number of families by this name in Sandymount). There was a family of Quigleys at Belton Terrace, just off the South Circular at Dolphin's Barn. And Mrs. Stoer could be the wife either of F. H. Stoer, Esq., 83 Tritonville Road, Sandymount, or of John Stoer, manager of the Dublin Tar Company, Newgrove House, Sandymount. Paddy Dignam went to confession to Father Bernard Conroy, supposed to be the brother of Gabriel (the journalist, who is protagonist of "The

Dead"), at the Sandymount church. Bernard Conroy was indeed and in real life curate at the Star of the Sea church—a real curate of a real church, with an imaginary brother.[6]

Thus Paddy Dignam is an imaginary creature, surrounded by and related to all sorts of very specific social reality. In terms of the novel, it matters not at all who Mrs. Stoer is; Joyce evidently cared only to associate Dignam with a specifically Sandymount family. Much of his information about Sandymount society doubtless came from his Aunt Josephine, who had spent years in it; he used his names and circumstances carefully to set Paddy Dignam in his exact milieu. Yet Paddy himself remains a most shadowy creation. One reason for this is no doubt the fact that the materials for his character were derived from another character in *Ulysses*, the man who is shown making himself most responsible for poor Paddy Dignam's surviving children. This was Matthew F. Kane, who is Martin Cunningham in the novel.

Kane was Chief Clerk of the Crown Solicitor's Office in the Castle. On July 10, 1904, he went swimming from a boat off Kingstown, and suffered a stroke, dying in the water. His body was recovered by his companions, and buried in Glasnevin out of Kingstown; thus the funeral cortège proceeded through Dublin from southeast to northwest, along the lines of that in the novel. Like Dignam (p. 100), Matthew Kane had five children, all of whom were very young (he himself was not yet forty). He also had a great many friends, who assembled for the funeral. Among them, according to the *Freeman's Journal* (Thursday, July 14, 1904, p. 2), were J. S. Joyce, J. A. Joyce, A.B., and Charles P. Joyce—as well as John Wyse Power, Alf Bergan, Alfred H. Hunter, Tom Devin, Long John Clancy (Fanning

6. Gabriel Conroy's brother was named Constantine in "The Dead"; Joyce, finding a Conroy at the Star of the Sea, altered the name he had already given, and rebaptized Gabriel's brother as Bernard.

in the novel), J. H. Menton, and Sir Frederick Falkiner, all well known, of old, to students of *Ulysses*. Prayers were said at the graveside by the Reverend Father Coffey. After the funeral, a meeting was held, at which a sum of money was subscribed to take care of the dead man's children. Unlike its counterpart in the novel, Matthew Kane's funeral was well attended, and the fund for the support of his children was generously subscribed. Matthew Kane had been widely popular, and was much respected by his associates and superiors in the Castle, as well as in the community at large. In adapting his funeral to that of Paddy Dignam, Joyce's chief problem was exclusion, diminution, and reduction; one sees that he has succeeded in producing a kind of ghost-figure, a literary vestige which retains nothing definite in its personality except Elpenor's fiery face. Having used up Matthew Kane's real-life wife in the dipsomaniac figure of Mrs. Martin Cunningham (Stanislaus Joyce, *My Brother's Keeper*, pp. 225-6), he was obliged to create a sorrowing widow for Paddy Dignam; and here too his imagination did not extend much beyond the conventional. He gave her a snub nose, a sniffly manner, a brood of brats—and nothing else.

The mournful ghost of little Paddy Dignam, created only in the article of death, and most poignant in the fading, characterless, condescending affection he evokes, haunts the world of *Ulysses*. While Stephen mourns his mother, Bloom mourns Paddy Dignam; and the black clothing, which is the outward and visible sign of a shared inner awareness, unites them symbolically long before their minds actually meet. Baudelaire has said, with a rare insight which may have more to do with Paddy Dignam than Matthew F. Kane ever had, that "nous célébrons tous quelque enterrement." Bloom celebrates in Dignam a death which is, in every sense of the word, common; Joyce celebrates in both of them the lot of the ignobly decent, the universality of the unmemorable. The death of Matthew F. Kane, because it was a better "subject," a more striking incident in itself, with more "points," was for the novel an impossibility. Not only the narrative, but also the symbolic "points" of the episode had to be deliberately subdued. We note with passing curiosity that Joyce blithely deleted from the novel a death by water, such as an alert archetypalist would have gone far out of his way to introduce. (Not that he discarded it permanently; the drowning of Martin Cunningham found its final resting-place in *Finnegans Wake*, p. 387 ff.) For the special purposes of *Ulysses*, he converted Paddy Dignam into a low-keyed preachment on temperance themes. The compulsive drinkers who populate the novel, and whose mores are so carefully studied in the "Cyclops" chapter, exist against the background of Paddy Dignam's instructive demise.[7] Richie Goulding and Myles Crawford are next in line, and Molly Bloom, with her usual instinctive, female prudence, sums up the matter concisely: "and they call that friendship killing and then burying one another" (p. 758). For Joyce's own ambivalent attitude toward drinking, see Mr. Ellmann's biography, *passim*.

## Music, Musicians, and Some Other Performers

Even when he alters their names, Joyce rarely fails to leave some sort of clue to the originals of his characters; whether it leads anywhere in terms of the novel, in terms of the biography,

7. A psychological mechanism, almost didactic in its baldness, and so most unusual for Joyce, is that which leads Stephen to translate his feelings of inferiority before Daniel O'Connell into an offer to buy drinks for the whole newspaper office (p. 142). And—given the circumstances under which the song is sung in *Ulysses*—one is almost bound to think that Joyce intended an ironic counterpoint on the last stanza of "The Boys of Wexford," which begins, "My curse upon all drinking—'twas that that brought us down."

or in terms of Dublin as a city, is another matter. Ben Dollard
is described as having been a ship-chandler before he went
bankrupt drinking #1 Bass (p. 279). Out of three original firms
of Dublin ship-chandlers open for business in 1880, only one
went bankrupt; that was the firm of George and William J.
Merritt, which disappears from *Thom's Directory* between 1887
and 1888. Not only does the firm disappear as a firm; a Mrs.
Merritt disappears in the same year from her address at 55
Rathmines Avenue. Bloom thinks, anachronistically, that Ben
Dollard is living in the Iveagh home in 1904 (the Iveagh hostel,
which would have been a natural refuge for a penniless man,
was not opened till 1906; it served for a while to shelter John
S. Joyce—see the letter in the Cornell University Library from
Charles to Stanislaus Joyce, September 6, 1912). In fact,
whether his name was George or William J. Merritt, and wherever or however he survived, the original of Ben Dollard left no
other record of himself—as Dublin paupers usually neglect to
do. Probably his fictional name comes from the Dollard Print-
ing House, a landmark of central Dublin in 1904 as it is today.

Our search for the original of Ben Dollard thus peters out
in the slummy side-streets of a derelict's Dublin. But some hints
for his singing of "The Croppy Boy" may have been gleaned
from a concert given by William Ludwig, the celebrated Dublin
basso, on June 8, 1897; for next day, the *Freeman's Journal*
described the occasion in its best lyrical prose. "The effect of
his singing a ballad of '98, 'The Croppy Boy,' was electrical.
The rude and simple ballad became in his hands a highly
dramatic episode. Tender, soft, and beautiful were the opening phrases in the song, but full of fire and vehemence was the
dramatic conclusion. The pent-up feelings of the audience could
not be fully controlled, and burst after burst of cheering went
up at the concluding verses" (*Freeman's Journal*, June 10, 1897,
p. 6). At this concert also appeared a young tenor named

Melfort D'Alton. Mr. Ellmann is doubtless right in thinking one of the originals of Bartell D'Arcy to have been Barton McGuckin, who admired John Joyce's voice, according to fond family tradition, and had misgivings about his own. But for all his inner misgivings, Barton McGuckin was a prime favorite with Dublin opera audiences, and a first-string professional, whom the Carl Rosa management engaged for special performances when they visited Dublin. The pictures of him which survive (there is one on page 10 of the *Weekly Freeman* for March 11, 1911, and a better one in E. MacDowell Cosgrave, *Dublin and County Dublin in the 20th Century*, London, 1908, p. 243) show a man as magisterial in his port and expression as William J. McKinley himself. This is most unlike our image of Mr. Bartell D'Arcy. But Mr. Melfort D'Alton, aside from the resemblance of names, striking in itself, was just about on the professional level assigned to Mr. Bartell D'Arcy. He sang the sort of Irish folksongs which Bartell D'Arcy is represented as singing, whereas Barton McGuckin was an operatic tenor; and he was never a top-flight singer, though he continued to teach music in Dublin for many years.[8] Molly would have been critically most unfair in referring to Barton McGuckin's voice as "tinny" (p. 730), but not if she were thinking of someone like Melfort D'Alton. Condescension from a singer of Molly's professional standing (see below, p. 75) implies something close to downright incompetence.

One final particular, which points in a different direction altogether, at least as far as Bartell D'Arcy's last name is con-

8. A poem of Gogarty's suggests that he was also something of a ladies' man:

> Melfort Dalton, I knew you well
> With your frozen eyes and your spastic stance;
> Ah, but your voice was clear as a bell
> When you tenored the ladies into a trance.

"To an Old Tenor," *Collected Poems* (London, 1951), p. 103.

cerned. At the opening of the Dublin Cycle Show, January 22, 1894, there was a grand miscellaneous concert, announced on p. 4 of the *Freeman's Journal* for that day. Among the artistes, mostly amateurs, were Mrs. Charles Chance under her performing name, Madame Marie Tallon (she is recognized as having contributed something to Molly Bloom), and Mr. F. P. D'Arcy. So it may be that the original of Bartell D'Arcy was another D'Arcy, who sang. But if this is so, the details of F. P. D'Arcy's musical attributes are concealed in the obscurest corners of the history of Dublin's musical amateurs; for he was a very minor musician indeed.

When asked who is going on tour to Belfast with Molly, Bloom nervously invents eminent associates for her. " 'Louis Werner is touring her,' Mr. Bloom said. 'O yes, we'll have all topnobbers. J. C. Doyle and John MacCormack I hope and. The best, in fact' " (p. 92). These are all real people. Louis Werner is Herr Louis Werner, well-known conductor and accompanist, who was appearing on the evening of June 14 with Mary Anderson, in Belfast. John C. Doyle, the baritone, had won the Feis Ceoil award in 1899, and was widely regarded as a top vocalist, while John MacCormack was just now on the threshold of his international career as a singer. Joyce appeared with both these men at a concert in the Antient Concert Rooms on the last night of Horse Show week, August 27, 1904. This was the last of a series of farewell concerts for MacCormack, which had in fact stretched out over a period of more than four months. Apparently he had first intended to depart for the Continent at the end of April, "to study," as the *Freeman's Journal* for April 16 put it, "under the best continental masters." The August 27 concert is nicely described by Ellmann (*JJ*, p. 174), but the two earlier concerts, which took place on April 14 at the Rotunda and April 23 at the Mansion House, have an interest of their own. At both these concerts, Rossini's *Stabat Mater*

was featured; and these events, either or both of them, may
well have suggested Molly's singing of the same piece in the
Gardiner Street church (p. 81). Aside from MacCormack's
contributions, the success of the piece at the Rotunda was
largely attributed to a new choir, assembled and directed by
Mr. Vincent O'Brien; but special note was also taken of the
duet, *Quis est homo?* which lingers vividly in Bloom's recollection (p. 81). This selection, said the *Freeman's Journal* (15
April, 1904, p. 6), "is a piece with great traditions. It was sung
over the grave of Rossini in 1868 by Madame Patti and Signor
Albini. Last night it was sung by Miss Mollie Byrne and Miss
Mary Durkin, and their rendering of it, with the horn accompaniment, was most pleasing, and was heartily applauded." This
Mollie Byrne is no doubt the same soprano who placed third
in the 1904 Feis; she lived at 6 Islington Avenue, Sandycove,
and evidently has a claim to share in the creation of Mrs.
Bloom, if only to the extent of her name and one of her musical
numbers.[9] The horn accompaniment, which with proper deter-
mination might be twisted into an ironic commentary on Bloom
the cuckold, had best be written off as mere coincidence.

Mr. Ellmann's success in running down the several originals
of Leopold and Molly Bloom contrasts with his difficulties in
the matter of Blazes Boylan. Ted Keogh may claim a part in
the making of Boylan in that he wore a straw hat and managed
a prizefighter (Ellman, *JJ*, p. 389); but he was not a billsticker
or a singer, and though his father dealt in horses, he did not
live in Islandbridge, as Boylan's father is said to have done.
Presuming that Boylan (like Bloom and Molly) is a composite
figure, we need not expect to find every one of the identifying

9. Joyce seems to have given Mrs. Bloom the first name of "Marion," which
can be either masculine or feminine, to suggest that she is a manly woman,
as Bloom is a womanly man. "Molly" as a nickname would more naturally
derive from "Mary" than from "Marion."

characteristics in any single individual. But a man with the name of Boylan, known to Joyce, with some pretensions to tenor singing,[10] who came from the Islandbridge area, has some claim to a place in the fable. The man in question was named A. J. Boylan, and, after gaining second place in the tenor competition of the 1901 Feis Ceoil, he sang in the 1904 Feis (in which Joyce also participated), as one member of a quartet which sang the prize anthem. His associates were listed in the program as Miss M. Shinkwin, Mrs. Krall, and Mr. P. Conroy; J. C. Doyle sang the solo part. It seems a fair guess to identify this singing Boylan with the A. J. Boylan who lived at 2 Mayfield Villas, Kilmainham, from 1908 to 1916. Either he or his father occupied the same address (it was a section of the South Circular Road) in 1906 and 1907 under the listing of J. A. Boylan. And it would not have been hard for Joyce to incorporate Kilmainham with Islandbridge; the two communities, lying side by side on the southwest bank of the Liffey, were absorbed together into the municipality of Dublin in 1900. Boylan's persistent association in *Ulysses* with D'Olier Street is also worthy of remark, as a clue to his identity. On p. 91, he is seen lounging in the door of the Red Bank Restaurant, at #19; and on p. 525, the Sins of the Past accuse Bloom of having mentally telephoned unspeakable messages "to Miss Dunn at an address in D'Olier Street." This is no doubt Boylan's secretary, Miss Dunne, as her name is spelled on p. 226; [11] and the address sug-

---

10. Boylan's singing activities in the novel are, confessedly, a little dim. Bloom says (p. 270) "he can't sing for tall hats," but we hear on p. 727 that he "was in great singing voice." This expression may be a metaphor for sexual enthusiasm, yet one notes on p. 691 that some literal singing of "Love's Old Sweet Song" was evidently done during the afternoon of June 16, at #7 Eccles Street. Other songs associated with Boylan are the "seaside girls" song (p. 62), and "The Young May Moon" (pp. 165, 725).
11. An early notebook for the "Wandering Rocks" episode, in the University of Buffalo library, gives Miss Dunne's name as Miss Parker.

gests that Boylan is associated with the only advertising and
bill-posting company in D'Olier Street, The Advertising Co.
Ltd., 15 D'Olier Street (*Thom's Directory*, 1904). But present
officers of the company, including its historian Mr. W. E. D.
Allen, can think of no one who resembles the figure of "Blazes"
Boylan very closely.

The name of the prizefighter whom Boylan managed (Myler
Keogh) might conceivably have been derived from Ted Keogh,
supposing that individual to have been a manager of pugilists;
but it is far more likely to have been taken from an advertisement in the *Freeman's Journal* for April 28 and 29, 1904 (on
page 4 each day). The ad called attention to a great civil and
military boxing tournament to be held at Earlsfort Terrace
Rink on Friday and Saturday evenings. Clancy, from America,
was to face Salters of the 21st Lancers, in the main event; in the
supporting ten-rounder, M. L. Keogh of Dublin was matched
with Garry of the 6th Dragoons. The *Freeman* of April 30 reported on page 7 the outcome of this bout, which readers of
*Ulysses* could predict without difficulty; Keogh knocked out
Garry early in the third round with a right-hand punch to the
mark. The *Independent*, reporting the same events, was under
the impression that the fighter's name was McKeogh; this was
evidently an error of transcription involving misread initials.
Garry of the 6th Dragoons, his name suggesting "Garryowen,"
that anthem of Irish belligerence, was gratefully removed in
favor of Percy Bennett of the Zurich consular staff.

To return to music and musicians, a legitimate and rewarding subtlety appears in Joyce's handling of the text of a Mozart
aria. The situation requires some explaining. For Joyce, as for
most right-thinking people, Mozart was the supreme musical
genius. He shows this, in characteristically indirect fashion, by
having the Blooms equate Mozart with the most ordinary musical trash. In answer to Bloom's question, Molly says casually

that she is singing *Là ci darem* with J. C. Doyle and "Love's Old Sweet Song" (with Boylan, understood); she has no notion of the gap between these two musical worlds. When Joyce is reducing Bloom to the ultimate fatuity, he describes him as "favouring preferably light opera of the *Don Giovanni* description, and *Martha*, a gem in its line," but as having "a *penchant*, though with only a surface knowledge, for the severe classical school such as Mendelssohn" (p. 645).

Condescending as his interest is, Bloom nonetheless lives Mozart throughout the day; and one of his most intense preoccupations is that when Molly sings *Là ci darem* she shall pronounce the word "voglio" correctly. On p. 119, Bloom contemplates asking J. P. Nannetti how the word is pronounced, but decides not to risk embarrassing him. In fact, however, Bloom is concerned (as so often) over nothing; the word "voglio" does not have to be pronounced in the course of *Là ci darem*. The phrase Bloom is thinking of (as he recalls of his own accord on p. 92) is "Vorrei e non vorrei," "I would and I wouldn't." The phrase is sung by Zerlina in response to the blandishments of Don Giovanni. Bloom has this aria significantly mixed up with that sung early on in the opera by Leporello, "Non voglio più servir." For the idea of being in service to Molly bulks large in his mind, and is intimately connected with the idea of sexual solicitation. He feels sympathy for the cabmen who, like himself, are at the beck of others (p. 76); he responds to Molly's apparition in his fantasy with an obsequious "At your service" (p. 432); and he complains to the mournful nymph, "I have sixteen years of black slave labour behind me" (p. 540). Thus Bloom's error in the matter of *Là ci darem* serves, as Bloom's errors do not always serve, to make a pretty distinct point about his character.

The euphonious name of Almidano Artifoni, who in the novel takes the part of Stephen's singing master (pp. 225, 246,

251), was derived, as we learn in Mr. Ellmann's biography (*JJ*, p. 191), from the director of the Berlitz school in Trieste. Translated into a Dublin environment, he gives Stephen Dedalus kind and fatherly advice; then, after making his way across town, by tram and afoot, to the intersection of Northumberland and Lansdowne Roads, he disappears into a doorway, and we must look in *Thom's Directory*, 1904, to discover that at #14 Lansdowne Road lived the chevalier Benedetto Palmieri, professor of singing, R.I.A.M. The prize for a choral work at the 1904 Feis Ceoil (in which Joyce himself participated) was won by this same Benedetto Palmieri. His winning composition was a cantata called *Exodus*, and Part I ended with a chorus of angels singing "Alleluia Adonai!" in a manner very reminiscent of Handel's *Messiah* and the Black Mass in *Ulysses* (p. 584).[12]

A curious error occurs in one of the parody passages in "Cyclops," where the arrival of Rumbold on the scaffold is being celebrated. A high double F, we are told, was heard—"recalling those piercingly lovely notes with which the eunuch Catalani beglamoured our greatgreatgrandmothers" (p. 303). The eunuch Catalani is unknown to musical history. There was a famous soprano, Angelica Catalani, but she was warranted female. Possibly Joyce was thinking of the tenor Campanini, of whom J. S. Joyce was once supposed to be the destined successor (Ellmann, *JJ*, p. 14). But that there is an error, and likely a

---

12. Though he is "Father Artifoni" in *Stephen Hero* (pp. 169-71), because modeled after Father Charles Ghezzi, who taught Joyce Italian at University College, Dublin, Almidano Artifoni is a layman and a musician in *Ulysses*. Ghezzi appears in the *Portrait* under his own name (like Nash, who bitterly resented being publicly stigmatized as the class idler); and Joyce, having published Ghezzi there, had no hesitation about shifting the name of Artifoni (which he liked) to the character of Palmieri. Either he did not think his whole canon was one controlled composition, or he did not include *Stephen Hero* in the canon (cf. below, p. 225).

pointless one, is very probable. The reference to Catalani was introduced in a late stage of proof, when many private complexities found their way into the novel.

Mr. Walter Bapty, about whom a dramatic story of seduction, betrayal, and revenge is told on p. 276, also makes his first appearance as an addition to page-proofs. Historically, he was a professor of music in Dublin, and one of the main organizers of the first Feis Ceoil. He not only sang in the second one (1897), but continued to teach music, sing in the choir of St. Patrick's Cathedral, and ultimately achieved the office of Senior Vicar Choral there, before his death on April 2, 1915, at the age of 65. If he lost his voice under the assault of an irritated husband, it was evidently only a temporary loss. Whether true or false in the world of fact, the story of Walter Bapty serves in *Ulysses* to underline a connection between tenors and sexuality which is overt in the novel, and to remind Bloom of his marital complacency. As for a proper fictional reason why it had to be attached to the name of Walter Bapty, or any actual man, we seek in vain.

A vague reference on p. 648 to "the usual hackneyed run of catchy tenor solos foisted on a confiding public by Ivan St Austell and Hilton St Just and their *genus omne*" bears no weight in the fable but calls for explanation, simply to avoid annoyance. Both these splendidly titled gentlemen (their names seem to come from Cornish towns) sang during the 1890's with the Arthur Rousbey Opera Company. Mr. St. Austell's real name was W. H. Stephens, and Mr. St. Just no doubt concealed an equally plebeian title under his superb stage pseudonym (see *FW*, p. 48).

Eugene Sandow, who briefly inspired Bloom to a program of muscular development, appeared at the Empire Theatre in Dame Street, as reported in the *Freeman's Journal* for May 7, 1898, p. 9. According to the same newspaper's issue of February

3, 1894, a benefit was held at the Queens Royal Theatre for Mr. J. W. Whitbred, at which Mr. Pat Kinsella played Rory O'More from Sam Lover's novel, and Miss DuBedat sang "Going to Kildare"; all these persons, if not this particular incident, have left marks on Bloom's memory (see especially pp. 165 and 173). Martin Cunningham's wife is said to be very fond of "The Geisha" from which she twice (in Bloom's imagination) performs numbers (pp. 95, 554); the show was in Dublin and was reviewed in the *Weekly Freeman* for December 28, 1901, p. 9. Poole's "Myriorama," remembered by Molly (p. 724), was also recalled by Miss Delia Moore, in a letter headed "Memories of the Nineties" and published in the *Evening Herald* for January 3, 1941, p. 4; the show (it appears) used to come once a year, generally at the Rotunda, and was both entertaining and instructive. The Bohee Brothers, Tom and Sam, who turn up in Bloom's nightmare (p. 436) appeared in the Leinster Hall, giving banjo solos, songs, choruses, and dances (*Irish Independent*, August 28, 1894, pp. 4, 5). When "Simon, Cardinal Dedalus" makes a dramatic appearance in Stephen's fantasy under the impulsion of phrases by Kitty and Lynch (pp. 512-13), he recites two numbers. One is a verse of the well-known comic ballad, "Nell Flaherty's Drake," the other is less familiar. It is a curious, unrhymed, rhythmic chant:

> Conservio lies captured.
> He lies in the lowest dungeon
> With manacles and chains around his limbs
> Weighing upwards of three tons.

We are partly relieved of the necessity to seek the original version of this poem, or to explore its multiple thematic interconnections with the rest of the novel, by the knowledge that it was one of John Joyce's favorite recitations. James recorded his father's fondness for it in a notebook, several pages of which were devoted to reminiscences of "Pappie" (Cornell University Library, Bound MS 35). Finally, the Coffee Palace concerts, at which Molly used to strum (p. 738), and the Clarendon Street concert at which she sang a year ago (p. 733), define very precisely the range of her musical endeavor. The interests of both institutions were strictly focused on the promotion of total abstinence, and performers were held to no very lofty standards; concerts at both addresses customarily offered a potpourri of comic and sentimental songs, recitations, imitations, ballads, sketches, "coon" songs, jigs, juveniles, and assorted amateur vaudeville acts.

All these details of musical and theatrical Dublin in the 1890's serve to enrich Joyce's picture of a town in which music and drama were the most popular of the arts. It will be observed that Joyce says little, and that little in sardonic vein, about the Abbey Theatre. He was interested enough in vaudevilles, melodramas, and pantomimes to remember and discuss them—but not in the plays of Yeats, Moore, Martyn, Hyde, Synge, or Lady Gregory. There were no doubt good reasons for this preference. At best, authors are easily drawn to look on their contemporaries with jealous eyes, and Joyce liked to think of himself as an outcast. Besides, the whole tonality of Joyce's novel required that it deal, not with subtle and self-conscious acts of creation (except Joyce's own), but with the ignobly decent.

In the matter of music, Joyce's limitations are still more striking. He represents only vocal music, and knows no instrumental performers; his interest in the tenor voice is practically obsessive. His taste is pretty much the eclectic taste common to Dublin in his youth; "The Croppy Boy" and "Good Bye, Sweet Heart, Good Bye" rub shoulders with *Lá ci darem* and *Qui sdegno*; it is the taste of people whose music is an integral part of their lives, who hear more amateur than professional performances. Except for the major innovation of "Sirens,"

Joyce uses his musical and theatrical materials in no startling
ways; thematically, he now and then reinforces a point with
the words of a song or a reference to the theme of a play.
Anstey's play Vice-Versa, in which he acted at Belvedere with
Albrecht Connolly, made a considerable impression on Joyce,
partly because of its theme (son and father exchange positions),
but it does not bulk very large in Ulysses, and one would have
to know the original to understand why Joyce was interested
in it. On the whole, he uses his materials mostly for adornment without reference to large-scale symbolic structure. Don
Giovanni serve its purpose relatively early in the novel, and is
largely allowed to lapse thereafter; Bloom is Lionel while he
listens to the aria from Martha, but lapses into Bloom again
immediately thereafter.

### Sinbad: Phantasmal Mirth

Stephen's mother had "heard old Royce sing in the pantomime of Turko the terrible, and laughed with others when he
sang:

> I am the boy
> That can enjoy
> Invisibility." (p. 11)

There is a good deal about these pantomimes throughout the
novel; and indeed their popularity in Joyce's Dublin was remarkable. Immense preparations went into the production. The basic
pantomime, imported with script, props, and principal players
from London, was augmented by local talent, filled out with
local allusions, and enriched by specialty acts locally booked.
Puffs appeared in the local papers for weeks in advance; the
billboard notices were glittering and splendid; special trains
were scheduled for the convenience of rural and suburban audi-

ences; the viceroy and his lady themselves were sometimes known to attend; and the pantomimes ran for six or seven weeks consecutively. They usually opened on the afternoon of St. Stephen's day (December 26th) at the Theatre Royal or the Gaiety, and continued as long as the supply of fresh audiences held out. Indeed, pantomimes are still a prime attraction in Dublin; the manager of the Gaiety reports that some 70,000 Dubliners saw *Aladdin* during January and the first weeks of February 1960.

Varying as they did from year to year, week to week, and even from night to night, replete with topical jokes and vaudeville turns devoid of verbal content, the pantomimes never did get written down in anything like their full form. The basic pantomimes survive in printed versions, but the curious will find them pretty drab and infantile productions. They are usually built about a fairy story—Aladdin, Cinderella, Robinson Crusoe, Sinbad, Dick Whittington, or whatever; and this basic fable is then embroidered with all sorts of horseplay and buffoonery. Part of the humor is transvestite; the "principal boy" is always a girl, the "principal girl" a boy. Children, animals, clowns, knockabouts, jugglers, and bits and pieces from other pantomimes are freely imported, as occasion offers. Both in Dublin and in London, they seem to have had rather the character of stage carnivals.

Now the fact that there was a pantomime known as *Turko the Terrible* might set us off in search of this text; but I think there is reason to suppose that Joyce, and Mrs. Dedalus, saw another one, which has also left its mark on *Ulysses*. This was the performance of *Sinbad the Sailor* which is described in considerable detail on p. 662 of *Ulysses*—the one which opened on December 26, 1892. On this occasion Mr. E. W. Royce was one of the featured performers; and his appearance was billed as the first since his return from Australia. He took the part of

Turko the Terrible, not that this part was an invariable feature
of *Sinbad the Sailor* (the pantomime was often put on without
introducing Turko at all), but because, as an old Dublin favorite, he had to be worked in somehow. Thus Turko the Terrible
was built into Sinbad. There was a special evening for Royce,
on February 17, 1893, just before the pantomime closed; his
work was specially mentioned by the critics; but the basic pantomime remained that *Sinbad the Sailor* to which Bloom contemplated contributing a topical song. One notes that Bloom, as
well as Stephen, has his recollections of Turko the Terrible
(p. 57).

Joyce's description of the *Sinbad* pantomime on p. 662, being
taken entirely from an advertisement in the *Freeman's Journal*
for December 24 and 26, 1892, p. 4, offers an interesting study
in his use of details. Almost all the performers are omitted
from Joyce's account of the pantomime; this is certainly a most
striking omission. Messrs. T. W. Volt, Willie Crackles, F. J.
Little, Jess Smith, the Three Ottos, and (of course) E. W.
Royce disappear incontinent; so also do Mlles. Ida Logan, May
Hazlewood, Annie Teesdale, Dorothy Denis, Kathleen Morgan,
Little Katie Wallace, and Violet Evelyn. For purposes of euphony as well as transparent disguise, the names of two star
performers are run together—Kate Neverist and Nellie Bouverie
being combined to make Nellie Bouverist. The pantomime was
advertised as being written by Greenleaf Withers, Esq.; Joyce
altered this to the grotesquely improbable name of Greenleaf
Whittier (suggesting John Greenleaf Whittier, the American
poet, who did not work on *Sinbad the Sailor*), presumably
because he found the alteration wittier.

There are a good many passing omissions in his transcription
of the *Freeman* ad. He sacrificed to economy such dazzling
items as, "Machinery by Mr. G. Armstrong," and "Gas and
Limelight Effects by Mr. Boucher." But Mrs. and Miss Whelan,

George A. Jackson and Cecil Hicks, ballets by Jessie Noir, harle-
quinade by Thomas Otto, and "under the personal supervision
of Mrs. Michael Gunn" are all from the *Freeman* ad of December 24/26. A significant variation is that neither of the two
components of Nellie Bouverist was principal boy; historically,
that role fell to Miss Violet Evelyn. To summarize, Joyce drew
on the *Freeman* for all his material about the pantomime,
omitted excess identities very freely, and altered emphases in
moderation. He omitted, in fact, some of the best parts of the
ad, which drew a dramatic picture of the

GRAND BALLET
of
DIAMONDS
and
SERPENTINE DANCE

in Scene 6, and the culminating scene of

THE GRAND TRANSFORMATION
Entitled
WINTER AND SUMMER [13]

Bloom's association with the pantomime is dated in a characteristically enigmatic, but ultimately rather confused, manner.
The first "edition" of the pantomime opened at the Gaiety on
December 26, 1892; the so-called "second edition" is correctly
dated by Joyce, January 30, 1893; it included new acts and songs
by Miss Evelyn, Miss Neverist, Miss Bouverie, Miss Hazlewood,
Mr. Volt and Mr. Crackles, the Ottos, Mr. Royce, and Mr.
Fred Little. But Bloom's prospective work on the pantomime
was not of this period at all; it was done at least four and perhaps five years later. The dating is provided by references to

13. Like so many other leftovers from *Ulysses*, fragments of this ad found
their way into *Finnegans Wake*, p. 222.

the "posticipated opening of the new municipal fish market"
(p. 663), which took place May 11, 1897; and to the "antic-
ipated diamond jubilee of Queen Victoria" (June 22, 1897).
Bloom apparently could not decide which of these matters to
work into his topical song, and this of course opens the way for
a satiric Joycean equivalence. Overtly, Joyce is trying to date
the duration of Bloom's efforts. But the dating itself does not
work out. At the period indicated, Dan Tallon had not yet been
elected Lord Mayor, Thomas Pile elected high sheriff, nor
Dunbar Planket Barton appointed solicitor-general. They duly
achieved these posts in the fall, but Bloom would have had to
enjoy second sight to know in May and June the outcome of
the elections and the action which the Viceroy was going to
take. Nor is this the only oddity about the situation. Bloom is
supposed to have been working on the version of the pantomime which was produced for Christmas, 1897. Yet he is confused about his loyalties as between the Grand Lyric Hall on
Burgh Quay and the Theatre Royal in Hawkins Street, although
the Lyric Theatre opened for the first time on Monday, December 12, 1898. In any event, it is perhaps just as well that he
never made much headway with his song for the sixth scene of
Sinbad; since the pantomime produced for Christmas, 1897,
was Aladdin.[14]

One last detail from the pantomimes. Among the characters
in Sinbad the Sailor are, naturally, Sinbad; not quite so naturally, Mrs. Sinbad; and two additional enchanting personalities,
known as Tinbad and Whinbad. Perhaps they have something
to do with the dreamy, going-to-bed litany of p. 722. Xinbad

14. Material on the Christmas pantomime was originally included in the
"Cyclops" episode, where O'Madden Burke was to have asked an unnamed
figure whether he was not going to write a script about Brian Boru or Finn
MacCool. U. of Buffalo MSS, "Cyclops." Additional material on the panto-
mimes may be found in J. S. Atherton, "Finnegans Wake: the Gist of the
Pantomime," Accent, Winter 1955, pp. 14-26.

the Phthailer, though he is not here *in esse*, is clearly present *in potentia*.

On the obvious level of a mythological parallel, Sinbad is almost bound to have a function in *Ulysses*. Bloom is Orientally minded, and Sinbad is an Oriental version of the great ocean traveler whose main accomplishment is to get back home. Joyce mentions a number of other sea-voyagers in the course of his novel, including Robinson Crusoe, the Ancient Mariner, the Wandering Jew, the Flying Dutchman, and Captain Nemo. It may fairly be presumed that the thought of Sinbad was agreeable and useful to him in writing *Ulysses*. On the other hand, he did not go far out of his way to insert ocean travelers into his novel, for he never mentions Gulliver (only Houyhnhnms), Magellan, Marco Polo, Captain Cook, or Phineas Fogg—not to mention a long list of others. What is more, he does not obtrude parallel Ulysses-figures on our notice; he hides Captain Nemo in a burlesque list of celebrities and the Flying Dutchman in a distant performance vaguely suggested to Bloom by the appearance of W. B. Murphy. In fact, Bloom, the great traveler of *Ulysses*, is only once directly related to one of these assorted mariners, when he is described as mimicking, along with thirteen other historical personages, Robinson Crusoe (p. 485). It is evident that Joyce's method of handling parallel myths is simply to mention names wherever they make or reinforce surface relatedness, and allow the reader to make his own symbolic connections. This certainly is his procedure with the Sinbad story.

Are we then forbidden to suppose that the phrase "Darkinbad the Brightdayler" makes subtle reference to Max Müller's theory that Odysseus was originally a sun-god? I do not suppose we are. So far as he represents mankind, Bloom contains all the archetypes; being already a hero with a thousand faces, he may as well be a sun-god too. But few of these identities are suggested in the writing. Most of the appearances of Sinbad in *Ulysses* are straight theatrical history, simplified to meet the needs of Joyce's story. The going-to-bed litany is a piece of inspired stupidity, like Charles Bovary's famous hat, containing layer after layer of meaninglessness—an unfathomable depth of mental void. Relaxing its hold on external reality, and on its own thought processes, the mind is shown drifting off into a mechanical word-cuddling, and so into complete darkness. The more we project conscious intellectual meaning into the process, the less it serves its overt purpose. Like a Rorschach-blot, the passage will absorb anything we want to put into it, but there is a point at which our insertions, by expressing "us" all too richly, frustrate the ends of the novel.

# 4

## Surface or Symbol?

In a broad sense, the choice between surface and symbol is the most important one a reader of Joyce must make. Surface in fiction invites us to repose in the object itself as represented; symbol invites us to transpose, to see the object as a key to some meaning other than itself. Surface may be imaginary, even fantastic, symbol perfectly matter of fact; the difference is not one of degree but of kind. The root idea of symbol is that of the broken shard of which two men hold each a half; their fitting together is token of a larger agreement. Thus Joe and the Citizen, rehearsing the passwords and gestures of the ribbon-men (p. 290), are putting symbols to one of their original uses.

It is perfectly clear that surface and symbol are not exclusive alternatives. The shard is no less a shard because it represents an agreement, and a man who asks, "What's your opinion of the times?" may really want to know. Generally, in the effort to explain physical phenomena, one explanation is better than

two. If we have satisfactorily accounted for a flat tire by means
of a tack, we outrage a law of logical economy by attributing
it to a devil as well. But the world of literature is unlike that
of nature in that a literary element's existence as symbol does
not rigidly preclude its existence as surface, or vice versa.

Yet, if only to prevent thought from bogging down in uncontrollable multiplicity, some limit must be placed on the recognition of symbolic correspondences. Their use as literary symbols
may impose on words a radical new dimension of meaning,
evoking latent or implicit connections over which the author
has only limited control. Even symbols as stylized and conventional as "cross" or "rose" may have several orders of meaning,
according to context and individual associative patterns. Just
as we have to select among the everyday meanings of words on
the basis of context (only consider the possible meanings of
the simple monosyllable "rose"), so we must admit some symbolic meanings and reject others, also according to context.
What shall this context be? Without trying to abridge the rich
variety of possibilities, I suppose the unity of the individual
work of art is a natural and prudent control for symbolic interpretations. Literary criticism proper takes little interest in systems of correspondence beyond the formal pattern of the literary
work, assigning them rather to biography and social history. So
far as the work of art is pure, formal esthetic pattern, this divid-
ing line can be a clean one. Aristotle's complementary common-
places, magnitude and harmony, work very well under these
circumstances to justify symbolic enrichment while controlling
symbolic excrescence. One is intent to recognize the largest
possible harmony within the artistic framework, to realize as
taut and energetic a complex of tensions as can subsist without
discord. But major complications arise when we turn to books
like *Ulysses*, which are something other than formal pattern,
which fit into no clearly defined esthetic framework. The pres-

ence of the artist or the work of art within its own framework, opens the way to a host of theoretical difficulties. Elements in the novel may be taken to represent the novelist in the act of creation, episodes in the creative process, incidents from the author's biography, or fragments from other books of the author, at will. Once away from the concept of a limited esthetic whole, each part of which contributes structurally to the total effect, we lose control of a standard of relevance; and the admission of a single curious trifle from outside the esthetic scheme paves the way for a thousand others, at the whim of the symbol-monger. In the purely quantitative sense, this may be called an enrichment. It may also result in clutter, disorder, and extraneous multiplicity, so radical as to undercut all notions of artistic unity and economy.

So far as I can see, theory offers us no way out of this complexity, at least while we think it legitimate for works of art to be "impure"—and it is hard to deny them a right which they have already vigorously assumed. But theory, as frequently happens, is a good deal too refined here to be useful in ordinary, finite critical practice. Whatever the context in which we may elect to see the work of art as an object generated by causes or directed to ends, we must, as participants in an esthetic transaction, impose an elementary economy, if not on the author, at least on ourselves. All experiences of complex structures are bound to be partial; at any given moment, one eye cannot assume more than one perspective. Thus we are, in a sense, "composing" a picture in the simple act of selecting a perspective from which to view it. The picture without a frame, without a boundary, merely offers us a little less guidance than we are used to in performing a task which all pictures impose. Hence a very rough sense of appreciative economy may save us from the distraction (not to say humiliation) of appreciating flyspecks and pursuing the accidents of our own astigmatism. The justification of such an economy is simply our need as appreciators, only secondarily a presumed intent of the author. I can see no better ground on which to take a stand.

### Erin's King

One of Mr. Bloom's gayest family memories is of a trip he took with Milly around the Kish lighthouse on a boat called the *Erin's King*. Everyone else was sick and scared, because of the rough weather, but not Milly; Bloom recalls with warm paternal affection her pale blue scarf loose in the wind with her hair (p. 66), and thinks also of how he gave stale cake to the seagulls (p. 150). Among earnest readers of *Ulysses*, the name of the vessel has given rise to some determined symbol searching. Erin, to be sure, had many kings in the historic past from Partholon to Roderick O'Conor. But Parnell was known as Ireland's uncrowned king—to Mrs. O'Shea, more effusively, as Her Own King—and Joyce's particular devotion in politics (verbally, at least) was to Parnell. Thus the name of the boat has been supposed to involve a transient, poignant recollection of Parnell, perhaps on Bloom's part, certainly on Joyce's. It is a subtle allusion, to be sure, and therefore flattering to the wily critic who discovers it; but there is no denying that Joyce was a subtle man. One senses just a single major oddity about this reference to Charles Stewart Parnell; it is apparent only to a reader who is quite ignorant of the Dublin scene at the turn of the century. Most of Joyce's symbols work quite the other way; they imply some knowledge of the social milieu. But the only people to whom *Erin's King* suggests Parnell are those who do not know that it was a real boat, the only boat one could take on expeditions of this nature. Just as Bloom recalls, it was an old tub; it plied from Custom House Quay during summer months, taking

tourists for a shilling a head around Ireland's Eye or around the
Kish lighthouse. On the occasion of regattas in Dublin Bay, it
sometimes took people out to watch the races. Advertisements
indicating its schedule appeared regularly in the *Freeman's Journal* and other papers during the 1890's. If Bloom had chosen to
recall a brief two-hour excursion by water (and one of the points
about Bloom is that he has traveled widely in Dublin), he
could have sailed on no other vessel than the *Erin's King*. If
Joyce had any respect at all for the surface texture of his facts
—and the available evidence indicates that details of this sort
were of passionate interest to him—he could have given the
boat no other name.

Of course the really earnest symbol-seeker will urge that the
mere physical existence of a boat by this name does not detract
from its symbolic significance. Joyce (like his readers) found in
the world without, as actual, what was already in his world
within, as possible. Thus, if one's mind runs on Parnell, there
is every justifiable reason to see the *Erin's King* as a Parnell
symbol. Its being an old tub is a symbol of the degradation of
Parnell's name; Bloom's feeding the gulls off it is a symbol of
humanitarian impulses associated with Parnellism; and Milly's
youthful fearlessness in facing the open sea of vital political
action is contrasted with the craven cowerings of the average
Irishman. This is all arrant nonsense, to be sure, and no one
with a grain of common sense would accept it for a minute. But
once we are embarked on a symbol search, I can see no reason
in theory to disqualify even leaden-footed allegories like this
one. Of course we may stipulate that every proposed symbol
should serve a demonstrable purpose in the structure of the
book or the pattern of our responses to it; but that is a sharp
razor indeed, and would probably slice even the basic reference
to Parnell out of the passages describing the *Erin's King*.

In the general economy of *Ulysses*, the *Erin's King* is a rela-

tively strong spot of color. Unlike Odysseus, Bloom is not much
of an ocean voyager; the one occasion when he gets on a boat
ought to be rich in import. Given Erin's political history, the
name of the boat might well be significant; given the paucity
of domestic incident *chez* Bloom, the participation of Milly
seems particularly promising. On the other hand, the names of
stores passed by characters in *Ulysses* do not seem like much of
a field for symbol hunting. For one thing, there are so many of
them. The butcher, the baker, the candlestick-maker are all here,
fresh from the pages of *Thom's Directory*; and the sane reader
of *Ulysses* does not bother his head with the myriad municipal
details by which the progress of the characters through the Dublin streets is charted. Yet these names are occasionally manipulated for patent symbolic purposes. When Simon Dedalus has
just finished haggling over pennies with his hungry and shabby
daughter Dilly, he passes a shop known in the novel as Reddy
and Daughter's (p. 240). Richard Reddy, antique dealer, did in
fact have a shop at 19 Ormond Quay, lower; but the addition of
"and Daughter's," an ironic parallel to the usual "& Sons" as
well as a possible but mythical partner, draws an emphatic line
beneath Simon's unfatherly attitudes. The French translation
confirms our sense that the relationship is more important than
the name by translating the store's name as "Reddy et Fille."

Another buried symbol appears in the "Sirens" chapter, where
Boylan rides to his assignation with Molly in "hackney car,
number three hundred and twenty-four, driver Barton, James of
number one Harmony avenue, Donnybrook" (p. 275). Boylan
is in supreme harmony with his surroundings, and the art of the
section ("Sirens") is music, so the address is quite properly em-
phasized. Actually, *Thom's Directory* for 1904 does show a
James Barton living at Rose Cottage, Harmony Avenue, in
Donnybrook; whether he was a cab-driver or not, and whether,
if so, he drove cab #324, are matters which do not appear. It

seems hard to suppose, however, that Joyce has not assigned Boylan this particular driver on account of his useful address. It is also hard to suppose that Joyce intended his buried and incidental symbols to carry any more weight than that of a buried and incidental meaning in the novel's total structure.

On the other hand, a deliberate and important symbol in the book often receives multiple reinforcement. The drowned man in Dublin Bay, of whom Stephen and Bloom are both aware, is not historical in the narrow sense. Nobody was drowned on June 7 or pulled out of the waters on June 16, 1904; neither C. P. McCoy, Joyce's imaginary assistant coroner, nor Louis A. Byrne, the real coroner, had occasion to identify a drowned body on that day. Matthew Kane was drowned in mid-July, but he was swimming off a boat with a number of companions, who rescued his body and hauled it aboard the boat before it had a chance to sink or drift away. Joyce's invention was not radical on the face of it, for people did get drowned in Dublin Bay, and did float ashore from time to time. But Joyce wanted to ensure that the reader would look for the symbolic import of this significant corpse (it finds a place in an early cast of characters under the allusive name of L. Annegato: *British Museum Additional MSS #49975*, "Cyclops"). Consequently, he had the victim drown off Maiden's Rock (p. 46), which is a real but tiny feature of Dublin Bay—with Lamb Island and Clare Rock, it comprises a little string of rocks just to the north of Dalkey Island. Its physical reality is, however, only the tiniest of *points d'appui* for the name; its real function is to suggest disaster at the hands of sirens. Sirens are the theme of a song which Stephen sings (p. 647), and one of the topics of his conversation with Bloom (p. 649), as well as central figures of an entire episode in the novel. The drowned man is associated with the drowned father of Shakespeare's song from *The Tempest* (p. 50), and so has a remorseful, reminiscent significance for

Stephen. He is associated with the protagonist of "Lycidas" (p. 50), and so becomes a potential redeemer. As a man whom Mulligan might have saved but whom Stephen could not, he becomes an occasion for self-reproach.[1] All these layered and complex relationships serve to reinforce the figurative and symbolic significance of the drowned man, and to strengthen the reader's assurance that he is in fact essentially symbolic.

## Tom Rochford

A first principle of Joycean technique is to use what comes to hand; if it does not serve as symbol, it may at least be

---

1. Still another possible innuendo about the drowned man in this passage derives from an old tradition that about the turn of the eighteenth century, extraordinary annual revels used to be held on Dalkey Island. They were presided over by "His facetious Majesty, Stephen the First, King of Dalkey, Emperor of the Muglins, Prince of the Holy Island of Magee, Elector of Lambay and Ireland's Eye, Defender of his own faith and Respecter of all others, Sovereign of the illustrious Order of the Lobster and Periwinkle" (F. Elrington Ball, *History of the County Dublin*, I, 79-80). Stephen's link to the drowned man would clearly be strengthened if he were a drowned mock-monarch named Stephen. On the other hand, this story does not joint very snugly with that of the sirens, and Joyce evidently opted to let the King of Dalkey lie latent to be picked up by anyone who knew about him. (Joyce must have known about the King of Dalkey, for he uses him in *FW*, pp. 87, 582, 616.) Maiden's Rock was named for some girls who drowned there while gathering an edible seaweed called "dilisk" (D. A. Chart, *The Story of Dublin*, p. 353), and the eager maze-maker will connect this with the circumstance that on p. 240 Dilly Dedalus is shown (imaginatively, by Stephen) as drowning in seaweed. On the other hand, it is accepted that "Dilly" Dedalus gets her nickname from a sister of Nora Barnacle.

Finally, there is an untidy possibility of identifying the drowned man with Denis Breen, who at one o'clock has just "blown in from the bay" (p. 157). This phrase was added after the publication of "Lestrygonians" in the *Little Review*, i.e. January 1919, and fulfills a cryptic, semi-anonymous prophecy on p. 23 of the novel.

turned to account as surface. But some materials fall somewhat uncomfortably between these two stools, having too much character to be mere surface and too little to be consistent symbol. Taking for granted that the reader explores symbols at his own risk, Joyce has provided a deliberate minimum of explanation. Thus, as in traversing Milton's *Paradise Lost*, the reader of *Ulysses* threads his way through a wilderness of allusions, metaphors, and concrete facts, the significance of which depends on outside knowledge. But Milton takes for granted—and draws one into—the world of classical knowledge, which has beauty and significance of its own; Joyce leads one mainly into the holes and corners of the Dublin in which he grew up. The parallel with Dante is somewhat closer than that with Milton. Dante too expects us to be familiar with the complexities of a very small and special community; but unlike Joyce, he enjoys the advantage of an over-all intellectual structure. Even his occasional lapses into autobiography (like *Inferno*, XIX, 15-21) involve a self-justification which entitles him to make a particular judgment in the body of the poem. The point about Dante's characters, including his own character, is often terribly clear merely from their present position and action; the point about Joyce's characters is often so private that its very existence in the reader's mind depends upon a set of far-fetched accidents.

A classic instance of indeterminate meaning is provided by Mr. Tom Rochford, whose character is limned in *Ulysses* by three or four widely separated touches. He appears in Davy Byrne's pub, complaining of dyspepsia (pp. 175-6); he demonstrates to Lenehan a machine he has invented for keeping count of music-hall turns (pp. 228-9); and he is praised as a hero for having rescued a man from a sewer (p. 229). He wears a claret waistcoat (pp. 175, 228), described as a booky's vest (p. 229); and so, being somehow connected with horses, is set down by Mr. Richard Kain as a jockey.

But it is not difficult at all—if one finds oneself at liberty to pursue slight symbolic clues—to claim a rather more exalted position for Tom Rochford. He is robin-red-breasted as a harbinger of spring and rebirth; his two-columned machine represents a form of spiritual accounting ("the golden opes, the iron shuts amain"); and his saving a man from a sewer establishes him as a prototype of the resurrection, a Christ-figure. The first part of his last name reminds us of "Tu es Petrus," and the second part of St. Christopher. In the apocalypse scene he resurrects Dignam from the dead (p. 465) and leads mankind in the act of throwing away his life and thereby saving it (p. 583). He is evidently a Redeemer of some sort.

Pursuit of symbolic hints like these (and they are a good deal clearer than many others which have been put forward in all simplicity and good faith) is doubtless rousing good fun; but some literal facts may be useful too, and the sewer-rescue episode leads toward them. Anachronistically enough, from the standpoint of the novel, the incident occurred on Saturday, May 6, 1905; and Tom Rochford took part in it, though not quite the part represented by Joyce. A man named Fleming, whose profession it was to do such things, went down a sewer at the corner of Hawkins Street and Burgh Quay (just outside the Scotch House), and was overcome by sewer gas. A fellow worker, John Coleman, went down to rescue him, and was also overcome. Tom Rochford, of #2 Howth View, Sandymount, was the third man down the manhole. He was described in Monday's *Independent* as having been for eight and a half years in the employ of the Corporation, but for the past few weeks out of work. Early accounts of the episode described him as having been a "clerk of works"; in later stories he rises to the dignity of an "engineer." The Sandymount address suggests (though it is not substantiated by any more positive evidence) that Joyce was acquainted with him.

In any event, Tom Rochford descended the manhole, and was overcome by gas. He was followed by Kiernan Fitzpatrick, a cab-driver; Martin Lambert, a fireman; and Patrick Sheahan, a police constable. All in all, twelve men went down the sewer and were dragged out unconscious. Two of them died, Fleming, the original victim, and Constable Sheahan. Tom Rochford's eyes are described as having been severely injured by the fetid gases of the sewer, and he also had a few abrasions; but he was never in danger of his life, and after a few days was released from the hospital.

From this rather too gaudy story, Joyce blithely discarded all the eleven rescuers except Rochford, with whom he was very probably personally acquainted. In the process of getting rid of these others, he had to invent a rope to put around Rochford; he had also to angle sharply his view of the event itself. As far as the general public was concerned, the hero of the day was Constable Sheahan, whose burial was impressively ceremonious, and whose name may be read on the badly weathered monument which stands, to this day, in the middle of Hawkins Street at its intersection with Burgh Quay. Constable Sheahan was discarded from *Ulysses*, with ten other heroes, in favor of Tom Rochford. For several weeks after the event, nagging little letters appeared in the Dublin papers, asking what would be done to reward a newsboy who had spread the alarm; but nobody ever directed a public thought to Tom Rochford, or for that matter to the other volunteers.

Joyce chose this neglected hero for inclusion in his novel, partly, it seems likely, on the elementary ground that he knew him (there is no better instance of his calm assumption that "Ireland must be important because it belongs to me"). He also had, or may have had, artistic purposes which can perhaps be reconstructed. For Tom Rochford's career did in fact exemplify a quality dear to Joyce and thematically important to the novel. He was an ideal "hero," loaded with volunteer courage, but quite ineffectual in the practical grind of getting ahead— a Pyrrhic victor, one might say, in the race of life. This, as Joyce saw it, was the Irish character; it was the charm of his father, and a grounds for despising the cold, prudential, successful English. The race of life leads only to the grave; but Tom Rochford, casual and volunteer, will brave even the grave to bring back Paddy Dignam. So far the symbolic interpretation goes fairly obediently hand in hand with the literal facts; but how about such a trifling detail as the dyspepsia in Davy Byrne's pub? It is available to a rather portentous symbolic interpretation; Tom Rochford, who forced the sewer to disgorge its victim, is now tormented by an analogous ailment, he is a mute, inglorious Orpheus with indigestion, a hell-harrower who is being vigorously harrowed himself. This symbolism sounds silly, but in fact there are some indications that it is intended.

—How is the main drainage? Nosey Flynn asks (p. 176), with his usual perceptiveness—and his question incorporates with its solicitude a reference to Dublin's perennial sewage-disposal project. Diving into repugnant holes is an action recurrently characteristic of Tom Rochford in the novel; that he should have difficulties with his own main-drainage system is too direct a parallel to be accidental. But what effect does it actually have? Heartburn and acid indigestion are not afflictions dignified enough to "stand for" anything very portentous; nor do they relate to anything else in the symbolic structure of the novel. We should be tempted to write them off as surface realism, along with various other animal noises which the novel depicts, did the author not seem to lay undue weight on them. Where the general economy is so sparse, it seems particularly distressing that the reader's energies should be left suspended between an extended perception which relates to nothing else in the book and the recognition of a mere accident.

Or, perhaps, the point of Tom Rochford's dyspepsia is, once more, only that it has no point. Joyce, like God the Father, gives us signs to interpret; and part of their virtue (for him, and perhaps for us) is that they do not yield too easily. But this is a virtue all too easily overdone. The Joycean symbol does not admonish, it tantalizes; and exerts thereby a lengthier and more active fascination—so long as it does not seem willful. How long can mystification seem deliberate and yet not willful? It is a hair-line decision, and Joyce in the matter of Tom Rochford may seem to have provoked the reader's impatience by an indecisiveness over the import of his materials which leaves him dangling interminably between varieties of meaning, varieties of meaninglessness.

### Blephen/Stoom

"The lutenist Dowland who lived in Fetter Lane near Gerard the herbalist, who *anno ludendo hausi, Doulandus*" pops up on p. 646 of *Ulysses*, as Stephen is recounting to Bloom his enthusiasm for Elizabethan music. Clearly, this is John Dowland (1563-1626), who was living in Fetter Lane in 1603 and 1606; the Latin anagram does not make much sense as given, because it was based on the Latin form of Dowland's name which Joyce does not give in full, Iohannes Doulandus, and he has misquoted it from "*Annos ludendo hausi.*" It is attributed to Ralph Sadler and Henry Peacham, and a rough translation would be, "I used up my years in playing."

Having dug through the difficulties, adventitious and inherent, of the passage on p. 646, we may turn to previous appearances of Fetter Lane in *Ulysses*. When Stephen is expounding his Shakespeare theories in the National Library, he thinks, apparently in an unspoken monologue between spoken passages, of Shakespeare living richly in Cheapside, while poor Penelope, his wife, remained in Stratford.

> Do and do. Thing done. In a rosery of Fetter Lane of Gerard, herbalist, he walks, greyedauburn. An azured harebell like her veins. Lids of Juno's eyes, violets. He walks. One life is all. One body. Do. But do. Afar, in a reek of lust and squalor, hands are laid on whiteness (p. 199).

This passage too has its obliquities, though they are not very complicated. Amid semi-quotations from *Cymbeline* (IV, 2, 222) and the *Winter's Tale* (IV, 4, 121), Stephen reflects on Shakespeare, surrounded by sexually inviting flowers, composing sexually alluring images, and justifying his infidelities with the thought that he has only one life to live; while in Stratford, amid lust and squalor, his wife is unfaithful to him. The situation nicely parallels that of Bloom, who has just passed by, uncomprehending and uncomprehended. What warrant Stephen has for making Shakespeare acquainted with Gerard the herbalist we cannot tell; for Joyce in his novel, as for Stephen's special brand of criticism, mere proximity would be enough. The feeling Stephen attributes to Shakespeare, that we must hasten to have adulterous affairs because our time on earth is limited, is not one to which the Bard himself gave notable expression. But the mixture of feelings is very effective nonetheless, implying as it does Stephen's psychological identification with Shakespeare.

Why, then, does Bloom think practically the same thoughts at the Ormond Bar concert, when Stephen is nowhere in the vicinity? Bloom has just finished writing his philandering letter to Martha Clifford, ending on a melancholy, plaintive note.

> Too poetical that about the sad. Music did that. Music hath charms Shakespeare said. Quotations every day in the year. To be or not to be. Wisdom while you wait.
> In Gerard's rosery of Fetter lane he walks, greyedauburn. One life is all. One body. Do. But do (p. 276).

The first paragraph is characteristic Bloom-thought. The irrelevant half-quotation from Congreve is blithely misattributed to Shakespeare; the practical uses of worldly wisdom to be absorbed from partially misapprehended literary clichés are generously insisted on. How is it possible for a man who thinks of Shakespeare in these terms to be aware of Gerard's rosery of Fetter Lane? Somehow or other Stephen's thoughts, Stephen's phrases, have been mislaid in Bloom's mind. Our first assumption is bound to be that Joyce intends to demonstrate some kind of telepathic communication between Bloom and Stephen; and indeed, their situations are crucially similar. Bloom is driven to walk because aware of Molly and Blazes, Stephen to talk because tormented by remorse and resentment. Both express their urgent need in blunt, self-directed imperatives. On the other hand, Joyce never enforces thematic parallels of this sort so crudely as by transferring one man's thoughts to another man's head. There are a number of instances in the novel where Bloom and Stephen think along vaguely parallel lines. Stephen dreams about meeting Bloom in the street of harlots (pp. 47-8); they are both briefly aware of Turko the Terrible (pp. 11, 57); they both think briefly about the problem of dating the career of St. Patrick (pp. 167, 650-51), they are both Hamlet-conscious. But, looked at a second time, these are seen to be tangential and fleeting similarities, growing out of the fact that Stephen

and Bloom have lived for the last twenty-two years in the same
medium-sized city, at about the same social level. Turko the
Terrible was a familiar fellow around Dublin, who could be
discovered in the pages of Dublin's comic newspaper *Zoz*, as
well as on the Gaiety stage. Bloom doesn't really think about
the problem of dating St. Patrick, till it is brought to his attention by Stephen; and Stephen's dream about Bloom is an interesting presage, but in no sense a meeting of minds. Actually, it
is more remarkable that the thoughts of Bloom and Stephen are
so disparate than that they are so similar. Bloom, for instance,
thinks continually of *Don Giovanni*, and assigns himself the
part of Leporello in this opera; but Stephen never thinks of
himself as a Don Juan. He applies phrases from the opera to
Shakespeare ("he would but would not," and "assumed dongio-
vannism," p. 194), but never to his own predicament. When he
is out of their presence, Stephen never thinks of his father's (and
Bloom's) friends, Martin Cunningham, Ned Lambert, Tom
Kernan, Jack Power, and so on. Long acquainted with Stephen's
father, his uncle Richie Goulding, and Mrs. Dante Riordan,
who was Stephen's governess, Bloom still knows remarkably
little about the young man's history and opinions. I do not
complain here of lack of verisimilitude; the point is simply that
Joyce has kept Bloom and Stephen intellectually distinct and
socially remote, with the deliberate purpose of rendering their
conjunction more significant. Thus the incident of Bloom's thinking Stephen's thoughts on p. 276 is one which interrupts strikingly the prevailing tenor of the novel; if it cannot be given narrative or symbolic significance, it will have to be written down
as an arbitrary authorial intrusion, perhaps an authorial accident.
It does not appear in either the manuscript notebook or the
first typescript of "Sirens" at the University of Buffalo Library;
neither is it found in the manuscript held by the Rosenbach
Foundation. It first turns up, not as an insert, but as an estab-

lished part of the printed text, on the proofsheets at the University of Buffalo. How it got there, whether by accident or design, and what function its presence is supposed to serve, no can say with confidence. Neither symbol nor surface, its actual effect is mainly to disquiet; whatever our other uncertainties, this at least is plain.

## Bloom as Hungarian, Bloom as Jew

In making the chief protagonist of *Ulysses* a renegade Jew, Joyce had several points to make, several effects to gain. Aside from his Continental and Irish prototypes, sketched in their impressive variety by Ellmann, Bloom is a product of several general ideas, widespread throughout the late nineteenth century, about modern urban life in general, and Jews in particular. "There is a new sort of nomad," says Spengler, "cohering unstably in fluid masses: the parasitical city-dweller, traditionless, utterly matter-of-fact, without religion, clever, unfruitful." [2] One could scarcely ask to have Bloom hit off more precisely; by having him stand outside the traditions of all faiths, just as naïve about the Haggadah (p. 121) as about the ceremonies in All Hallows (pp. 79-82), Joyce gains at once ironic perspective on the various religious formulas and a wonderful sense of Bloom himself as a malleable, formless, indeterminate piece of human clay.

2. *Decline of the West*, tr. C. F. Atkinson (New York, 1945), I, 32. These ideas about the inchoate and depersonalized masses, more or less mixed with anti-cosmopolitan, i.e. anti-semitic, feeling, were widely diffused, and Joyce could have picked them up in many places. See, for example, Alfredo Oriani, *La Rivolta Ideale*, Part I, Chapter viii. The notes for *Exiles* (New York, 1951), p. 113, cite Part III, Chapter ii (titled "Femminismo") of Oriani's book. See also the fascination and disgust of Joyce's association-patterns regarding Jews, below p. 146.

There are, however, some limitations and difficulties in which this portrayal of Bloom involves his creator. Joyce once explained why Bloom was of Hungarian origin by saying simply, "Because he was." The reference is doubtless to Teodoro Mayer, the Triestine newspaperman and publisher of the *Piccolo della Sera*, who certainly served as one of the models for Bloom (Ellmann, *JJ*, p. 385). In the novel itself, however, some further justification of Bloom's Magyar background is called for. Part of this justification appears when Bloom is said by Martin Cunningham (who works in the Castle, and claims to be in the know) to be responsible for "all the plans according to the Hungarian system" (p. 331). Here the allusion is to Arthur Griffith's little pamphlet *The Resurrection of Hungary*, published serially in the *United Irishman* during 1904, and printed as a pamphlet at the end of the year.

That an imaginary character should be credited with responsibility for an actual historical event is no sin in a novelist. In having Bloom invent political policy for Arthur Griffith, Joyce may seem to be veering close to the Lanny-Budd syndrome, but the test is not historical fact, it is authenticity of character. And just here a complaint is in order. Arthur Griffith's Hungarian policy is not, in fact, within the range of Bloom's character. He was not born in Hungary; he knows (from what we can tell) very little about the country, in fact he hardly ever thinks of it; and he has no Hungarian acquaintances. Whatever Hungarian background one does find in *Ulysses* seems to have been imported, and from no great distance. For instance, "The Royal and Privileged Hungarian Lottery" which is said to have got Bloom into so much trouble till the freemasons got him out of it, was picked out of a single paragraph in the *Irish Independent* of June 16, 1904, p. 4. The episode in question took place in London; a printer was summoned into court by the Treasury, on charges of having published announcements

describing the "Privileged Royal Hungarian Lottery." Joyce
simply moved the episode to Dublin, placed it some years in
the past, and attributed the experience to Bloom.

The renegade Jew Dlugasz who appears momentarily in
"Calypso" and the few words of pidgin-Hungarian inserted toward the end of "Cyclops" are almost the only other reminders
of Bloom's Hungarian background. Bloom does not think himself Hungarian and scarcely Jewish; quite innocently and unself-
consciously he calls himself (and not only in public, but in
his deepest and most inward thoughts as well) an Irishman.
His ideals are vaguely bourgeois-international; he thinks no
Hungarian thoughts and makes no Hungarian comparisons,
even when one might think them appropriate. For example,
Griffith's pamphlet makes much game of an Austrian emperor
known as "Leopold the Wily"; Bloom makes just one reference
to the house of Hapsburg, and then does not know whether
he is thinking of Leopold or Otto (p. 172).

More important than his deficiencies of Hungarian information are Bloom's discrepancies of character. Griffith did not
have by any means the sort of personality to accept major policy
suggestions from such a man as Bloom; Bloom did not have,
in any particular, the sort of personality to suggest to Griffith
the Hungarian policy which Griffith himself said was imitated
from the program of Francis Deak. Bloom has no such inflexible
patriotic motivations as Griffith's pamphlet and Griffith's policy
predicate. Whatever else one thinks about Arthur Griffith, his
Sinn Fein policies were passionately, even chauvinistically,
single-minded. Bloom is not a fellow of this kidney at all.
Joyce goes far out of his way to show that he is not.

—And after all, says John Wyse, why can't a jew love his country
like the next fellow?
—Why not? says J.J., when he's quite sure which country it is?
(p. 331)

The second remark is attributed to Stephen Dedalus and applauded by Professor MacHugh [3] in one manuscript fragment of
"Cyclops" which brings both these personages out of "Aeolus"
into Barney Kiernan's; its origin lies in a remark made by James
Joyce in his own person about Amalia Popper (Ellmann, *JJ*,
p. 355). It ties in with a contemptuous view of Bloom in particular and Jews in general as opportunistic and self-seeking.[4] On
another occasion, Bloom is made to cite, in perfect seriousness,
the selfish and unpatriotic man's motto. It comes out "Ubi
patria, vita bene," but muddled Bloom is evidently striving for
"Ubi bene, ibi patria" (p. 628).

Joyce's own politics were, of course, as complex as the next
fellow's; he claimed, simultaneously, to be utterly apolitical as
an artist and an ardent Irish Nationalist, devoted to his country's welfare, and only awaiting an incorruptible leadership to
spring into action. He described John S. Joyce as an ardent
Parnellite, associated, inexplicably, with underlings of the Castle
and the municipal administration. Which view he took of himself and his family seems rather to have depended on which
notion gave most scope at the moment for his native hauteur.
This triple confusion, without the hauteur, is duly transferred
in *Ulysses* to Mr. Bloom. He not only imitates Joyce's favorite
anti-hero, Mr. Dooley, in being indifferent to all causes except
his own well being; he is also on vague good terms with the
Castle gentry, Martin Cunningham and Jack Power; and he is
said, further, to be a great admirer and intimate adviser of

---

3. "That's Gallic," says he. "Paris did that for you." "Talking about
Gaelic," says Ned. . . .

*U. of Buffalo MSS*, "Cyclops."

4. The idea that Bloom has a "soft hand under a hen" (implying slyness
and greed) is first expressed by the narrator of "Cyclops," recurs on pp.
382 and 549, and perhaps relates to O'Madden Burke's six-word summary
of Bloom's social program, "Free fox in a free henroost" (p. 480).

Arthur Griffith—who despised both Mr. Dooley and the Castle gentry immoderately. Bloom is a known freemason in a country where the masonic lodges are the spearhead of anti-Catholic feeling; and simultaneously, he is an inspirer of the Sinn Fein policy, which was stridently pro-Catholic. Arthur Griffith seems to be the only person in Dublin who does not know that Bloom is a freemason; the freemasons, if they knew half as much about Bloom's alleged relations with Arthur Griffith as Martin Cunningham and the boys in Barney Kiernan's do, would have expelled him in a minute. For all Arthur Griffith's known liberality in his choice of associates, and Bloom's obvious mushiness of intellect, this is carrying political open-mindedness to an extreme. Bloom might well be ignorant of some of the political attitudes in question, or indifferent to them, or confused among them; he might have vague leanings toward all of them successively, depending on the influence he was under; but to represent him as being firmly committed to them all simultaneously is to spread him unbelievably thin, and to represent skillful politicians as childishly naïve. Bloom might well be illogical, but the novel gives us no adequate perspective on his illogicalities; it implies that they are everyone's illogicalities. Just possibly one reason for this may be that they were very close to James Joyce's own.

Another difficulty of representation has to do with Bloom's Jewishness, his own sense of himself as a Jew or ex-Jew. A superficial difficulty which Joyce has blandly ignored, but which his mention of Arthur Griffith obtrudes on our notice, is the fact that Griffith was openly and vigorously anti-semitic. He was particularly so in 1904. The occasion of his hostility was that succession of anti-semitic outbreaks in Limerick which has already been described as having some influence on *Ulysses* (Marvin Magalaner, *PMLA* (December 1953) LXVIII, 1219-23). In this matter, Father Creagh, the local priest, had taken the lead by denouncing Jewish usurers, Limerick Jews, and the Jews who killed Christ, with the strong imputation that these were birds of a feather. Griffith seconded Father Creagh in the *United Irishman*, demanding freedom for the Irish peasantry from the international moneylenders and profiteers. Fred Ryan, the economist who wrote for and edited *Dana* (pp. 31, 211), rebuked Griffith's anti-semitism, and declared in the first issue of that magazine that Irishmen who were claiming freedom for themselves could ill afford to refuse it to others. Griffith replied, embarrassed by some of the more rabid quotations from Father Creagh's sermons, but generally intransigent; and there the controversy petered out. Despite the overtones which anti-semitism has since acquired, the issue was not a serious or significant one. Griffith was anti-semitic, not on principle, but through a characteristically simple-minded and short-sighted suspicion of whatever was not Irish. Joyce coped with the problem characteristically too, by allowing the Citizen and the nameless narrator in Barney Kiernan's to express the anti-semitism on their own which was in fact Griffith's as well. But it is certainly clear that, in making Bloom responsible for Griffith's policy, Joyce does not want the ideal reader suffering from an ideal insomnia— on the contrary, he will fare much better with one whose sense of fact is dozing.[5]

Bloom, one knows, is supposed to be an elastic, amorphous personality; he absorbs and assimilates experience uncritically, as Stephen rejects it uncritically and on principle. The trouble is that attitudes and degrees of innocence which would be un-

5. Sentimentalists who simplify Bloom the Jew into a pathetic and admirable little man who forgives his enemies and is so apotheosized into the perfect Christian hero would do well to face the sizable element of anti-semitism in Joyce himself (see below, p. 146). This element is not distinct from powerful feelings of masochistic self-loathing; it involves also a shrinking from excessive self-awareness and a scorn of prudent self-interest.

thinkable in a man of Bloom's experience are rendered necessary by his neutral role in the novel. Joyce has to some extent sacrificed his character to his function in the fiction. This becomes particularly evident when he unquestioningly accepts Sir Frederick Falkiner's vision of Reuben J. Dodd as "a dirty jew" (p. 180). Sir Frederick had in fact become so irritated by an epidemic of window-breaking that when a Jew named Henry Kahn was guilty of this offense, in January 1902, he broke out into unrestrained language about Jews in general—oblivious of the fact that few Jews were window-breakers and that the shopkeeper whose window Kahn had broken was himself Jewish. The Recorder's language aroused widespread indignation; a question was ultimately asked in the House of Commons, and the Recorder was generally understood to have expressed regret and withdrawn his wilder charges. That is the factual background for the "great strawcalling" that Sir Frederick is said to have inflicted on Reuben J. Dodd (p. 180). Reuben J. Dodd was in bad odor with James Joyce because he had loaned money to John S. Joyce, and, curiously, expected repayment.

Now of course Joyce was at liberty to alter historical events as he chose, and in fact he chose to minimize Sir Frederick's anti-semitism as much as he could, so that Bloom could be made to see Sir Frederick as a fine, decent old man who did not object to Jews as a group, just to Reuben J. Dodd, the "dirty Jew." [6] In the context of real life, Bloom's attitudes are quite impossible; in the context of the fiction, they are merely wooden and improbable. For Bloom, as a Jew among Gentiles, adopts the alien point of view with quite unnatural ease, and takes the

6. Mr. Ellmann tells me that Reuben J. Dodd was probably not a Jew at all. It is curious that Bloom and all his companions in the funeral cortège should be mistaken in such a matter, though less unlikely perhaps that Joyce should be. But my point regarding Bloom's lack of fellow feeling for his fellow Jews still remains.

appalling Gentile distinction between "white Jews" and "dirty Jews" with all the seriousness of an Englishman.

It is hard to be sure of one's perspectives in these matters, but Bloom seems totally and unnaturally deficient in a kind of wry, self-mocking humor, such as one finds pre-eminently in Heine, but which also seems to me characteristically Jewish. Bloom has, in fact, no sense of involvement. In part this is doubtless an artistic option, but in part it also represents an imaginative deficiency. The Jews of Dublin are not semi-Oriental nomads, wandering the face of the earth under the curse of having crucified Christ. Neither are they ordinary Irishmen with Catholicism subtracted. The ghetto experience has made its own funny, rueful, derisive wound in them, which Joyce would have had to be a much more perceptive and adaptable man than he actually was to have captured. In fact, Bloom is a magic-lantern Jew, as he is a cut-out Hungarian.

Or, to speak more analytically, Bloom's Hungarian character was a surface to which Joyce tried (not very hard) to give a semblance of substance, and for which he tried (not very successfully) to find a function. On the other hand, Bloom's Jewish character was a symbol into which Joyce tried to project, not only his social reflections about modern man, but some rather intimate and complex psychic responses of his own. Bloom's Jewishness served, for Joyce, as a vehicle for his own self-pity; his moral complacency; his loneliness; his deep sense of sexual injury; his guilt; his self-loathing. As a Hungarian, Bloom has hardly any fictional functions; as a Jew, he has almost too many. This is only one of several circumstances which, taken in conjunction, make him seem more like a verbal device than a proper literary character.

## Dog-God

Joyce, who feared and hated dogs, represented a number of them in *Ulysses*, with various intent. Here at least we are almost free of the temptation (should it be called an obsession?) to look for real-life originals; not many of the dogs in 1904 Dublin left memorials of themselves which can still be traced. There is, to be sure, an exception. The Citizen's dog, Garryowen, is evidently modeled on a hound owned by Aunt Josephine's father; he is "old Giltrap's dog" (p. 307), and "grandpapa Giltrap's lovely dog Garryowen" (p. 346), with perhaps a hint of a performing dog which appeared, in January 1904, at the Tivoli. (This act was called, enchantingly, "Harry Edson and His Wonderful Dog 'Doc,' the Dog With the Human Brain and Gold Teeth.") But his origin is the oddest thing about Garryowen.[7] The other dogs in *Ulysses*, particularly the one which threatens Stephen on the strand and the one which follows Bloom into Nighttown, call for more exalted exegesis.

In the first place, both dogs are Protean in their transformations. Stephen's looks at first like a rabbit, then like a buck, a bear, a wolf, and a calf; only when he finds the corpse of the drowned dog does he pause, "sniffling rapidly like a dog" (p. 47). Later on the same page, he will be a fox burying his

7. Among the details loosely associated with Garryowen is a review of his poetry in an evening contemporary by D.O.C., initials which, read backwards, describe the incident (a "cod" is a joke). "Little Sweet Branch," whose work has been mentioned with Garryowen's, is Douglas Hyde with his Gaelic pseudonym translated (see Yeats's *Autobiography*, p. 132); Donald Mac Considine, with whose work the dog's poetry has also been compared, eludes identification entirely. The reference in his *rann* to "Lowry's lights" shows that Garryowen has been appearing on the stage of Dan Lowry's Music Hall, the Empire Palace, along with Great Marie Kendall, no doubt.

grandmother, a pard, and a panther, vulturing the dead; so it is evidently significant that his dog nature recurs just when he encounters the dead dog. The corpse forces upon him and upon Stephen the recognition of his dogginess, and causes a most unequivocal phrase to recur in Stephen's mind. "Dogskull, dog-sniff, eyes on the ground, *moves to one great goal*" (my italics). Mr. Deasy has said, on p. 35, that "all history moves towards one great goal, the manifestation of God." This is certainly the manifestation of dog, toward which the mongrel Tatters,[8] the silted dog corpse, and Stephen have moved.

The scene also relates thematically, and by overt statement, to the wholly imaginary and deliberately symbolic man drowned off Maiden's Rock, of whom Stephen has been thinking. As the dog recognizes himself manifested in the body of the drowned dog, Stephen may find himself manifested in the body of the dead man. This parallel is made partially explicit by Stephen's applying to the dead dog the epithet which has previously been applied to him, "dogsbody" (pp. 7, 8). In this epithet, it seems clear, the overtones are more important than the literal meaning. For the only recognized public meanings of the epithet, first applied to Stephen by Mulligan, are ludicrously irrelevant—midshipman or pease pudding. Even if we suppose it used loosely and in derision, the epithet in this sense has very little point. Its overtones, however, are very rich and complicated. Dogs, being often scavengers, are generally considered unclean beasts, hence represent outcasts and pariahs. Sexually shame-

---

8. His name derives, no doubt, from the famous dog Tatters, belonging to Conn the Shaughraun in Boucicault's play—a dog who, though he takes some part in the action of the drama, never appears on stage.

The dog on Sandymount strand is Mulligan ("a primrose doublet") and Ireland ("For that are you pining, the bark of their applause?"), as well as one of Ireland's many pretenders ("Paradise of pretenders then and now") (p. 46); hence, an incarnation of Proteus.

less, they provide the material for insults like "son of a bitch"; often fawning and obsequious, they carry the implication of servility and cowardice. Finally, in English at least, the reversal Dog-God is a handy plaything for ironists, especially those obsessed with the enormous distance between God and Man. In the passage of "Proteus" presently under discussion, there seems no reason to exclude any of these meanings from our consciousness. Stephen's reflections throughout the chapter have concerned the place of God in the universe, whether behind particular phenonena or within them. The dead dog, being a part of the natural universe, is a manifestation of God as legitimate as Stephen Dedalus, the landscape ("Sir Lout's toys"), or anything else. On the other hand, this is not the only or even an ultimate view of phenomena for Joyce, who like a good Aristotelian generally saw the texture of things as more substantial than the image of a transparent veil or curtain would imply. God as Joyce conceives him is evidently more a shout in the street—intrusive, irrelevant, confusing—than part of the continuing texture of things. Perhaps the abrupt dogginess of the dog, confronted with his own kind, suggests the shock and terror of unmediated vision, as the kick he gets from his master is its reward. At least we have some legitimate reasons for finding significance in the crossing of live and dead dogs in the "Proteus" scene. There is here a texture of symbolic relations demanding to be borne in mind—not, surely, as an ultimate philosophic position, nor, necessarily, as a key for future interpretations, but as one of several philosophic positions with which Joyce plays dramatically in *Ulysses*. Perhaps even this reflexive vision is included in the scene, the full richness of which unfolds only gradually. Being emphatically a live dog, Stephen (Joyce) can play several roles, adopt various poses, see life under numerous unreconciled aspects (as he is doing in this book, and above all in this chapter); but death will reveal, as it cancels, identity.

If we suppose, then, that Proteus the *Ding-an-sich* reveals himself only in this elusive and partial way, it is also clear that the scene does not confer on its properties (dogs, either live or dead) any fixed symbolic character. Their sniffy, inquisitive, metamorphic nature clearly reflects an aspect of human behavior. But they are no more likely to reflect, recognize, or be irradiated by the Divine Nature than anyone or anything else in the cosmos. Garryowen is a surly mutt, not a representative of Immanuel. Bloom is fool enough to think the dog likes him, but actually Garryowen has growled at him a couple of times, sniffed at him with suspicion, and finally chased him with murderous intent—behaving in none of these instances like anything but an ill-natured cur.

The dog which follows Bloom into Nighttown is more interesting. Like Stephen's dog, he metamorphoses continually, being a spaniel on p. 425, a retriever on p. 430, a terrier on pp. 434 and 440, before entering on a complex series of quick changes on pp. 445-6. On these two pages he is successively retriever, wolfdog, setter, mastiff, spaniel, bulldog, boarhound, and greyhound. These multiple appearances pretty well exhaust his potential; and, having popped up briefly on p. 463 as a beagle, a dachshund, and Paddy Dignam, he subsides for better than a hundred pages.

The crucial passage is therefore that on pp. 445 and 446, where Bloom, in pursuit of Stephen, finds himself at fault. Here the dog appears, nuzzles Bloom's hand, and begs of him, wriggling obscenely. Bloom is about to give him the crubeen, but holds back and feels the trotter. "Sizable for threepence," he thinks. "But then I have it in my left hand. Calls for more effort. Why? Smaller from want of use. O, let it slide. Two and six." The trotter did indeed cost threepence, but the pig's

foot was only fourpence, so "two and six" must refer to something else.[9] Whatever it is, and whatever the reason for which
Bloom is worried about his left hand, nothing comes of the
encounter. The dog eats his food (fulfilling thereby a Cerberus
parallel) but does nothing to help him find Stephen or forward
his faltering purpose. Accused by the watch (they carefully con-
jugate his name as far as the accusative), Bloom protests that
he is doing good to others, but only the seagulls testify to his
virtuous intentions, the dog dribbles rabid scumspittle and
growls at Bob Doran. "Let it slide," indeed; one is only too
happy to.

On pp. 585-6, after Stephen has been struck by Private Carr,
the retriever reappears, but all he does is echo the last syllable
of the previous speaker. "Salute!" cries Major Tweedy, and the
dog repeats eight times "ute." "Blow," shouts the bawd, and
the dog repeats three times "wow." Private Compton asks "who
owns the bleeding tyke," but quite properly gets no answer,
and the dog disappears. There is a bark in the distance on
p. 593, but no further token of a canine presence. Of course,
the very indifference of the crowd and ineffectuality of the dog
may be read, if one wishes, as a pathetic picture of God in the
modern world, where truth cries out in the streets and no man
regards it. But there is no reason to think the dog speaks truth,
or contains truth, or has any truth to convey, one way or another. The chorus of the damned repeats backwards a phrase
containing the word "God" and so inevitably produces "Dog"
but this may or may not be related to the dog in the scene.
The effect was introduced only in the last proofs, and the
French translation simply inverts "Dieu," to give us "Ueid."
Bloom's action in rescuing Stephen is that of a retriever (the

9. Even if Bloom, like Reuben J. Dodd redeeming his son, paid "one and
eightpence too much" for his food (pp. 93, 445), that would still give us
only two and three. Cf. also p. 696.

dog's present incarnation), and Bloom is a consistent retriever, having once retrieved a lame dog (pp. 641, 753); so that the confrontation of Bloom and Stephen is in effect the confrontation of dog and dog. But it has no such effect as the confrontation in "Proteus"; nobody discovers anything in particular and so far as the two protagonists behave in a doggy manner (they sniff, walk suspiciously around one another, finally urinate together), this is precisely the least remarkable and interesting thing about them.[10]

Elsewhere, the dogs of *Ulysses* are surely random. Mrs. Conway's Skye terrier (pp. 172, 665, 723, 745) may or may not be symbolic of anything, but if he is, it is in a most torpid and inactive way. Odysseus came home to a dog named Argos, with interesting mythological connections, but there is no parallel dog in *Ulysses*, and Athos, Bloom's father's dog, is no more than a name (pp. 89, 708). Mrs. Stanhope calls Molly "Doggerina" on a postcard (p. 740), which may be an elaborate roundabout for "bitch" as well as a backwards way of saying "little goddess," but does not strike Molly as peculiar, given the fact that the lady calls her husband "wogger." A couple of dogs were copulating in the street when Bloom and Molly managed to beget Rudy (pp. 88, 763), but if there is crucial symbolic significance in this event, it is grotesquely embodied in a dramatic shape, and buried in an oddly out-of-the-way corner of the book's structure.

In this whole matter of dogs and their function in the novel,

---

10. If there are going to be any climactic symbols of Bloom's communion with Stephen, they must be sought in "Eumaeus" and "Ithaca." The ceremonial micturition and the drinking of ceremonial cocoa have been put forward. The latter convinces more than the former. But neither left much trace in the planning of the book. There is a single enigmatic phrase in *British Museum Additional MSS* #49975, "Ithaca," which reads: "SD = cocoa 'creatura.' " But this could mean many things. There is nothing whatever about the ceremony in the garden.

it seems best to assume that Joyce started with certain "given" properties of his story and actors, and worked them into the fiction wherever they seemed to fit on one level or another. He did not start with a categorical Dog-God relation or equation, and deliberately exploit it by working gods and dogs into all the significant juxtapositions he could discover. If anything, it seems probable that he started with the figure of Ulysses, which he probably investigated (to begin with) in some such commonly available handbook of mythology and symbolism as that which Selig Korn published in 1843 under the reversed name of S. Nork. Looking up "Ulysses" in the splendidly named *Etymologisch-symbolisch-mythologisches Real-Wörterbuch zum Handgebrauche für Bibelforscher, Archäologen und bildende Künstler* (Stuttgart, 1843), one would discover immediately, not only that Odysseus is his own son and that Penelope is typologically "the veiled one" [11] but that three animals in particular are associated with Odysseus, the pig, the dog, and the fox.

The career of Odysseus is indeed strikingly bound up with pigs, from the boar which marked him on Parnassus, to the beasts of Circe's palace, to the charges of Eumaeus. As the deadly boar which almost killed Adonis-Odysseus, the pig is a symbol of death, sacred to Pluto and Persephone, to whose country Odysseus journeys. But it is also, because of its splendid rate of reproduction, a symbol of fertility and growth. Finally, Eumaeus the swineherd, who comes of royal stock in a far-distant land and possesses 360 pigs in 12 pens, is identified with Odysseus (who brought 12 ships to Troy, killed 12 Trojans, shot his arrows through 12 axes, and killed 12 slave-girls who

11. Molly Bloom is seen only once in *Ulysses* when she is not in bed, and then only briefly (p. 222). The bedclothes drawn up over her face remind Bloom of the word "yashmak," a word doubtless brought to Joyce's attention as the title of an 1897 musical comedy.

misbehaved with $9 \times 12 = 108$ suitors). Both are gods of the solar year; and both, being descended from Persephone (who is Maya the weaver and therefore intimately related to Odysseus' three weaving women, Penelope, Calypso, and Pallas), are aspects of Hermes. In this capacity, Odysseus is regularly represented (says Korn) with staff, hat, and dog; his faithful hound Argos is related to the two solstitial dogs Argos and Scylla, as well as to another cosmic canine, Sirius; in his hermetic capacity as conductor of souls, he is familiar with Cerberus too.[12] Finally, and this appears notably far-fetched even in a generally far-fetched treatise, Korn declares that Odysseus' skill in deceiving his own wife entitles him to the badge of fox, like Hermes his progenitor.

I am not arguing here that Joyce was specifically acquainted with Korn's dictionary. If he had been, he might have found (in addition to the themes already adumbrated) some useful hints for Bloom as *Lingamzwerg* (phallic dwarf), as *Vegetationsfeind* (enemy of fertility), and as *Selbstgegenübersteller* (self-encounterer: he meets himself not only in the figures of Eumaeus and Hermes, but in Irus and Thersites). By spreading out from Korn's article on "Ulysses" he might have picked up a good deal more, not only of curious lore, but of complex interpretation, at once appallingly naturalistic and highly esoteric. The natural processes of changing weather, vegetable growth, and sexual reproduction are everywhere invoked to explain the tangled complexities of mythology and religious practice. Korn himself merely reproduces in capsule form the work of a thousand poets, scholiasts, mythographers, anthro-

12. David Hayman argues interestingly if briefly that "Mercurial Malachi" becomes identified through hat, staff, and "his my sandal shoon" with Stephen (*Joyce et Mallarmé*, Paris, 1956, I, 100-101). But a satisfying, systematic study of the established hermetic symbols in the book is still to be made.

pologists, and students of comparative religion. If Joyce had wanted to study a more staid and conservative compilation (an unlikely supposition in itself), he might have consulted Dr. Oskar Seyffert's *Lexikon der klassischen Alterthumskunde*; or he might have gone to the work of Max Müller, Salomon Reinach, Pauly & Wissowa, W. H. Roscher (whose studies on the *omphalos* no doubt influenced his interest in the word), Jane Harrison, O. Gruppe, Lewis Farnell, Percy Gardner, or C. V. Daremberg & E. Saglio.

From all or any of these sources, so available to a man with Joyce's interests, attitudes, and linguistic ability as to be practically unavoidable, he could within a week's time have acquired a list of properties and symbolic relationships sufficient to have stocked his novel twenty times over. Obviously, the selection which he made among these themes was almost as significant as the act of creating them would have been, if he had had to create. Yet, for all this, the two processes are different. The traditional properties of Odysseus and Telemachus, the traditional relations between them, do not have to pay a symbolic tax to gain admission to the novel. They can be taken as givens. Usurper, web, whore, prudence, exile, fidelity, navigation, home, revenge, the underworld—these are concepts without which one could not recite the most primitive version of the *Odyssey*. Pig, dog, staff, hat, moly, and other assorted properties of Hermes are not quite such inevitable modalities of the fable, but they are pretty hard to avoid.[13] Their presence in the pattern of the fiction does not necessarily serve immediate, specific objectives. Like the chin-whiskers of Uncle Sam or the gaiters of John Bull,

---

13. Just as Joyce neglected Martin Cunningham's **death by water** in favor of an archetypally less interesting death by strong liquor, so he neglected all sorts of available dogs which might have been inserted in his novel. The real parallel in the Bloom ménage for Odysseus' elderly hound Argos is Bloom's nameless cat. This may be a point in itself.

they are properties traditional to the characters. Joyce sometimes found brilliant applications—parodic, serious, symbolic,
superficial—for these properties within the complex texture of
his own tapestry, but sometimes he did not. Quite sensibly he
continued to use them anyway, whether or no; and left the
reader to find or neglect the application, according to his temperament.

# 5

## Scholar, Poet, Wit

### Stephen's Originalities

In the course of his somewhat casual educational efforts at
Deasy's school, Stephen Dedalus propounds to his scholars a
curious riddle:

> The cock crew
> The sky was blue:
> The bells in heaven
> Were striking eleven.
> 'Tis time for this poor soul
> To go to heaven.

—What is that? (p. 27)

Not surprisingly, none of the young gentlemen in the class can
find an answer to a problem so enigmatic; nor, I dare say, have
many of the readers of *Ulysses* solved the riddle on their own.
As they read, they must, therefore, set it down as just another of
the obliquities of this very oblique young man. Even when
Stephen announces the answer triumphantly as "The fox bury-

ing his grandmother under a hollybush," things are not exactly crystal clear. Why, we ask, a fox? Why a fox's grandmother? Why under a holly bush? For that matter, why eleven? There may be answers to all these questions, but as they are merely possible, perhaps we had better face immediately an even broader question. The riddle may be in effect a shaggy dog riddle, the point of which would be simply that it has no point. Or, more intriguing still as a possibility, the answer which Stephen proposes to his own riddle may be in some way revelatory of his inner impulses. Not to prolong the matter, the riddle is a traditional piece of tomfoolery based on folklore, which is recorded —both question and answer—in P. W. Joyce, *English as We Speak It in Ireland*, p. 187. There is one weak evasion in Stephen's version of the answer; he changes the original "mother" of the response to "grandmother." But in his inner thoughts, he returns immediately to the original version, and while in fantasy he reverts to the transparent "grandmother" disguise (pp. 544-5, 557-8), we shall not be much exercised to find or create a private, personal meaning for the riddle in Stephen's mind. He sees himself as the fox, savage and ravenous, yet in the race of life a predestined quarry.[1] He has buried his mother, a poor soul trodden underfoot, that he might live. Her burial under the evergreen holly is her hope of resurrection; at eleven o'clock the sun (Son) is rising to its highest point.

But these are, or might be, only the riddle's purely private

1. When Bloom is turned upon by the mob, which was lately adoring him, they cry, "Lynch him! Roast him! He's as bad as Parnell was. Mr. Fox!" (The last two sentences were added in a late stage of proof.) When Parnell was in hiding with Mrs. O'Shea, "Mr. Fox" was one of the names he used; he also called himself Smith, Preston, and Stewart, so Joyce's choice of "Fox" is apparently significant—as it may well have been for Parnell himself. See also Stephen's phrase (p. 191), apparently descriptive of Shakespeare, "Christfox in leather trews." For the folklore analogues of Stephen's riddle, see F. J. Norton, "The Prisoner Who Saved His Neck with a Riddle," *Folk-Lore*, LIII (March 1942), pp. 27-56.

connotations for Stephen; and when we know that the riddle is not original with him, or peculiar to him, the impact of these connotations is considerably lessened. Stephen has not invented or altered the riddle for any fictional purpose, except in the minor detail of substituting "grandmother" for "mother." Since the riddle was a stock, prefabricated bit of foolishness, it can have just the sort of meaning attaching to an *objet trouvé*, that is, a meaning defined by its artistic context. That artistic context can be taken as the classroom situation within which it is asked, and the enduring guilt over his mother's death which intimately enfolds Stephen's mind. In the first aspect, Stephen is and remains a forbiddingly negative person; the riddles he propounds have answers, but his hearers have to know them beforehand or independently, so that instead of involving the mind in a labyrinth, they repel it by means of a glassy surface. Under that glassy surface spread out the personal connotations which the riddle may have for Stephen; they are largely undefined, and limited only by the reader's ingenuity in looking for them. This is a frequent quality of the novel.

One of the standard points about the *Portrait of the Artist as a Young Man* is that Stephen is not much of an artist. On pp. 77-8 he writes a pseudo-Byronic poem to E. C., which (perhaps fortunately) we never see; and on pp. 254-62 he composes a pseudo-Dowsonian villanelle, which we do. For the rest, he wanders about, lecturing his instructors, reciting before his fellow students, cuddling fine phrases in his mind, and feeling grandly sensitive. The young man generates a disproportionate amount of dark rapture and languid hauteur for the amount of literature he actually brings forth; and, it is often argued, we are supposed to feel this as a satiric "point" made by Joyce against Stephen Dedalus. The artist being represented is indeed a very young man; and Joyce, instead of playing Stephen Dedalus off against Dublin, may be thought almost to have equated them.

Dublin is a dreary, decadent city, and Stephen is the sort of callow, rebellious young crocodile who is bred out of it.

But the Stephen Dedalus who enters upstage left in *Ulysses* is only two years older than the young man who set out on his travels at the end of the *Portrait*; his experience of the world has been increased simply by a couple of months' starvation in Paris, the death of his mother, and a few more months of discontented inanition in his father's house in Cabra. Hence it should not surprise us if the poem he writes in the "Proteus" section, on a scrap torn from Mr. Deasy's letter about the hoof-and-mouth disease, is less than great art, perhaps even less than original creation. It is adapted, in point of fact, from one of Douglas Hyde's *Love Songs of Connacht*. Stephen's contribution is a bit of somber tempestry, and the demonology implied in the words "pale vampire":

| HYDE | DEDALUS |
|------|---------|
| And my love came behind me, | On swift sail flaming |
| He came from the south, | From storm and south |
| His breast to my bosom, | He comes, pale vampire, |
| His mouth to my mouth. | Mouth to my mouth. |

There is no question, of course, that Joyce could have provided Stephen with an original poem, had he chosen to do so, and one a good deal better than this turbulent little quatrain, in either version. If he was making a "point" against Stephen, why did he bury it so deeply, and what did he expect to gain by doing so? For Stephen's act of creation in *Ulysses* is clearly intended to be a real act of creation. It is described with the same sort of reverence as surrounds the creation of the villanelle in the *Portrait*. Stephen plays with his rhymes, compares them with Italian rhymes, seeks (just as in the *Portrait*) for some paper to write on, damns Deasy's bank notes to make evident his Bohemian values, and talks of his lovers in the poem as if they were his own creatures. "Mouth to her kiss. No. Must be

two of em. Glue 'em well. Mouth to her mouth's kiss" (p. 48).
We are plainly supposed to see this as the very act of artistic
decision and choice; it is exercised, curiously, on the one line
which is almost word-for-word identical with Douglas Hyde's.
Perhaps the motive here, as in following Hyde at all, is conceal-
ment, an inner reservation on Joyce's part against displaying the
creative act; perhaps it is an ironic hedge against the accusation
of self-display; perhaps it is a satiric assault upon Stephen. The
first two alternatives make some sense psychologically, if we
think of Joyce as a peep-show artist; but not very much if we
think of him as literary craftsman. The third alternative under-
cuts Stephen almost completely. The villanelle of the *Portrait*,
with its hothouse atmosphere of Dowson-cum-Swinburne, is a
rather flimsy verse, and there is good ironic character-delineation
in having Stephen produce just this sort of mannered, characterless poem. He is not a very good poet, but he is not a plagiarist; nor is there any evident reason why he should be a
plagiarist. For in a novel, which operates perforce within a limited representational scale, if Stephen is too silly or too rascally
a fellow, then the Ireland with which he quarrels will stand out
too brightly, and the reader will be left indifferent as between
them. Within *Ulysses* there is even less point in Stephen's being
a naïve plagiarist, ignorant even of *The Love Songs of Connacht*,
or—alternatively, and rather worse as an alternative—ignorant of
the fact that he knows them. For a man who proudly announces
himself as a "judge of impostors" (p. 576) [2] it will scarcely do to
be an abject impostor himself, unless somewhere in the novel
there is a center, a focus, of the relatively genuine. Of course
one can argue that it is not in Stephen at all, that it is in the

2. In all fairness, it must be granted that the phrase in which Stephen lays
claim to this position had a somewhat battered history, and should not,
perhaps, be taken too seriously. An early MS describes O'Madden Burke
as "Gentleman, patriot, scholar, and judge of malt" (*U. of Buffalo MSS*,
"Cyclops").

later Joyce, the author of *Ulysses*, the man who in 1922 climactically published. This view has some sizeable inconveniences, as it reduces a good part of the novel to a series of exultant leers —"Look how much smarter I am now than I was seventeen years ago!"—and indeed it is downright incompatible with some of the author's proceedings in his own person. But these points will emerge.

Stephen the student has in general the indirect and enigmatic manner which delights in enunciating conclusions without grounds. On p. 209, he very kindly and uncharacteristically refers us to "my lords bishops of Maynooth" as the source of his words, when he declares that original sin was known to Shakespeare: it "darkened his understanding, weakened his will, and left in him a strong inclination to evil." Without much trouble, we may find the appropriate passage in the *Maynooth Catechism*, Chapter V, No. 56: "Because of Adam's sin, we are born without sanctifying grace, our intellect is darkened, our will is weakened, our passions incline us to evil, and we are subject to suffering and death." This is straightforward paraphrase, and Stephen's citation of source is as dutiful as one could want. A rather subtler use of a more elaborate catechism appears in the *Portrait*, in that scene where Stephen and Cranly are talking over the relative advantages of being damned and redeemed. Stephen speaks with some bitterness of having to spend an eternity in the company of the dean of studies.

—Remember—Cranly said—that he would be glorified.
—Ay—Stephen said somewhat bitterly—bright, agile, impassible, and, above all, subtle (*Portrait*, p. 283).

Cranly's next remark, a famous one, is that Stephen's mind is supersaturated with the religion in which he says he disbelieves. It gains its point from the circumstance that Stephen's four adjectives are taken from the *Catechism of the Council of*

*Trent,* "On the Eleventh Article of the Creed," where the souls of the dead are described as "impassible, bright, agile, subtle," with a paragraph devoted to justifying each adjective. Though this scene is sketched out in *Stephen Hero* (pp. 141-2), the four adjectives do not appear, and Cranly's summary remark is not made.

To see that Stephen makes use of the catechism in order to attack the Church is to gain a new perspective on his quarrel with Rome. The borrowing is creative on Joyce's part and doubtless on Stephen's as well. But not all his borrowings are so clearly motivated. In the course of their morning conversation atop the Martello Tower, Stephen and Mulligan are much exercised by the mirror which Mulligan is using to shave; their conversation regarding it consists largely of borrowings from Oscar Wilde. Mulligan holds it forth, bidding Stephen look at himself; and then, when Stephen seems displeased at his own image, Mulligan laughs gaily:

—The rage of Caliban at not seeing his face in a mirror, he said. If Wilde were only alive to see you (p. 8).

The phrase is, of course, from the Introduction to *The Picture of Dorian Gray:* "The nineteenth century dislike of Romanticism is the rage of Caliban not seeing his own face in a glass." The quotation is not very apposite; Stephen in fact *has* seen his face in the mirror, and does not much like what he sees there. He is not, in this scene, anti-Romantic; nor is he generally much concerned with problems of Romanticism versus Realism, such as Wilde was happy to play with. The phrase is evidently a flip borrowing.

In any event, Stephen responds by drawing back, pointing at the glass, and declaring with bitterness:

—It is a symbol of Irish art. The cracked lookingglass of a servant.

This epigram is greeted by Mulligan with considerable respect. He suggests that Stephen go downstairs, repeat it to Haines, and touch him for a guinea (p. 9). In fact it does get repeated while breakfast is preparing, and on p. 17, Haines remarks, "That one about the cracked lookingglass of a servant being the symbol of Irish art is deuced good." What none of them seems to recognize is that this epigram too is based on one of Wilde's—quite as closely imitative as the previous remarks on Caliban.

"I quite understand your objection to art being treated as a mirror," says Cyril in *The Decay of Lying*. "You think it would reduce genius to the position of a cracked looking-glass." Stephen's contribution is simply the equation of Ireland with a serving-maid; it raises his conversation above that of his companions, but the eminence is a low one, and his contribution to the epigram would be generously paid at a guinea.

Who is deceived in all this passing back and forth of "tame essence of Wilde" (p. 196)? Mulligan and Haines, certainly; they take second-hand, warmed-over Wilde for first-hand Dedalus, and reward him, in their frank admiration, more richly than with guineas. But is he, in relation to them, a naïve or a deliberate counterfeiter? It makes some difference to our view of his character whether we suppose him to be acting out of weakness or malice. No doubt it is better for the novel if we suppose his borrowings deliberate and malicious. His telegram to Mulligan at the Ship is cribbed from Meredith, and he knows it, and (p. 418) says so. He is alleged to be in a society of knaves so a measure of counter-knavishness on his part is tolerable. On the other hand, when we discover that Stephen's creative acts are so largely assisted, a certain shadow is cast on his suspicion that people are out to "pick his brains." This is a biographical fact of recurrent significance; it is an element in the novel which we are apparently supposed to take seriously, and Bloom independently confirms on p. 605 Stephen's buried suspicions in this regard.[3] But where so much is borrowed, what sort of property rights can anyone assert?

Joyce makes much of Stephen Dedalus as a student of esoteric literature poring nightly over ancient tomes in Marsh's Library, near St. Patrick's Cathedral. Joyce's own acquaintance with this picturesque collection was not quite so extensive. Since all readers must sign into the library, his acquaintance with the books there can easily be judged. Just twice, on October 22 and 23, 1902, Joyce visited Marsh's Library to read the *Vaticinia* of Joachim Abbas (Venice, 1589). From the first of Joachim's prophecies, he selected the first part of the picturesque first sentence, "Ascende, calve, ut ne amplius decalveris, qui non vereris decalvere sponsam, ut comam ursae nutrias." The passage is itself based on II Kings, 2:23, where the little children are described as mocking Elisha on his way up to Bethel, by calling out at him, "Go up thou bald-head." Joyce may have been aware that the passage derives from II Kings and the story of Elisha and Elijah; had he known this, he would doubtless have welcomed it, as another father-son relationship to set alongside Kendal Bushe and Seymour Bushe, Dumas *père* and Dumas *fils*, Hamlet the elder and Hamlet the younger, and that in Anstey's *Vice Versa*. Stephen, on the other hand, seems to take the passage as a warning against entering the Church; indeed, to fortify this meaning, he alters, no doubt consciously, "ascende" to "descende" and "amplius" to "nimium." [4] We may take for granted that his reading of the prophecy has little or nothing to do with

3. The quixotic idealist who cared to see justice done in this intricate posthumous quarrel between Gogarty and Joyce might be interested in a report from Charles to Stanislaus Joyce (letter in Cornell University Library, 12 April, 1906) to the effect that Gogarty had a comic act consisting of a rapidly spoken description of Jesus as a wandering bill-sticker. Do we have here a hint for Bloom where Joyce would be the debtor?

4. The second change ("amplius" to "nimium") was made some time after "Proteus" appeared in the *Little Review* (May 1918).

its original intent; the reference to "ursa" in Joachim's sentence is supposed to point toward a member of the house of Orsini, which produced, among other Popes, that simoniac Nicholas III, whom Dante encountered in Hell. As a matter of fact, though the phrase is picturesque enough, Joyce seems to have had some trouble deciding where in his work it would appear to best advantage; a letter to Stanislaus Joyce, dated around August 10, 1906, requests the Latin quotation from the writings of Joachim of Flora; they were apparently to be used in rewriting "A Painful Case"! (letter in Cornell University Library).

The origins of Stephen's lecture on Shakespeare have been very adequately discussed by William Schutte in his thesis *Joyce and Shakespeare* (New Haven, 1957), but some of the twists that Joyce imposed upon his materials may perhaps need emphasis. In summary, it seems clear that Joyce took most of the materials from which he framed Stephen's discourse out of biographies by Georg Brandes and Sidney Lee (New York, 1898, and New York, 1916) with a liberal powdering of adventitious speculation from Frank Harris and Oscar Wilde. He worked this material over pretty carefully, incorporating it first in a notebook chronicle of Shakespeare's life from 1593 to 1616 (now in the University of Buffalo Library), and drawing on this, with modifications as needed, for the lecture. In general, Lee contributed facts on Shakespeare's family connections and business circumstances; Joyce read him carefully, simplifying radically where it suited his convenience, and pinpointing any word in Lee, however trifling, which served his novelistic purposes. For instance, Stephen says of Shakespeare (p. 202), "he sued a fellowplayer for the price of a few bags of malt"; the notion itself comes from either Brandes or Lee, both of whom report, however, that Shakespeare actually sued the Stratford apothecary, Philip Rogers. Joyce records the fact correctly in his notebook, but Stephen simplifies irrelevant details, and alters the relation in order to show Shakespeare's sense of property as stronger than his sense of good fellowship. On the other hand, Lee ordinarily refers to a house in London owned by Shakespeare as "the house in Blackfriars." Only once does he give its exact location, in a footnote on p. 457; it is "the house in Ireland yard," and Stephen, with his special eye for the verbal curiosity, picks it up under this name, and so refers to it on p. 201. Lee reports (*Life of Shakespeare*, p. 88) that Gilbert Shakespeare saw Will play Adam, in *As You Like It*, wearing a long beard; Stephen, attracted by younger and more active roles or desirous of giving the Bard a better part, allows him to play Orlando, or at least to take part in the play's wrestling scene. Stephen follows Lee and Brandes in reporting that a "gospeller" stayed at New Place, but omits the date (spring, 1614; it is distinctly and correctly recorded in Joyce's preliminary notebook) in order to give the impression that it happened after Shakespeare's death. At that time (according to Stephen's argument), Anne Shakespeare took up with puritans, and once more, spiritually and perhaps physically, cuckolded her dead husband. The curious titles of the tracts which she began reading in her dotage are anachronistic to the seventeenth century: *Hooks and Eyes for Believers' Breeches* and *The most spiritual Snuffbox to Make the Most Devout Souls Sneeze* (p. 204), and in fact they are not of that period at all. Joyce derived them from a review article based on Octave Delepierre's *History of the Literature of Lunatics*; the article appeared in the *Irish Independent* of June 15, 1904, p. 4, and Joyce used nothing else in it.

Frank Harris is responsible for a number of Stephen's more blithe identifications as well as his notions of Shakespeare's sex life. The phrase "Chettle Falstaff" (p. 202) evidently derives from Harris's assertion (*The Man Shakespeare*, New York, 1919, pp. 372-3) that Henry Chettle was the original of Falstaff. The story that Shakespeare was supplanted as the lover of Mistress Mary Fitton by the Earl of Pembroke is also repeated by Harris (*The Man Shakespeare,* pp. 202-11); it was originated by Thomas Tyler, and Stephen repeats it (pp. 194, 199). Of course Harris also accepts the story of Sir Will Davenant that he was Shakespeare's bastard son (*The Man Shakespeare,* pp. 386-7), and Stephen dutifully follows suit (p. 199). Karl Bleibtreu, though his name bulks large in *Ulysses,* did not contribute anything very substantial to Stephen's Shakespeare lecture. One of his letters (in the Cornell Library) reminds Joyce that Sidney Lee was really named Simon Lazarus; but the picture of the Earl of Rutland writing Shakespeare's sonnets from the Tower of London ("When in disgrace with fortune and men's eyes") proved a little fantastic even for Stephen.

As might be expected, Stephen makes very casual use of his historical materials. On p. 185, he declares that Robert Greene called Shakespeare "a deathsman of the soul"; Greene does use the phrase in the *Groatsworth of Repentance,* but he uses it of the abstraction "Lust," not of Will Shakespeare. The words with which Stephen tries to show that Shakespeare's art is the "art of surfeit" (p. 199) mostly do not occur at all in Shakespeare's writings; "marchpane" does occur just once. Most of the Elizabethan expressions which color Stephen's discourse were Joycean afterthoughts, added in late stages of the proof. Among these are, for example, such expressions as "bloodboltered" (p. 185), "sirrah" (p. 187), "nookshotten" and "God ild you" (p. 190), "lakin" (p. 199), "giglot" (p. 200), and "meacock" (p. 207), as well as the greater part of Gilbert Shakespeare's broad Warwickshire dialect (p. 206). These additions suggest an effort to impress as well as to divert. Mr. Schutte investigates interestingly Joyce's liberties with the firedrake, the date of which Stephen alters radically in order to dramatize

Shakespeare's cosmic importance. A pseudo-Miltonic quotation on p. 182 is mixed with half a line of real Milton and a line of real Dante; a phrase from *Macbeth,* "As happy prologue to the swelling act / Of the imperial theme" (I, 3, 127-9) is twisted, for Joyce's or Stephen's own comic purposes, into a reference to pregnancy (p. 189). The parallel between Shakespeare and Socrates is urged on the grounds that they both had shrews to wife and midwives as mothers; but Mary Arden, who married about the age of twenty and had plenty to occupy her after that, is most unlikely to have practiced the midwife's art, and there is no evidence that she did. Stephen makes a curious, and, for all one can tell, a deliberate error in discussing *Hamlet* when he says (p. 185) that in the play nine lives are taken off for his father's one. Gertrude, Claudius, Ophelia, Laertes, Polonius, Rosencrantz, Guildenstern, and Hamlet himself add up to only eight; who is the ninth?

Stephen has a curious habit, in this section, of seeming to quote others, while actually advancing ideas of his own. For example, he mentions "the new Viennese school Mr Magee spoke of" (p. 203). Not only has Mr. Magee made no such reference in the novel, he does not seem to be thinking in Freudian terms at all. Though less impatient than A.E. with the idea of prying into the poet's private life, he has said nothing more distinctively Freudian than the one word "doctor" (p. 202). This is no doubt a conscious confusion on Joyce's part; if Magee is the Freudian in the discussion, the obviously Freudian aspects of Stephen's theory are less explicit. On the other hand, an interesting connection is suggested by Stephen's misremembering (on p. 191) of John F. Taylor's "Language of the Outlaw" speech, which he heard on p. 140 from Professor MacHugh. *In painted chambers loaded with tilebooks*—the phrase does not occur, either in Professor MacHugh's version, or in any other version of Taylor's speech which we possess. In context it suggests that Stephen (through association with Thoth the bird-god of books and libraries) accepts identification with the Egyptian high priest, and so declines the language of the outlaw (Gaelic-Hebrew), in which the Word of God will be spoken. The inexactness of Stephen's quotation makes this declaration of apostasy a good deal less explicit than it would be if more neatly connected with "Aeolus."

The details of the Shakespeare chapter, which is Stephen's most concentrated display of historical scholarship, are thus seen to be very freely handled. The overriding objective of the scene is to display Stephen's mind in action. Here, by contrast with his various foils, he is made to shine. Not only does he provide all the new materials for the discussion, by ranging freely and securely through the maze of Shakespeare's social and domestic circumstances; he alone deals with vivid particulars and provides new meanings. Whatever others contribute to the discussion is either irrelevant, muzzy, or trite. In order to make his case seem stronger and his ideas more defensible than they actually are, Stephen is allowed a free hand with his sources; he strains the interpretation of his facts, and sometimes the facts themselves, very hard indeed. But he is allowed to be aware of his distortions when it seems that the reader may be so too (witness the picturesque firedrake). Thus Joyce has provided him with a built-in hedge against the reader's criticism; he knows what he is doing, the structure of his discourse is precarious, he is alone and sensitive amid a community of boors (the repeated invitations to social occasions from which he is excluded draw directly on our sympathy), and he uses all the interesting words and ideas which occur in the scene. In all these ways, the use of the scholarly materials in this section is made to serve the general end of marshaling the reader's unqualified support for Stephen.

The other concentrated area of Dedalian erudition is in the

field of Aquinas, Aristotle, and scholastic philosophy. Here again we need say the less on the topic since another fine book, Father Noon's *Joyce and Aquinas* (New Haven, 1957), enables us to estimate very closely the extent and quality of Joyce's acquaintance with Aquinas—particularly the degree to which the esthetic philosophy of Stephen Dedalus, as enunciated in the *Portrait*, can be called "applied Aquinas." There is little doubt that Joyce was generally familiar with the intellectual system of Aquinas, and that, indeed, it was the only major intellectual system with which, in his world, thinking people were concerned. But Father Noon dispenses sharply with Stephen as a purveyor of Thomistic esthetics (*Joyce and Aquinas*, pp. 11, 17), only salvaging a little from the lectures in the *Portrait* and the theory of epiphanies with the left-handed suggestion (*Joyce and Aquinas*, p. 73) that Joyce's intent may have been ironic. This is no more than kind, and it raises the awkward question why Joyce, who worked so hard to win our sympathy for Stephen in the library scene of *Ulysses*, should be thought to have undercut his character so radically in the *Portrait*.

It is apparently true that as Joyce proceeded with work on *Ulysses*, he grew increasingly impatient of Stephen. But if this feeling controlled, one would expect the ironic assaults to grow steadily deeper. Whatever other rule they obey, it is not this one. In fact, arguments have been put forth to just the opposite effect, that Stephen grows steadily in maturity and understanding from *Stephen Hero* to the *Portrait* to *Ulysses*. One may feel certain reservations here about the propriety of making a judgment of artistic intention depend on the accidental survival of a MS (if Joyce thought this line of development important, why didn't he publish or retain a complete MS of the book which made it clear?) and yet concede that in the simplest sense the statement is right. Stephen is older and more mature in *Ulysses* than in the *Portrait*, and in the *Portrait* than in *Stephen Hero*;

but the question is simply whether Joyce views him more ironically in one book than in another. I am sure that the irony is deeper in the *Portrait* than in *Stephen Hero*, but I suspect it is less marked in *Ulysses* than in the *Portrait*. One reason for these variations is that Stephen was not for Joyce a constant, uniform object toward which he took varying attitudes, but a shifting complex of forces within larger complexes, a reservoir of qualities which might be drawn on, as needed, for the purposes of the two finished books in which he appears. He threatens to overbalance the *Portrait*, and to heavyhand the other characters to death, unless restrained by a little authorial irony. But in *Ulysses* he is very effectively controlled by Mulligan, Bloom, and the established complacency which dominates the National Library; there is no need for ironic authorial undercutting.

Broadly speaking, I think we will understand "Joyce's" attitude toward Stephen better, the more we divide it into the attitudes of the *Portrait* and *Ulysses*. Joyce's attitude toward his subject is generally, like a painter's attitude toward "green," what the composition of his picture demands. But I do not think the critics who at every turn invoke ironic views of Stephen are really interested in forming coherent patterns at all; they mostly want to save Joyce from being identified with Stephen's naïvetés. There is no need to oppose to this view the amply documented biographical fact that Joyce did identify to a considerable degree with Stephen Dedalus, and sometimes with Stephen Dedalus in his more imposturous moments. He was particularly proud of his theory about Shakespeare and his esthetic theories—out of both of which he contemplated making separate treatises. But indeed, the argument need not depend on biographical facts at all. The fact is that within the works of art where Stephen appears he has no serious intellectual competitors. James Joyce blithely erased from the account of his university days the school's outstanding figure, Tom Kettle—no doubt for other reasons as

well, but partly because he threatened the intellectual suprem-
acy of young Dedalus. Father Butt says in *Stephen Hero* that
Dedalus doesn't know enough Aquinas to interpret his esthetic
position "practically" (*Stephen Hero*, p. 104); the adverb makes
the charge comic, but it is close enough to a larger truth so that
nobody is allowed to make it, or come close to making it, in
the finished *Portrait*. Stephen is consistently safeguarded from
invidious comparisons in matters of scholarship and intellect;
the second term of the comparison has to be imported, or remains undefined. (Mr. Hugh Kenner makes free use of a kind
of universal cosmic skepticism which he seems to think is the
Truth, and by contrast with which Stephen Dedalus is unfail-
ingly callow.) Stephen does indeed know remarkably little Aquinas, compared with Father Noon; but Joyce knew his business
well enough to keep people like Father Noon far outside the
representational scale of the *Portrait*. Had he really wanted to
make Stephen appear petulant, pretentious, and brash, he need
only have introduced for a moment one man possessing a touch
of Father Noon's scholarship and urbanity. He has not done so;
and we can only conclude that Stephen Dedalus represents the
highest range of intellectual hills that Joyce wants us to see in
his novel.

This whole matter of learning in fiction reinforces our perception of how arbitrary the scale of values in a literary work is
bound to be. In *A Streetcar Named Desire*, Tennessee Williams
has his protagonist read Whittier and Longfellow. On the side,
he is trying for pathos; this is the intellectual life of a provincial
high-school teacher. But it is also, in the context of the play,
the intellectual life, period. Nobody else reads anything more
exalted than comic books and racing forms; so that Whittier
and Longfellow stand within the drama for the life of the intellect generally. When Blanche DuBois is crushed and driven
into the asylum, modern culture goes with her; only animals are

left behind, gorged and contented. So with Stephen's esthetic theories in the *Portrait*; they do not produce great works of art, but they produce more vitality (of mind, of feeling, of language) than any other feature of Ireland depicted in the novel. It has often been remarked that the Dedalian esthetic is derived only remotely from Aquinas, but much more directly from the late nineteenth century. Oscar Wilde, Arthur Schopenhauer, Stéphane Mallarmé, Henrik Ibsen—from these four authors, it seems clear, one could derive much more of Stephen's conclusions than one could ever deduce from St. Thomas. Why, then, does St. Thomas bulk so large in the intellectual life of Stephen Dedalus, while these actual and immediate influences bulk so small? Obviously, not because Joyce wanted us to see Stephen's esthetic theories ironically, but because he wanted us to take them seriously. Aquinas is Joyce's *point d'appui*; he prides himself on being "steeled in the school of old Aquinas." Joyce's strategy propounds that modern authors, like Wilde, the hermeticists and symbolists, are posturers; they pretend to believe in anything which enables them to gain a good literary effect; they are clever, subjective, and private, and intellectual rigor is not in them. Stephen's thought, on the other hand, is rigorous and authentic; it forms itself on a clear and coherent intellectual system, which has withstood the test of the ages; it stands foursquare on the fact of external reality. (Joyce in *Ulysses* (p. 38) has Aristotle repeat, with his head, Dr. Johnson's famous experiment, with his foot, to prove the solidity of the external universe.) Aquinas authenticates Joyce and Aristotle authenticates Aquinas. It is a chain forged, precisely, to prevent the thin edge of irony from entering our view of Stephen. There is additional relish in the fact that Stephen the freethinker quotes Aquinas to the dismay of the dull and respectable who have always thought they understood him. One reason for Stephen's playing the role of hedgerow schoolmaster to Lynch and Cranly instead of lecturing to the literary society (as he did in *Stephen Hero*, and Joyce did in real life) is precisely to shield him from ironic attack, as well as to emphasize his habit of using whetstones. Dull themselves, the whetstones sharpen Stephen—it would serve no clear purpose in the novel to have us reminded that there are still other people in the world, in Dublin, compared with whom Stephen himself is pretty dull.[5]

Perhaps this view of the novel makes Joyce look less like the dean of studies in glory than one would prefer—there is no accounting for tastes. On the other hand, there may be readers who will gladly dispense with that agile, contemptuous, glittering, pervasive ironist who is always sneering at us for taking his characters and his ideas seriously. If all Joyce is doing in *Ulysses* is setting up with his left hand a series of cheap triumphs for his right, most of us will feel that his energies could have been better employed. Quite obviously, I am not denying that the ironic mode is frequent in *Ulysses*, only urging that in the matter of Shakespeare and Aquinas, the two largest ventures of Joyce's strictly intellectual life, the ironies are less sweeping and wholesale than they have appeared. Perhaps, indeed, they are less sweeping than we think they ought to be. But I do not think this is good warrant for reinterpreting the text in the teeth of its evident import.

5. My argument here runs tightly between Scylla and Charybdis. In urging that Joyce did not arrange Stephen's lectures on Aquinas and Shakespeare to look silly, I do not want to propose that either or both of them should be solemnly searched for the key to Joyce's career. The Son reconciled to the Father, the Sabellian heresy, and the rest seem to me remote and highly figurative metaphors for the processes of Joyce's intellectual and artistic development, which we can describe more exactly in its own terms than with fancy theological talk. I propose that the arguments are seriously intended as surfaces—using that term in the sense of a theatrical façade or flat, which we are not intended to see around. I reserve the right to feel grave doubts of their structural solidity.

## Joyce's Scholarship

When we have said so much to shield Stephen from the glittering ironies of incomplete comparison, there remain certain peculiarities in the handling of learning within the novel, qualities peculiar to Joyce rather than to his characters. One can describe them best by saying flatly that a good deal of the learning in the book is fake and at the same time genuine, like the quotation from Greene (above, p. 128), which is an accurate quote in itself, radically misapplied. Some of the variations on this theme involve a very high order of complexity; there is no better way to illustrate their diversities than by an almost random sampling.

On pp. 672-3, for example, there occurs a picturesque little section of historical philology, according to which both Hebrew and Irish were "taught on the plain of Shinar 242 years after the deluge in the seminary instituted by Fenius Farsaigh, descendant of Noah, progenitor of Israel, and ascendant of Heber and Heremon, progenitors of Ireland." In addition to Genesis xi:2, the source of this fanciful material is Geoffrey Keating's *History of Ireland*, Book I, sec. xv. Keating, in the process of deriving the Irish ruling house from Adam, describes Feinius Farsaidh as the son of Baoth, son of Magog, son of Japhet, King of Scythia and ancestor of the Phoenicians as well as the Milesians of Spain; and he dates the founding of the seminary precisely 242 years after the deluge. The translation of Keating's book published in 1908 by Father Patrick S. Dinneen [6] for the Irish Texts Society uses rather elaborate transcriptions of Gaelic names— Feinius Farsaidh, the plain of Seanair, Eibhear and Eireamhon.

6. No doubt it is this Father Dinneen whose request for a book distracts Mr. Lyster in the middle of the Shakespeare lecture (p. 208).

Joyce may have corrected and simplified these spellings himself or by reference to such transcriptions as those in John O'Hart's amazing book of *Irish Pedigrees*. The solemn, elaborate nonsense of these imaginary genealogies evidently amused him, and may amuse us; it is characteristic, however, that the joke is not random, and that Joyce copies with utmost accuracy from an ancient source material which is on the face of it fantastic.

Antisthenes, the Cynic philosopher, appearing first in "Aeolus" (p. 147), under the sponsorship of Professor MacHugh, recurs several times in the novel, and constitutes a strong touch of color in the representation of literary learning. He is a good author to cite; for not many people have read much Antisthenes, and nobody has read the book to which Professor MacHugh alludes, because it has been lost for over a thousand years. Its title survives among library lists as *De Helena et Penelope*, and there are traditions to the effect that the book defended a preference for Penelope over Helen. Professor MacHugh does not say specifically that he has read it; but he does not say, either, that he has not read it, and could not have read it. Joyce gets his chosen effects (which are, first, an unusual view of the Ulysses story, and next an erudition which everyone will feel to be uncommon) without actually committing himself or his character to a demonstrable untruth. The device is rather like that by which one cites in a casual, knowing way an unpublished fragment of Rilke's, or the title of a book by Lycurgus.

Joyce's tendency to dominate his reader with erudition which is real up to a point and then faked, takes many forms. When Stephen reflects on the "brood of mockers" suggested by his friend Mulligan, he lists (p. 195) three figures, all of whom sound impressive, but none of whom fits very exactly into his category. "Photius, pseudomalachi, Johann Most" are the names. Photius of Constantinople (815?-897), though in Western eyes a major heresiarch, was by no means a mocker. He was a man of immense learning and painful seriousness, as anyone who consults his *Homilies* will soon discover. He was not even a great heretic, for though the schism between East and West early became associated with his name, he was in fact a communicant of Rome at his death. Johann Most (1846-1906) also has a poor title to inclusion in a list of mockers. He was an anarchist leader, editor, martyr, controversialist; he was violently anti-clerical, but so far committed to his own creed and so far outside the Christian church as scarcely to count among the "mockers" of it. Joyce may have thought him a jester because he managed to die (of erysipelas, in Cincinnati) on St. Patrick's Day; but this is scarcely a major levity.[7] Finally, the name "pseudomalachi" is a total blank. The author of the Book of Malachi in the Old Testament is a shadowy figure, and St. Malachias the Irish prophet of the twelfth century is perfectly historical; but neither of them has a double or an imitator, and, in short, no pseudo-Malachi is known to ecclesiastical history. The word is formed on the analogy of the pseudo-Dionysius, and, if it makes reference to anyone in particular, doubtless refers to Mulligan, a fake radical who pretends to mock Christianity but retains a basic reverence for it. These three names are so ill-assorted, so diverse in their connotations or lack of connotation, and so obscurely connected (if they are connected at all) that their juxtaposition as "mockers" seems altogether perverse.

On the other hand, the three authors in whom one could find the person of the Saviour described (p. 674) are not only all historical, they all actually dealt with the person of the Saviour. Johannes Damascenus, Lentulus Romanus, and Epiphanius Monachus did not describe the Christ as "leucodermic,

7. Herbert Gorman (*James Joyce*, New York, 1939, p. 183) records Most among the "Marxists" whom Joyce had read.

sesquipedalian, with winedark hair," but they did describe him. Lentulus Romanus is available in several popular editions, and Epiphanius in the *Patrologiae Graecae*, but Joyce probably got their names somewhere else, for he shows no sign of having read the works within which their short and rather conventional descriptions of the Saviour occur. The third figure, St. John Damascene, probably supplies the link, for though he does not describe the physical person of Christ as do the other two, he is much exercised by the idea of "hypostasis" or the two natures of Christ as God and man. (One of his neater formulas is that they were combined in one person without the possibility of conversion, confusion, or separation.) It is probable that the juxtaposition of these names would give nervous indigestion to a professional theologian, and the actual terms used to describe Christ are silly on the face of them—yet, as often with Joyce, the mere fact of his possessing the names and being aware of a sort of common relevance among them suggests an erudition which is far from contemptible. It is as if, somehow, he felt impelled, wherever his learning is most considerable, to make an egregious blunder, in order to show that the learning is mere façade.

Rudolf Virag, in the course of his jerky, spastic apparition within the scene of Nighttown, makes abrupt and rather knowing reference to a number of far-flung heresies and heretics. He is "basilicogrammate" (p. 500), which, if I understand the word correctly, implies a lord of language; and certainly he flourishes big words with sesquipedalian virtuosity. Speaking of Christ, he mentions (p. 510) a fable that the Saviour was really a bastard son of Mary by a Roman centurion named Panthera. It is a tale familiar to Christian thought through rabbinical sources, as well as through its refutation by Origen (*Contra Celsum*, I, 32), and Thomas Hardy makes use of it in a poem; but without distinct

theological learning and interests, it would not be easy to lay hold of. Judas Iacchias, mentioned by Virag on p. 509, in the midst of his most enthusiastic blasphemies, is evidently a hermetic or occult version of Judas. The term Iacchus, originally a mystical appellation of Dionysus, was freely combined in hermetic circles with names of established religious figures (see, for instance, the term "Iacchus-Iesus" in George Moore's *Vale*, p. 167). Stephen's thoughts about Occam (p. 41) constitute a humorous extrapolation on a rather peripheral consideratio
 raised by *De Sacramento Altaris*, likely in Problem III; as a preliminary to more involved considerations, the *Venerabilis Inceptor* urges that the body of Christ need not be locally present anywhere in the sacrament. Stephen's joke is no less funny for being erudite. Lycopodium, to which Virag and Bloom make occasional reference, is a genus of cryptogams; their conversation is built on cryptograms, and occasionally on nonsense babble. Elephantuliasis (p. 505) is a nonsense-reference, like the consuls Diplodocus and Ichthyosaurus (p. 503); bubbly jock (p. 504) is Scotch slang for a turkey, just as it seems to be, and viragitis (p. 505) is a disease known only to Virag. Rualdus Colombus, on the other hand (p. 502), is an historical anatomist (1516-59), and the "bachelor's button" he is supposed to have discovered is the clitoris. Joyce was much impressed with an imaginary statistic, which he attributed to Colombus, to the effect that the "dorsal nerve" of the clitoris is four times larger than the corresponding nerve of a man (*U. of Buffalo MSS*, "Notes for the Episodes," Circe).

All this illustrates the random, almost perverse use of learning coupled with nonsense that is characteristic of Joyce. Mastiansky and Citron, accusing Bloom of apostasy, fling at him (p. 487) the names of two obscure Jewish heretics from the Middle Ages. Laemlein of Istria, the false Messiah, was Ascher Laemlein, an obscure Jewish prophet residing near Pola, who about 1502 proclaimed himself the Messiah; and Abraham Ben Samuel Abulafia was another pseudo-Messiah, born in Saragossa, who lived from 1240 to 1291 (?). But neither the religious terror nor the erudition of Bloom's neighbors can invoke anything more than George S. Mesias, Bloom's tailor, who presents a bill "to alteration one pair trousers eleven shillings." (For eleven shillings Bloom could have got a new pair of pants at Kino's.) The story that Arius breathed his last in a Greek water closet is typical of Joyce's eye for the picturesque detail; he might have found the story, vigorously specific and with built-in moral, in Epiphanius *Adversus Haereses* II, ii, x, or, more reticently phrased but closer to hand, in a footnote to Gibbon's *Decline and Fall*, XXI. The material on Aristotle's will (p. 201) comes from Diogenes Laertius, IV, 1; the idea that he was a "millionaire" may easily be extrapolated from the same source, and the fact that he was "bald" is selected from an ancient and very widespread tradition that he was slender, bald, dressed elegantly, and spoke with a lisp. The bit-pictures of Dublin history on p. 46 (galleys of the Lochlanns and turlehide whales) derive from two different sources, as from two very different periods of Irish history. The Lochlanns (Scandinavians) invaded Ireland in the eighth and ninth centuries; their arrival in fleets (not specifically "galleys") is described, for example, in Geoffrey Keating's *History of Ireland*, II, xvi, with which we know (see above, p. 136) Joyce was familiar. The stranding of a herd of turlehide whales, which saved Dublin from famine, took place in 1331, and is described in Walter Harris, *History and Antiquities of the City of Dublin* (London, 1766), XI.[8] Both incidents are described in the "Dublin Annals" section of *Thom's Directory*, but we know

8. Harris's book was being reprinted serially, during 1904, in the *Dublin Penny Journal*.

he got the turlehide whales from Harris, because the telling adjective "cagework," applied to Dublin, plainly derives from Harris's description of that style of architecture (IV, 1). The snatch of unidentified verse on p. 189 is from a poem by Louis H. Victory, "Self-Perturbating Mimicry," in *Poems* (London, 1895), p. 54:

> In quintessential triviality
> Of flesh, for four fleet years, a she-soul dwelt.

Joyce has mildly misquoted to conceal the fact that the poem describes a child. James Lovebirch, the pornographic author (p. 232, etc.), though pseudonymous and anachronistic, was as real as Paul de Kock and Leopold Sacher-Masoch; during the period 1908-21 he published in Paris such works as *Les Cinq Fessées de Suzette*; but I have not found *Fair Tyrants*. The quotation from Brunetto Latini (p. 192) had to come from the *Tesoro*, translated by Bono Giamboni (Bologna, 1887), II, 137-8; the notion that the unicorn once in the millennium cometh by his horn (p. 383) also derives from the *Tesoro*, though tacitly; and the reference to Drummond of Hawthornden (p. 192) is odd in being unnecessary—the things which Stephen has been saying bear no such intimate relation to anything in William Drummond as to require acknowledgment.

Among the unlikely possessors of polite learning must be numbered the Citizen, who (apart from his long account of the glories of Irish culture, widely available, for instance, in A. S. Green, *The Making of Ireland and Its Undoing*) describes William Field, M.P., as "hairy Iopas, that exploded volcano, the darling of all countries and the idol of his own" (p. 309). The reference is not to an obscure Gaelic deity, but to *Aeneid*, I, 740. Another esoteric bit of lore from the Citizen is the tribal slogan, "Lamh Dearg Abu," which he recites as he lifts a medher of dark, strong foamy ale to his lips (p. 319). The Gaelic means "Up the Red Hand," and gets one of its points from the fact that the Allsop bottle carries a red hand on its label. That the slogan of the O'Neills is also "Lamh Dearg Abu" renders the joke less broad but does not undercut it.

## Prudence and Vision

When we talk of Joyce's learning as having certain qualities, which we estimate from the finished novel, we of course imply certain tacit, vague, and quite misleading things about the process of the book's composition. We suggest that Joyce had a certain number of information particles which he was concerned, as a prudential matter, to use in building a novel. On occasion this is certainly what happened. The phrase from Joachim Abbas, picked up in Marsh's Library in the autumn of 1902, was carried about the Continent for sixteen years before Joyce found a use for it; but he held onto it, watched and waited, tried it here and presumably there, and finally worked it into his mosaic. We can trace the passage of other phrases, stored in early drafts, notebooks, workbooks, letters, diaries, newspapers, and individual memories, from their source ineluctably to their final position. Joyce was a very tenacious and economical writer; once he had a memorable phrase or a useful name, he did not lightly let it go.

But there are also, in the background of *Ulysses*, certain curious papers known as note-sheets, the full peculiarities of which have not yet been realized. (The original documents are in the British Museum and the University of Buffalo Library.) Professor A. W. Litz, in his excellent study, *The Art of James Joyce* (New York, 1961), has described the characteristics of many of these note-sheets. Crowded with incoherent and ill-written phrases, hatched over with dark crayon-overlays, they are very hard to read, but they clearly contain a great deal of material which, in modified or unmodified form, was finally transferred into the novel. Professor Litz, judging from the fact that they contain so much trivial material, concludes that the note-sheets were compiled and used late in the writing of *Ulysses*. They seem to him to comprise chiefly "verbal insertions, cross-references, minor themes" (*The Art of James Joyce*, p. 13). This is certainly an apt description of many of the sheets. Yet I doubt that it is the whole truth about them, or that it supports the conclusion that the note-sheets were used only in the last stages of revision.

For, in the first place, most of the note-sheets do not have the look of documents created over an extended period of time and incorporating materials from a variety of sources and occasions. Joyce commonly worked on his manuscripts with whatever writing device came to hand. One can often distinguish corrections as being done with different ink, a different pen, and in a somewhat different hand, from the original MS. Variations of this sort are clearly apparent in the note-sheets when they occur; but in many of the note-sheets they do not seem to occur very often. Joyce's notes flow continuously along, the phrases sometimes connected by a perceptible logical string, sometimes quite unconnected. But the handwriting is fluent, headlong, and to all appearances largely uninterrupted. Some of the note-sheets do look like collections of random phrases, scrawled every which way with a variety of different inks, pencils, and pens. But others seem to represent coherent, connected work; they follow consecutive lines of thought, and appear to have been written almost at a sitting. Notes made over a period of time, as thoughts occur to one, simply do not look like this. Judging from the handwriting, as well as the internal coherence of many note-sheets, I should say that a good many of them represent primitive acts of creation, written down at high speed, without any attempt to express ideas fully or to indicate emphasis, subordination, or relation between them. Within the main stream, each phrase or theme or concept is separated from its neighbors only by a casual comma or a new line, yet even when there is no formal connection between the thoughts, impetus makes itself felt. In short, what we have here may well be a preliminary harrowing of the artist's mind, an almost random throwing up of concepts, images, and phrases freely associated with the themes of the action. As Mr. Litz points out, Joyce made elaborate associative notes of this sort for *Exiles*; they were made, and explicitly dated, in November 1913, when the general structure of the play was in Joyce's mind, but before it had started to take shape on paper—as a preliminary, precisely, to its taking shape on paper. For the play did not assume anything like final form till mid-1915.

Some of the note-sheets, then, are what Mr. Litz describes— the mosaic-worker's box of little colored cubes, to be drawn upon when filling in a pre-existent composition. Others include the materials out of which the episode was to be constructed. Even among the "mere" word-lists, one finds many general observations regarding the characters of the novel, and comments by Joyce for his own guidance in constructing the book. As one would anticipate, Joyce commenting on his own novel, is something of a wit. "Bl. Boyl.," as he defines him, is a "centre of levity." "Mockintosh" tells his own story. The Pope Joyce calls "Vicar of Christ (Bray)," and he summarizes the Trinity, inaccurately but wittily, as "J.C. = $\sqrt[3]{\text{God}}$." His capsule definition of "Vaccination: hair of dog that might bite you," is worthy of the variety stage. Playing with a moral theme like a metaphysical preacher, Joyce toys with the idea that the "human tangent thinks itself divine line." Nausicaa is a "pavement artist," that is, a prostitute, a faker and trickster, and an incompetent, sentimental draftsman. Or there will be a series of images on, for example, the theme of the Jews:

Jews and Irish remember past
Jew = cuckoo = profiteer                    the cuckoo's a fine bird
LB's son Messiah                            he sings as he flies
Jews fouled wells of thought
circumcized coins
LB: ex quibus Christus
                    (*British Museum Additional MSS* #49975, "Cyclops.")

Among the note-sheets in the British Museum are stylistic experiments in literal Latin translation: "Hannibal huge desire impelled of Tarentum to be captured," or "Among the Romans to those badly their affairs waging it was accustomed to be interdicted." But these games are exceptional. Most of the note-sheets consist of small free-association patterns, episodes in a state of radical compression, and phrases or words which were ultimately scattered freely through the book. When Joyce thought of a property useful for his novel, he did not generally indicate (or, probably, know) its ultimate dimensions or even its ultimate function. He threw it into the note-sheets, to grow and seek its attachments as it would.

Thus, though many of the note-sheets are essentially scaffolding for the construction of the episodes, they also show how little formal scaffolding Joyce used. He allowed the book to grow, in large part, by a process of accretion and cross-patching, which involved a huge ragbag of miscellaneous words and phrases. Some of these elements coagulated more or less spontaneously, either in the process of appearing or after their arrival. Joyce maintained a loose control òver them through a stock of general observations about book, characters, and life in general. These generalizations add up to no distinct tendency for the novel as a whole. Joyce, I would guess, deliberately refrained from defining his purpose "as a whole" because he did not want to narrow it. He thought of his book as a growth, a meadow of blooms, not a formal demonstration; and, instead of requiring that each element justify itself by serving a clear esthetic purpose, he merely pruned from the new growth elements which appeared tonally incongruous or misleading.

In fact, it is neither safe nor sensible to assume that a book like *Ulysses* could have been written by the mosaic method alone. Besides being an ingenious, intricate pattern, it is a cataclysmic plunge into the black pit of the self, into the darkness of the inarticulate. Joyce himself recognized this aspect of his art, and practiced assiduously the performance and analysis of dream-work, the pursuit of maddeningly subtle and elaborate association patterns. The note-sheets represent, at least in part, a stage of inchoate mind-exploration; sometimes an early and sometimes a late phase in the process of long juxtaposition leading to ultimate fusion, which Joyce described to Miss Weaver (20 July, 1919, *Letters*, p. 128).

Later, most of the sections were drafted in exercise books. From the nature of the afterthoughts, interlinings, and belated insertions, we can see that these episodes were in very different states of gestation during the notebook stage. Surprisingly, a deep, complex, and intricate chapter like "Proteus" is relatively complete in MS. The earliest version we have (*U. of Buffalo MSS:* Slocum & Cahoon 5, b, ii) represents almost the entire chapter. This I take to be the version which Joyce described to Miss Weaver (18 May, 1918, *Letters*, p. 113) as the "second" draft; he says he spent two hundred hours revising it before writing it out "finally." (One cannot be sure what "finally" means, but it seems likely that the Rosenbach MS was not too far from that which was written out "finally" to be typed up by Claud Sykes in late 1917 and early 1918. A comparison of these two texts would thus enable one to account nicely for two hundred hours of Joyce's time.[9]) Of all the elements in the second (Buffalo) draft, Joyce seems to have had most trouble with that blue-eyed Psyche whom he imagined Stephen picking up in front of Hodges, Figgis; her section is much re-worked. Once over this hurdle, however, his way was clear, and most of the changes which were subsequently made in the episode (in manuscript, typescript, and proof) seem to have been aimed simply at deepening the difficulty, and rendering more elliptical the course, of Stephen's thinking. Flat attitudi-nizing like "Why am I angered because disdained? A fool's wrath is heavier than them both," is replaced by dramatization. Verbs, connectives, and transitional phrases are freely excised; the mind of Stephen is depicted as leaping, not strolling. A Dublin address is disguised, and a couple of Parisian names are changed (Bride Street for Blackpitts as the address of the late Patk Mac-Cabe; Rodot's for Polidor's, and bar MacMahon for Minerva). Stephen's ashplant does not, in the original version, rest in any-thing so exotic as a "grike" (p. 45), and the "Lochlanns" (p. 46) were originally merely Danes. Thus, in summary, the printed version of "Proteus" differs from our earliest MS in relatively few prunings, omissions, and transpositions.

Elsewhere, the later stages of preparing the book (the stages of typescripts and proofsheets) involved a new and complex series of additions. Free association and wordplay fleshed out sections of interior monologue (about 4½ pages out of the 15½ in "Lestrygonians" were added after its appearance in the *Little Review*; deletions, on the other hand, were infinites-imal). "Cyclops" and "Circe," where elements of burlesque

---

9. The first paragraph of "Proteus" as it appears in the Buffalo MSS is given in Appendix A. The *Little Review* version of this paragraph is iden-tical with that which appears in volume form, except for one obvious typographical error.

and fantasy are conspicuous, ballooned and collapsed violently. "Circe," which Joyce said he rewrote nine times, underwent particularly violent transformations. The primitive version of "Cyclops" (*U. of Buffalo MSS: Slocum & Cahoon 5, c*) involves several different characters, different attributes of familiar characters (the Citizen, for instance, is violently anticlerical), some different digressions, fewer and different burlesques, and of course variant phrasings. Joyce's love of economy is often in evidence. For instance, the early version of "Cyclops" describes the efforts of Joe Hynes to get Cusack away from Barney Kiernan's before Bloom's return from the courthouse. "Come on, Michael. Come where the boose is cheaper." But, the narrator explains, "Cusack was blue mouldy for a fight." One notes that though the incident has disappeared, both phrases have been distributed through the finished episode (pp. 293, 324). "The Citizen" was a nickname which in real life belonged to Joyce's friend John Elwood; for purposes of the novel, Joyce transferred it to the figure modelled on Michael Cusack, who often called himself "Citizen Cusack." Much of Bloom's wit was added in proof; he was a good deal duller in the *Little Review* than in the finished volume. For example, on pp. 158-9, the mock classified ads, the descriptions of Miriam Dandrade and Mr. Purefoy, the phrase "Life with hard labour," and the discussion of Queen Victoria's nine children, all were added after the episode had appeared in *Little Review*. As Mr. Litz observes (*Art of James Joyce*, p. 29), many of the symbolic and structural elements (the Stuart Gilbert "correspondences") were added in late proof—the flowers, for example, in "Lotus-Eaters," and most of the foodstuffs in "Lestrygonians." [10] But

10. Many of the specific Odyssey parallels marked out in the note-sheets are either arbitrary, tentative, or trifling. Joe Cuffe may have been Melanthius in Joyce's mind (*British Museum Add. MSS #49975*, "Ithaca"), but no evidence of this intention remains in the novel, and a Schema at

a great many other things were added too—little chips of verbal and personal association in the "stream-of-consciousness" passages, larger chunks of parody and burlesque in sections like "Cyclops" and "Circe." The few excisions seem aimed at toning down what is too bold or too bald in a specific context. For example, the phrase "Blood is a sea, sea with purple islands" in the *U. of Buffalo MSS*, "Sirens" (Slocum & Cahoon 5, b, iv), was altered to a less direct assault on Phineas Fletcher: "Well, it's a sea. Corpuscle islands" (p. 277).

Generally, one gets the not-very-startling impression that the later chapters underwent more modification in typescript and proof than those which had undergone long preliminary gestation. "Proteus," though intellectually elaborate, rose from relatively primitive layers of Joyce's consciousness, and emerged almost perfectly formed. In "Scylla and Charybdis," also dealing with a topic of long standing in Joyce's mind, most of the late additions consist of single words, inserted or substituted with the evident aim of enriching the Elizabethan coloring. In other parts of the book, the late changes seem to be less distinctly motivated; sometimes they involve the addition of limericks, lists, songs, names, jokes, and miscellaneous material. At a random sampling, all the following items were added in proof: the triad ("Horn of a bull, hoof of a horse, smile of a Saxon") in which Stephen expresses his distrust of Haines (p. 24); the flower language on p. 77 ("Angry tulips," etc.); the controversy over Saint Patrick's birthday (p. 302), an episode which is annexed bodily from a poem by Samuel Lover; and the limerick on the reverend Mr. MacTrigger (pp. 169-70).

In making these late additions, Joyce seems frequently concerned to exercise the full range of his reference, and to dot

---

Buffalo assigns the parallel with Melanthius to "Corley." Mrs. Thornton may be Eurycleia, but she neither performs any action nor appears at the stage of the story which corresponds to the mythical prototype.

the novel with rocky little crystals of impenetrably private fact. But I think the work which he did on early versions of the book rose from a more intense and fusing vision, to which the conscious display of erudition was largely irrelevant. The processes of patchwork and mosaic, though they played an important part in the novel's composition, generally date from the late stages of its preparation. In its early manifestations, it was often an exercise in free association, artistically unstructured and only loosely directed toward an impact on an audience. Frequently, it would seem, the materials were allowed to proliferate and the structural emphases were, after a time, imposed on them. I think it is more common (not necessarily better) for the novelist to start with his controlling conception and attach his social or psychological details to it. The crustacean, exoskeletal quality of Joyce's book and some of the resistances which it offers to "vertebrate" interpretations likely derive from this special order and method of its composition.

## Lists

A distinctive feature of *Ulysses* is the long lists of names which Joyce every now and then pours across his page—names foaming forth in a grotesque, random array that stuns the reader's mind. The lists are a Rabelaisian as well as a Homeric device —they create a sense of lusty amplitude in the reader's experience of the novel. At the same time, their occasional relevance adds a mock-heroic dimension to the fable, moving the reader into realms of fantasy above and beyond the literal narrative. These are both definite uses for the word-and-name lists, above and beyond the simple pleasure of names picturesque in themselves or rendered picturesque by their neighbors.

I do not propose that there is any elaborate art for these lists, and I have no intention of discussing even one of them in full detail. Still, it may be possible to describe in brief how a couple of them work—how they veer and career from noble to vulgar, from public to private, from ancient to modern, from imaginary to real, from infant to adult personages, in a way to emphasize the full freedom of the author's associative fantasies. Yet, at its best, the list makes a sort of sense, too. For instance, the Citizen is introduced (in "Cyclops") as a manly muscular hero who wears at his belt a row of seastones, on which are graven the tribal images of many Irish heroes and heroines—and there follows, on pp. 291-2, a list of eighty-six names, most of which were added in page proof. The first eleven of these names, from Cuchulin to Red Hugh O'Donnell, are those of heroes familiar in the patriotic lore of Ireland. But Red Hugh O'Donnell suggests quite casually a twelfth name, Red Jim McDermott, an associate of Michael Davitt and O'Donovan Rossa, who betrayed them; in view of Joyce's recurrent concern with Judas, this placing seems significant. Soggarth Eoghan O'Growney is the Reverend Eugene O'Growney, author of *Simple Lessons in Irish* (he had died September 18, 1903); and then, sandwiched between two heroes of the rising of '98 (Michael Dwyer and Henry Joy M'Cracken), we find Francy Higgins, the sham squire, who took part in the betrayal of Lord Edward Fitzgerald. The list is Irish, we are intended to see—all too Irish.

Now the burlesque broadens; instead of Irish traitors sowed indiscriminately among Irish heroes, we get a Biblical heavy like Goliath, and the Village Blacksmith, out of Longfellow's poem. These musclemen are clearly intended to parallel the brawny Citizen. Captain Moonlight and Captain Boycott are Irish figures real enough in their concrete manifestations, but also symbolic and representative. They suggest, by no apparent logic, a couple of distinguished Italians, Dante and Columbus, with whose appearance we are fairly launched on the high seas of fantasy. A number of popular song-titles and a parody of a popular novel (*The Woman Who Didn't* derived from *The Woman Who Did* by Grant Allen, pub. 1895) mingle with historical types like Napoleon Bonaparte, Cleopatra, and Julius Caesar. Between Muhammad and Michelangelo, joined by their obvious familiarity and their alliteration, appears the abrupt and enigmatic name "Hayes"—whether Rutherford B., nineteenth President of the United States, Isaac Israel the Arctic explorer, Matthew Horace the authority on veterinary medicine, or one of the fifty-four entries under this name in *Thom's Directory*, 1904, we cannot possibly tell. Peter the Hermit, who organized the first crusade, is allowed to suggest Peter the Packer, Lord O'Brien of Kilfenora (1842-1914), Chief Justice of Ireland in the early twentieth century. These are followed by a group of four culture heroes freshly provided with Irish given names, evidently by way of satirizing the tendency to claim famous men for Ireland. Ballads and musicians provide the nexus for the next little group, which is followed by another based on geographical features around Dublin, before the whole process breaks down into a capering group of random names which deliberately have nothing whatever in common.

Looking at the list rather broadly, we note that of the eighty-six names used to invoke Irish heroes and heroines, somewhat fewer than twenty are names of characters openly imaginary—not figures from the legendary past, but characters like Dark Rosaleen and the Village Blacksmith. Of these imaginary characters, roughly half are Irish and half not. Of the non-Irish real-life characters listed, there are again about twenty, with no great concentration in any national grouping; we note three Italians, three Englishmen, a couple of Biblical figures, and a couple of Germans, the rest being scattered. Some six or seven names out of the list offer real resistance to our comprehension.

Peter the Packer is identified above; Hayes is probably beyond comprehension. There remain Horace Wheatley, Thomas Conneff, Waddler Healy, Acky Nable, and Joe Nagle. Some of these names are not quite beyond reach of a bold guess. Various Wheatleys seem possible, including the brewer of Wheatley's Hop Bitters, Wheatley the stationer on Sackville Street, and the author of a book about anagrams (*circa* 1860), but the Irish hero in question is probably a music-hall singer who played, among other things, Baron O'Bounder in the pantomime "Cinderella" which opened in the Gaiety on December 26, 1896 (*The Irish Playgoer*, Jan. 11, 1900, p. 16). Waddler Healy may very well be the Very Reverend John Healy, Archbishop of Tuam (1841-1918); the *Life* of this distinguished prelate by the Reverend P. J. Joyce (Dublin, 1931) quotes Dr. Walter McDonald as saying of his colleague, "he was tall, blonde, rough, strongly built, though inclined to waddle in his gait" (p. 59). "Acky Nable" and "Joe Nagle," as the Modern Library edition prints the names, offer some resistance to identification; but matters are somewhat improved when we find, in the Odyssey edition, that the first name is given as "Acky Nagle." The reference is evidently to two of three brothers Nagle who ran a well-known public house at 25 Earl Street North. Their names were James Joseph, John Joachim, and Patrick Nagle; and the first two were the men referred to as "Joe" and "Acky" (from Joachim) Nagle. Patrick and Joe ran the business; Acky died relatively young in life, about 1908. All three brothers lived at various times in the Phibsborough district, not far from the house of Joyce's father, at St. Peter's Terrace. Thomas Conneff, on the other hand, remains an impenetrable blank.

On p. 571 a hue and cry pursues Bloom through the nightmare streets; most members of it either have a previous character in the novel or in exterior reality, or announce in their names themselves that they do not pretend to an identity. Hornblower of Trinity leads the pack, by virtue of his tallyho cap and perhaps his name. After fifteen easily identifiable figures, there is a cluster of five indefinites (Whatdoyoucallhim, Strangeface, etc.); and then after another group of twenty-one people whom Bloom has seen or thought of during the day ("friend of Lyons" is perhaps Bloom himself in curious guise), we find a couple of men in the street, a fellow referred to simply as Footballboots, and a rich Protestant lady, none of whom (obviously) can, or are intended to, be identified. Making their only appearance in the novel are Superintendent Laracy, and Mesdames Gerald and Stanislaus Moran of Roebuck, who may be found in Thom's Directory for 1904 at Roebuck Hill, Dundrum. Why these ladies and gentlemen are chasing Bloom through his nightmare we can only guess; their names or addresses seem to have a remote connection with racing and hunting, though Joyce might easily have found more explicit ones (Foxhall Terrace, Ranelagh, or Gallopping Green, Stillorgan, for instance). Their association with Bloom the quarry may be even more indefinite or more private than this; but at least Joyce's names have verifiable public referents. If we discount the mystery man on the beach and the retriever as creatures who do not, and cannot be expected to, reveal similar tangibility, we are left with Mrs. Kennefick, Mrs. Galbraith, and Colonel Hayes, who need some explanation. Mrs. Galbraith appears in Molly's reflections on p. 736 as someone whom she had habitually seen, and an early MS substitutes her name for that of Mrs. Mastiansky in a discussion of intimate domestic habits (p. 734). She was probably the spouse of H. Denham Galbraith, Esq., 58B Rathmines Road; the guess would be founded on her relative proximity to Mrs. Bloom's former neighborhood. Colonel Hayes may or may not be related to the personage named simply "Hayes" on p. 292; the Army List for 1902 includes on its Active and Retired lists only one Colonel Hayes—Lt.-Col. Clarence Henry Hayes of the 1st Bengal Lancers and the Indian Staff Corps. He seems pretty irrelevant here. And Mrs. Kennefick, like Thomas Conneff, is a total blank.

The list of priests on p. 312 has every mark of being taken from a journalist's account of a public occasion; but I have not been able to discover the original. Twenty-six names are listed, with some tendency to put the more distinguished ones first; for example, William Delany, S.J., LL.D., was the President of University College, Dublin, and Gerald Molloy, D.D., was Rector of the Catholic University of Ireland. Of the twenty-six names, twenty-one are easily identified, mostly from p. 1366 of *Thom's Directory* for 1904; John M. Ivers, P.P., Peter Fagan, O.M., B. R. Slattery, O.M.I., and the two laymen (P. Fay, T. Quirke) elude positive identification. Similarly with the list of picturesque Irish sights emblazoned on the Citizen's handkerchief, or swab (p. 326). They are clearly intended to parallel the items on the shield of Achilles, and most of them are in fact familiar Irish sights. A few of them are quite unremarkable; the Henry Street Warehouse is merely a large warehouse and department store, as the Scotch House is but one pub of many on Burgh Quay, and the Rathdown Union Workhouse at Loughlinstown is in no way remarkable as a workhouse. The three birthplaces of the first Duke of Wellington are a mild local joke; several houses are indeed shown as the site of his birth, though that at #24 Merrion Street seems to have best claim to the honor. Kilballymacshona-kill is evidently a joke at elaborate Gaelic place-names. Generally, however, these two lists of priests and places seem to contain no covert allusions like St. Owen Caniculus (the dog, Garryowen) and St. Marion Calpensis (Molly) in the great ecclesiastical procession on pp. 332-4.

Two little lists, of embryologists on p. 411, and of astronomers on p. 685, raise curious questions. In the former instance, Bloom is asking what is responsible for the birth of males, and there seems to be some sort of point that his information is ludicrously out of date as well as ponderously pedantic; for he wavers between views propounded by Empedocles of Trinacria, and those of "most embryologists," by whom he means men such as "Culpeper, Spallanzani, Blumenbach, Lusk, Hertwig, Leopold and Valenti." Empedocles, of the fifth century B.C., scarcely belongs in a serious discussion of the topic; but neither does Nicholas Culpeper (1616-54), author of *The English Physitian*; or Lazzaro Spallanzani (1729-99), biologist and anatomist, who made some tangential contributions to embryology. Johann Friedrich Blumenbach (1752-1840) might very well be cited as a genuine embryologist, though his work was nearly a century out of date in 1904. Graham Lusk (1866-1932), of more modern date, was primarily an authority on nutrition; but Christian Gerhard Leopold (1846-1911), Oskar Hertwig (1849-1922), and Giulio Valenti (1860-19—) were genuine embryologists, whose names a man would not know unless he had looked into the literature. There are all sorts of absurdities in the specific content of the passage, which is characteristic of Bloom's jumbled pseudo-science; but though the ideas are silly, the names are all real and several are relevant. There is, in fact, just enough expertise in the passage to make us aware that the silliness is deliberate. This effect seems itself to be intended.

Finally, the astronomers on p. 685 are not properly a list, for they are adduced, in the course of a fairly elaborate discussion, to illustrate a minor but quite specific point. The author alludes to "independent synchronous discoveries of Galileo, Simon Marius, Piazzi, Le Verrier, Herschel, Galle"; and the order of the list, its punctuation, and its names are all odd. Galileo and Simon Marius were indeed contemporaries;

Galileo accused Marius (Mayer) of having pirated his "discovery" of the satellites of Jupiter from the *Sidereus Nuncius*. Le Verrier shared his discovery of Neptune (August-September 1846) with Galle—the former making the calculations and the latter the observations. That leaves Herschel and Piazzi as contemporaries who made more or less simultaneous discoveries—which ones we cannot be sure, since both were enormously prolific. In passing, we note that the phrasing of the list seems designed to obscure the parallels to which the author is drawing attention. The effect is to render his account of scientific history, like many of his other accounts, at once muzzy and precise, to mingle the painstakingly accurate with the altogether misleading after a quite distinctive fashion.

# 6

## Conscious Error, Unconscious Erudition

Joyce's tendency to slur the edge off his learning with a deliberate bit of inconsequence, absurdity, irrelevance, or privacy is,
I think, a recurrent trait. It is capable of defense on several
artistic grounds, and it is susceptible of a variety of psychological explanations. But these are beyond my present scope.
It is a piece of observable reality in the book—and, given the
quality of mind I sense in the author of *Ulysses*, it cannot
possibly have been an accident. I suggest merely that the act
of teasing, tantalizing, and provoking is very deeply built into
the texture of the novel—more deeply, perhaps, than has been
generally realized before—and that Joyce's intricate, perverse
way with small patterns may give us extra reason to hesitate
before large ones.

Indeed, the intricate mingling of privacy and absurdity,
fantasy and surface realism and exaggerated erudition, may
well be of the essence of his design. Joyce calls attention to

the mobility of the novelist's imagination—flourishing before us his freedom from time, space, physical possibility, logical consequences—to the effect, if not with the purpose, of suggesting that all reality within the book is mythical. Even his claims to authenticity are secretly fake. I think some of the letters when they are published will show a private, guilty sense of language as sham, and himself as forger, posturer, penman [1]— an awareness of the falsity of literature, for which there are excellent analogues in Ibsen. But Joyce, unlike Ibsen, combined with this mistrust of the intellect a special contemptuous yet affectionate feeling for the doggy average man. Hence, while he shows the pretenders to erudition (including himself) as consistently fake, he often shows the barroom philosopher and streetcorner sophist as unexpectedly right. And he expects the reader to see through surface inanity to underlying truth, as well as through surface pretensions (including, once again, his own) to underlying fraud.

## Myles Crawford and the Invincibles

Like Mr. Deasy, Myles Crawford the newspaper editor is supposed to be in the last stages of mental decay. We are not at a loss to learn this; it is made clear in the barking incoherence of his speech, through Bloom's interior comments, and from passing remarks by Ned Lambert and J. J. O'Molloy. "Incipient jigs" is the melancholy diagnosis of Ned Lambert

1. See especially letters to Nora, August 29, 1904; to Stanislaus, December 3, 1904; and to Nora, December 23, 1909; all in the Cornell University Library. Two curious observations on this point are found in the British Museum note-sheets (*Add. MSS #49975*, "Circe" and "Ithaca"): "They who live by the pen shall perish by the pen," and, more bluntly: "Fuck only time people really sincere." The importance of the forgery theme in *Finnegans Wake* needs no emphasis.

(p. 126); and it would be a shrewd dialectician indeed who could make much sense out of the editor's crowings about North Cork militia with Spanish officers in Ohio. But this is all surface incoherence, and there are a number of intriguing errors buried in his account of Ignatius Gallaher's journalistic coup, at the time of the Invincibles.

Myles Crawford's first, and in some ways his most interesting error, is in the matter of the date. "That was in eightyone, sixth of May," he cries, "time of the invincibles, murder in the Phoenix park" (p. 134). He has the day right, the year wrong. The murder of Mr. Thomas Henry Burke and Sir Frederick Cavendish took place on May 6, 1882; and some byplay is made with this error, since the editor goes on to say it was "before you were born, I suppose." He is right, of course, if his date is wrong, and wrong if his date is right. Joyce (who, in details of this sort, is regularly represented in the novel by Stephen Dedalus) was born February 2, 1882. (It is odd that we do not know from the author's explicit words when Stephen Dedalus is supposed to have been born, but there is nothing in the novel which precludes this date, and a good deal which would serve to confirm it. Let us call it a very fair presumption.)

Now so far as the editor's error about the year of the Invincibles is "dramatic," illustrative of Myles Crawford's jerky mentality, we need only appreciate it. Curiously, however, the error is repeated on p. 613 ("Eumaeus"), where Bloom himself, or someone very Bloomish, is supposed to be speaking. The murders in Phoenix Park, says this maundering personage, "took the civilised world by storm, figuratively speaking, early in the eighties, eightyone to be correct, when he [Bloom] was just turned fifteen." The phrase "to be correct" looks like, and doubtless is, an ironic offset. When Bloom says "to be correct," he is sure to be wrong. (This isn't invariable, however; Captain O'Shea, described as being "in the light dragoons, the 18th hussars, to be accurate" (p. 635), really was in the 18th Hussars.) To say the least, it is a curious coincidence that Bloom and Myles Crawford make the identical error; one cannot help wondering if it may not have been Joyce's error, as well. It is most improbable, to be sure, that so intense an egotist would have been mistaken in a date so closely approximating that of his own birth. But if he had personal motives for moving the date of the Invincibles' assassination to what would be in effect the day of his own begetting, they scarcely affect our awareness of what he is about in *Ulysses*.[2]

Historically speaking, though the murders took place in May 1882, the Invincibles were not identified, and the story of their conspiracy made public, till a year later. In the spring of 1883 their case collapsed through the treachery of James Carey. (Bloom's hesitation over his name (pp. 80, 161) is natural, since the informer had a brother named Peter Carey, though Bloom himself thinks he has the name confused with Peter Claver.) Consequently the great journalistic exploit of Ignatius Gallaher could not have taken place till that year. Treachery being Irish, all too Irish, Myles Crawford pegs out the route on a copy of the *Weekly Freeman* for March 17—of what year, we are not told. It could not have been 1904, for in that year, the *Weekly Freeman*, being published on a Saturday, came out on March 19; besides, the story would not have been news on St. Patrick's Day, 1883, for it was first revealed by Michael Kavanagh, the cab-driver who was on the stand when James Carey turned state's evidence, on Saturday, February 10. Furthermore, it was Michael Kavanagh, not "Skin-the-Goat" Fitzharris, who drove the murder (and getaway) cab. There were

---

2. It is possible, for example, that he identified the cold steel used by the Invincibles with his own favorite weapon, "the cold steelpen." If the ingenuity weren't too juvenile, one might also point out that his nickname was "Kinch the knifeblade."

two cabs and two drivers; "Skin-the-Goat" drove the decoy cab which went straight back to Dublin, Kavanagh drove the getaway cab which made a wide circle through the suburbs and entered town from the south.

Thus, the editor has all the actors in the drama mixed up (as well as the dates), and even when he accidentally gets a name straight—"Tim Kelly," for example—immediately corrects himself into error—"or Kavanagh I mean." His geography is also oddly oriented. "X is Davy's publichouse in upper Leeson Street," he cries, identifying correctly the place where the Invincibles stopped for a drink after the murder—J. and T. Davy, 110A and 111 Leeson Street Upper. But then, half a moment later, "X is Burke's publichouse." No doubt this is Daniel Burke, with four different licensed premises, none of them anywhere near Leeson Street. X, for the editor, marks any spot where you can get a drink. Yet, in his own gibbering way, the editor is prophetically right; X marks the spot of the crime, and it is to Burke's public house that Stephen inevitably gravitates, at the end of the "Oxen of the Sun" episode, on his way to betrayal. Myles Crawford's prophetic function (as bird he is omen in addition to augur) is confirmed in a late addition to the proofsheets, when he is made to prophesy (p. 131) the coming of the First World War; a similar but more elaborate prediction by O'Madden Burke was excised from the early version of "Cyclops" (*U. of Buffalo MSS*: Slocum & Cahoon 5, c). Cheap and easy from Joyce's vantage-point in 1921, this prophecy is so far outside the usual range of Myles Crawford's discourse, that its attribution to him can only have been made with pointed ironic intent. Like many prophets, he doesn't know what he's talking about, but is right anyhow.

Another innocent who commits a series of interesting errors is Patrice Egan, the dumb bunny known to Stephen in Paris (p. 42); he is represented as the son of Kevin Egan, the wild goose, i.e. the expatriate Irishman. His father being a bird, the son is a version of Jesus; by symbolic ricochet, that doubtless makes Kevin Egan a misplaced Joseph.[3] And in fact he was a Joseph in real life, Joseph Casey, as Ellmann declares (*JJ*, pp. 129-30). For fictional reasons, Joyce has given his son the name of another Fenian who took refuge in Paris. Patrick Egan, treasurer of the Irish National Land League, lived in Paris during 1881 and 1882, before he resigned, migrated to Nebraska, and eventually became American minister to Chile. Patrick Egan's ebullient good nature and naïveté are nicely described in the book of an English secret agent, Thomas Miller Beach, *alias* "Henri Le Caron" (*25 Years in the Secret Service*), and perhaps Joyce wanted to reflect on these qualities in making "Patrice Egan" such a simple young man. Or perhaps he was drawing from life. In any event, Joyce's intent cannot be misjudged. Patrice Egan's enthusiastic reference to the *Vie de Jésus* by M. Léo Taxil serves to demonstrate his shallowness. "Léo Taxil" was the pen name of Gabriele Jogand, who (in fulfillment of the "Proteus" theme) had a career as an intellectual quick-change artist. After a good Jesuit education, he had begun life as an anticlerical polemicist, and written voluminously and vigorously on this subject. But in 1885 (the year after his *Vie de Jésus* appeared), he did an about-face, and devoted the rest of his life to attacking freethinkers. In this capacity, his antimasonic enthusiasms and suspicions were so extreme as to inspire Gide with ideas for *Les Caves du Vatican*. In *Ulysses*, Patrice Egan has evidently read "Taxil's" book in complete innocence of the fact that his author has not been,

---

3. The Holy Family had a great fascination for Joyce, and a great deal of his recurrent concern with cuckoldry manifested itself in jokes about Joseph. See the disgusting story told by Kitty Ricketts on p. 509, of how one Mary Shortall (Short-tall = Everywoman) was seduced, infected, impregnated with an abortion, and deserted by one Jimmy Pidgeon.

for almost twenty years, the fellow he admires.[4] Imbibing his atheism from this source and his information about women from Michelet's feeble little essay on "L'Amour," Patrice Egan is evidently a milksop version of his father, who once had the capacity for dynamite and is still capable of absinthe.

Of course the whole technique of the buried error, inadvertent on the part of the character, but appreciated alike by the author and the knowing reader, rests on the presumption that the author himself is above suspicion. We cannot possibly think that *he* would be guilty of the infantile errors his characters commit—and if he is well advised, he will underline his immunity. Joyce is not altogether in the clear here. The eunuch Catalani (p. 303; above, p. 72) is an error so pointless that it may well have been Joyce's own. J. J. O'Molloy, repeating the oration of Seymour Bushe in the Childs murder case, describes the orator as mentioning "the Moses of Michelangelo in the Vatican" (p. 138). The statue stands in the church of San Pietro in Vincoli, and the original error may be attributed to Bushe, Molloy, or Joyce, as one chooses. The plain fact is that Joyce, like many men who are vain of their memories, was given to inexactitudes. They are mostly trifling in themselves, and the normal reader of *Ulysses* is never much aware of them; but then, of course, the normal reader has not been aware, either, of those passages where Joyce secreted significant errors for him to catch and appreciate. The village which Molly remembers as La Roque (p. 734) is San Roque; the title of Benedetto Marcello's hymn was *Coeli* (not *Coela*) *enarrant gloriam Domini* (p. 493); though Sir Hugo did win the Derby in '92 at 40 to 1 (p. 631), he was owned by Lord Bradford, not Captain Marshall, and Jeddah, which won at 100 to 1 in 1898, was an even longer shot. Accosted by the watch in Night-

4. For a fuller discussion of Taxil and Joyce's use of him, see Marvin Magalaner, *Time of Apprenticeship* (New York, 1959), pp. 50-71.

town (p. 448), Bloom murmurs what is described in all editions as the "past of Ephraim"; it is obviously supposed to be the "pass of Ephraim," i.e. "shibboleth," though for the unfortunate Bloom it comes out "Shitbroleeth." Bloom's error in pronouncing the word is token of his bad conscience, but what Joyce's error (in converting "pass" to "past") implies, we had better not guess.

Finally, the fact is clear that Joyce was not, and could not be, an impeccable corrector of proofs. His eyes did not permit it; and his compositional procedures would have rendered it impossible, even if he had had the eyes of a lynx. I am not sure that his errors matter much to our appreciation or understanding of the novel, and record a few of them here simply as several points out of many pertaining to the texture of the book. On p. 275, where Bloom is finishing his letter to Martha Clifford, he has just expressed the wish that she "Call me that other—" and adds that "it will excite me. You know now. In haste. Henry." The U. of Buffalo MS, the Rosenbach MS, and the *Little Review* version all read, and are obviously better for reading, "You know *how*." On p. 29, Sargent writes in "long shady strokes"; but the Rosenbach MS and *Little Review* reading of "shaky" strokes is better by a margin which only a specific proof-correction in the author's hand would overcome. On p. 38, Stephen thinks "my two feet in his boots are at the end of his legs"; but this is nonsense, the Rosenbach MS and *Little Review* read more sensibly, "*my* two legs." On p. 73, the question "What is he fostering over that change for?" should obviously be restored by replacing the good Irish word "foostering," as in the proofsheets at Harvard. On p. 81 occurs the absurd phrase, "Gloria and immaculate virgin," which makes more sense as it reads in the Rosenbach MS and the *Little Review*, "Glorious and immaculate virgin." (This has been described as a dramatic error of Bloom's but it runs precisely counter to his secularized character.) A careless interpolation on p. 83 destroys the sense of a perfectly simple sentence, which reads, in the Rosenbach MS and *Little Review*, "That orange-flower water is so fresh." The text now reads, as revised: "That orangeflower. Pure curd soap. Water is so fresh." Finally, on p. 179, Bloom is wondering how the blind stripling sensed that the van was in his way, and he thinks: "Kind of sense of volume. Weight would he feel it if something was removed." The Rosenbach MS and the *Little Review* make, at least, better sense than this. They read: "Kind of sense of volume. Weight or size of it, something blacker than dark. Wonder would he feel it if something was removed." Simply as a guess, I would think that the typist's or typesetter's eye slipped in this passage from one capital "W" to another, and nobody (including the author) had sufficient command of the difference between sense and nonsense to correct the error.[5] As a general caveat for future editors of *Ulysses*, it might be entered here that not even the best available text of the novel can be relied on implicitly, because over the years Joyce himself sometimes lost track of his own intent in matters of detail. Readers must invoke somewhat different resources to cope with this circumstance. Where Joyce's text violates plain sense, the editor must pursue its peculiarities with compensatory vigilance and explanatory enthusiasm; the reader who cares about the book as fiction would, I think, be well advised to cultivate a little fine indifference. Enigmas in novels may serve to distract as well as fascinate.

5. For a full analysis of the revision process which produced the text of *Ulysses*, we must wait for Professor Joseph Prescott's book, originally a Harvard dissertation, a chapter of which appeared in *James Joyce Miscellany II* (Carbondale, Ill., 1959), pp. 15-66.

## Bloom's Bloopers

Bloom makes so many errors in matters of fact, during the course of *Ulysses*, that there would be no point in trying to list them all. With an opinion about everything, he seems incapable of remembering the elementary facts about anything. But his gelatinous little mind is capable, now and then, of some surprising perceptions and imperceptions. Quite aside from his comic errors, Bloom knows some things he has no business knowing, and is ignorant of others which lie right under his large and sensitive nose. His mental outlines are very fluid indeed—which perhaps means no more than that Joyce found him a highly adaptable plaything.

For instance, Bloom is shown to be much interested in his own neighbors and neighborhood. He knows the valuation of the properties (a sure sign of a man well versed in *Thom's Directory*), and he has some shrewd business opinions on good locations for public houses and streets on which there should be tramlines. But his own house had a history, of which, apparently, it did not suit Joyce's purposes to have him aware. #7 Eccles Street had in fact been occupied by a man of some distinction in Dublin history. Thomas Braughall (1729-1803) played a man's part in the Catholic Emancipation Movement, and was forced into cruel exile by the Castle and its informers (*Dublin Historical Record*, XIV, 2, pp. 41-9). He had occupied #7 Eccles Street for many years, but Bloom gives no sign of knowing of his existence, no doubt because it would destroy the perfectly commonplace ordinariness of life in Eccles Street, as Joyce wished us to see it.

Bloom does not show himself much better informed about his next-door neighbor. At #8 Eccles Street was dwelling one

Woods—R. Woods, as *Thom's Directory* for 1904 informed Joyce, and will still inform us. Bloom, seeing Woods's servant-girl at the butcher's, thinks of his neighbor: "Woods his name is. Wonder what he does. Wife is oldish" (p. 59). But had Bloom opened his eyes, he would have seen that R. Woods was not a man at all. The "R." stood for "Rosanna," and in the *Evening Telegraph* of March 19, 1904, one might have read on p. 3 of Rosanna Woods's action against a man named Malone, who had first offered and then withdrawn his offer to buy her home. She was, however, determined to get rid of it; for J. F. Keogh announced in the *Irish Independent* of June 16, 1904, p. 4, that he would sell #8 Eccles Street "at public auction on the 22 of June next." Presumably none of this material suited Joyce's purposes, so he simply left Bloom ignorant of it.

Several matters, on the other hand, Bloom is made to remember, not inaccurately but far beyond the bounds of his possible experience. During the course of "Aeolus," he is made to compare the publisher Brayden with the tenor Mario (p. 116). But Giovanni Matteo Mario (1810-83) made his last stage appearance in 1871, at Covent Garden, when Bloom was just five years old; thus Bloom's remembering him in *Martha* is clearly a surface impossibility, and as it has no evident symbolic value, I suppose we must invoke some such term as "thematic parallel" to explain—if that is an explanation—its appearance in the novel.

Some of Bloom's other feats of memory, while less startling, reveal characteristic directions of his recall. When he is looking across the glimmering bay toward the Baily light on Howth, the words "Grace Darling" come to his mind (p. 369); they refer to a girl of that name, who in 1838, with her father James Darling, a lighthouse keeper, put to sea in a coble and rescued several passengers from the shipwrecked *Forfarshire* off the coast of Northumberland. Grace Darling is a figure of popular legend, not an erotic memory, as one might suppose. On p. 375 Bloom does incorporate her name in an erotic reverie, as he also converts the provocative name of Mrs. Bracegirdle, the Restoration actress; but these are the patterns in which Bloom's doggy mind works. The story of Grace Darling was nearly seventy years old in 1904, and was a story in the first place of rowing a boat in a stormy sea; but for Bloom, as perhaps for Joyce, the name alone is enough to set off erotic fantasies.[6]

Bloom's comic errors have met with such widespread appreciation that we need not do much more than call to mind some of the most obvious and funny ones. He thinks Gray's *Elegy* is by Wordsworth, Campbell, or somebody (p. 111); he thinks a phrase of Congreve's is by Shakespeare (p. 276); he thinks a love song by Robert Herrick is a Moody and Sankey hymn (p. 645); in the phrase from *Don Giovanni*, "*a cenar teco*," he thinks "*teco*" means "tonight" (p. 177). He thinks that seventy-two of Parnell's followers betrayed him (p. 634), though the final division in Committee Room 15 was 45 to 27. He

6. Long-range recall is not a dramatic characteristic of Bloom's so much as a recurrent characteristic of Joyce. He conflates Ned and Sam Lambert with Daniel Lambert the celebrated fat man who died in 1809 (see below p. 204 and p. 554 of the novel). Alf Bergan, who affects to be something of a connoisseur of prizefights, is made to compare (p. 313) the Keogh-Bennett go with that between Heenan and Sayers, which took place no less than forty-four years before, i.e. 1860. And Father Cowley compares Ben Dollard's singing (p. 282) with that of Lablache, i.e. Luigi Lablache, whose dates are 1794-1858. Even Blazes Boylan is oriented to the past. When he tells Molly that she could "give 9 points in 10 to Katty Lanner and beat her" (p. 730), he is paying no overwhelming compliment. Katti Lanner, the Austrian-born dancer, choreographer, and ballet mistress of the Empire Ballets, was born in 1831, and was consequently 73 years old in 1904. Boylan may be indulging in sardonic commentary on Molly's somewhat shopworn charms, but, if so, his delicate indirection is scarcely characteristic.

remembers (pp. 634, 638) the day when Parnell invaded the offices of *United Ireland* (December 11, 1890), and he was even on hand to return Parnell's hat when it was knocked off; [7] yet he does not recall whether the newspaper was called *The Insuppressible* or the *United Ireland*—that is, he has confused the Parnell paper with the O'Brienite organ set up to supplant it. Though he is interested in science, he fumbles at various physical laws, remaining uncertain throughout the book whether black reflects, refracts, absorbs, or conducts heat (pp. 57, 263). The reason why a man cannot sink in the Dead Sea is completely confused in his mind:

Because the weight of the water, no, the weight of the body in the water is equal to the weight of the. Or is it the volume is equal of the weight? It's a law something like that (p. 71).

The blurred margin of his mind is struggling with the rule that the weight of the water displaced by a floating body is equal to the weight of the body. Men sinking or not sinking in water seem to confuse him; he recalls that Mulligan saved a man from drowning but thinks it was at "Skerries or Malahide" (p. 605). Actually, Gogarty jumped into the Liffey between the Metal and O'Connell Bridges, on Sunday, June 23, 1901, to rescue a bookmaker named Max Harris—as the *Freeman's Journal* reported next day.[8]

7. Mrs. O'Shea remembers that Parnell lost his hat in the scuffle, which she witnessed: C. S. *Parnell, His Love Story and Political Life,* II, 168.
8. There are, of course, special circumstances surrounding some of these errors; they may or may not be "significant." Bloom as Ulysses-Odysseus was originally a sun god; therefore he wears black, which absorbs the sun's rays. He transfers Mulligan's lifesaving activities from the Liffey to "Skerries or Malahide" because he is vaguely aware, like Stephen, of a drowned man in the Irish Sea; and he gets the total number of Parnell's followers correct, but thinks they all betrayed him, supporters and overt enemies alike. In other words, he is in many of these matters right and wrong at the same time.
    For a further list of Bloom's errors, see Edward C. McAleer, "The

In matters of religion, Bloom is even more dim and inaccurate than elsewhere. He thinks INRI stands for "Iron Nails Ran In," and IHS for "I Have Sinned" (p. 80). He has only the most hazy impression of the teachings of the Haggadah, from which he significantly misquotes, "out of the land of Egypt and into the house of bondage" (p. 372). (He himself is out of the land of Egypt, but has found only new bondage in his "freedom.") His ideas of what is going on at the celebration of the Mass are ridiculously exterior and mechanical, above all for a man who was once baptized a Catholic; but of course the reasons for this are apparent.[9]

Constitutionally inaccurate, Bloom is usually lucky. His errors are generally close enough to the truth to serve the purpose. This is true, above all, because most of his associates are less well informed than he. Joyce has his own fun with Bloom's errors, and occasionally uses them to make or conceal a point of his own. For instance, as Bloom walks down Eccles Street, he finds "Number eighty still unlet. Why is that? Valuation is only twentyeight" (p. 61). In fact, #80 Eccles Street was valued at £17, and was let in 1904 to Mr. Timothy McKeon (as it was also in 1903 and 1905). But #7 Eccles Street, where Bloom himself is supposed to have lived, was valued at £28, and stood vacant in 1904. Joyce has merely transposed a touch of reality, significant to him perhaps, to an address where it reveals

Ignorance of Mr. Bloom," in *Studies in Honor of John C. Hodges and Alwin Thaler, Tennessee Studies in Literature Special Number* (Knoxville, 1961), pp. 121-9. Mr. McAleer, perhaps because of his chosen angle of vision, attributes to Bloom some errors which have no dramatic function at all, and which might just as probably be attributed to Joyce himself.

9. Note, however, that Bloom, when he sits down in the Ormond dining room, is made to observe (p. 266) the "mitres of napkins." This is no doubt merely a slip, Joyce's habitual thought-patterns glancing inadvertently through the character, but there is a curious phrase in the British Museum note-sheets for "Circe" which reads "Poldy (Saul! Saul!)." Did Joyce contemplate a conversion-scene for Bloom, the latter-day apostle to the gentiles?

no dramatic secrets. Proofsheets as late as those at Harvard still retain "Number seven" in the sentence. To realize that Joyce is playing this sort of private game adds nothing directly to our pleasure in reading the novel; but it may render more elastic our definition of what he thought relevant to the pattern of his fiction.

Bloom's absurd appetite for useless information of a dimly practical character amply motivates his thinking in this passage. He is the sort of man who would want to know all about his neighborhood, and what he knows is "wrong" only in the narrowest and most literal of senses. It is absolutely right to show him knowing property valuations; whether his figures are correct or not is a relatively minor emphasis. On the other hand, it seems pointless and out of character to have Bloom attempt feats of virtuosity with his memory, above all when fairly elaborate research is required to establish whether he is right or wrong. Looking at the houses of the parish priests in Sandymount, he invites himself to "remember about the mistake in the valuation when I was in Thoms. Twentyeight it is. Two houses they have" (p. 371). The houses were at #3 and #5 Leahy Terrace, and were indeed valued at £28 apiece; but, so far as *Thom's Directory* goes, this valuation held steady from 1884 to 1904, with no variations at all. So where was the mistake in valuation? If there was one, it must have been in the rates office or in the memory of L. Bloom; and if the matter was worth bringing up in the first place, I suppose it makes a difference which. But Joyce gives us no grounds whatever for deciding; and however far we go into the matter, on either assumption, we cannot hope to learn anything very surprising about the mind of Bloom or the financial affairs of the Sandymount priests. Fictionally, Bloom's excursus into this matter leads nowhere; we learn nothing definite about Bloom or Dublin.

Even in making a simple telephone call, Bloom is bound to

have memory troubles; having decided that Keyes's phone number is 2844 (by a complicated association with Citron's fictitious house-number), he finally calls 2044 and gets his man (pp. 121, 126). But the whole matter is imaginary, since neither number is listed in the Irish telephone directory for 1904, nor does Keyes appear in the book under any number.

A last passing oddity, of the sort which is bound to occur when a writer imports historical materials wholesale into a work of fiction. If Bloom had had a chance to chat with Alexander Keyes, he would have discovered that Keyes was a member of the jury which tried the Childs murder case (*Irish Independent*, Monday, October 23, 1899, p. 6). Either Joyce did not know this himself, or he found it too involuted a circumstance to use even in a novel as involuted as *Ulysses*.

## Nosey Flynn, Polymath

Because he is so regularly inaccurate, and unremarkable when accurate, Bloom surprises us only in exceptional circumstances. Even Stephen fakes his learning often enough that no great importance attaches to his being wrong. A more interesting and unexpected source of curious lore is Nosey Flynn, whose brief appearances in the novel are crowded with various, fresh, and generally accurate information. Aside from his jackdaw mind, Nosey Flynn is one of the more disgusting of the rounders, bounders, loungers, and cadgers with whom Joyce's Dublin is so liberally populated. A raw, wet Dublin day is a test for the most continent nose, but even in the bland midsummer warmth of June 16th, Nosey Flynn drips and snuffles incontinently. In Davy Byrne's pub, however, he is as good as an almanac. He tells us immediately the inside story of how Boylan got to win money on the boxing match, before we have heard anything else about it. He gives a quick but literally accurate account of a number of horse-races and race-horses, with a poignant summary of his own ill luck; and tops off his conversation with an odd bit of masonic gossip out of the eighteenth century and the heart of a great Irish house.

His horse-lore is vivid, particular, and highly compressed; it is obviously a major interest of his life. Lenehan, he says, is giving Sceptre today (for the Gold Cup), in preference to Zinfandel, the favorite, belonging to Lord Howard de Walden, which had won the Coronation Cup at Epsom, the day after the Derby race, with Sceptre second. The prices on these horses for the Gold Cup were 6 to 4 on Zinfandel and 7 to 4 on Sceptre. As in the Coronation Cup, M. Cannon ("Mornington," his first name, was popularly abbreviated to "Morney") was listed to ride Zinfandel, O. Madden was the jockey for Sceptre. Abruptly, Flynn now shifts to another race, the Derby itself, run on June 2, 1904, and won by St. Amant (sired by St. Frusquin out of Lady Loverule) at 5 to 1 over John O'Gaunt. St. Amant was owned by M. de Rothschild, and won the Derby in the manner described, in the midst of a violent rainstorm. Nosey Flynn is rightly impressed by the fact that a week before the Derby he could have got 7 to 1 against St. Amant. The going price was 6 to 1 on May 20; the odds shortened on May 30, to 85 to 20 (only a little better than 4 to 1), before lengthening again slightly before the race. "Blue jacket and yellow cap" (p. 171) is the sort of detail one gets from Nosey Flynn; and it is confirmed in a newspaper account of the Derby, which refers to St. Amant as "The Boy in Blue." But, as this epithet indicates, Joyce or Nosey Flynn has altered one detail in the story; St. Amant was not a filly but a colt.

Joyce has gone to such pains to establish Nosey Flynn as a knowing amateur of the running horse that a mistake of this nature seems utterly out of character. So, indeed, it is. Few fillies have won the Derby, and no serious horseman would make such an error about so big a race, run only two weeks before. There is no reason at all for Nosey Flynn to alter the sex of the Derby winner; but Joyce himself may well have had an interest in doing so. In his world the females do, often enough, come out winners in what he persistently thinks of as the race of life; and a filly named St. Amant winning the Derby corresponds after a fashion to Molly winning what she wants from existence with the help of Boylan. Simply as a name, St. Amant cannot help suggesting Boylan's capacity *vis à vis* Molly; and the fact that the filly was owned by M. *Leopold* de Rothschild must have suggested to Joyce even further subtleties of parallel, though he has left them carefully out of sight around the corner of his opaque page.

For if Nosey Flynn's little lapse of memory really was intended to suggest all this elaborate parallelism, it suggests it only very hazily. Nothing is more convenient from the author's point of view than a symbolism just dim enough to be vaguely recognizable as possibly symbolic, but for which the reader alone can be made responsible. This sort of situation recurs continually in life, particularly in Joyce's life; it has usually been thought one advantage of art that the significant could be distinguished from the insignificant detail. But evidently we are dealing, in *Ulysses*, with a special variety of art.[10]

Taking for granted that it was not a mere error, I have guessed at a Joycean motive for altering the sex of the horse St. Amant;

10. How literal and accurate Joyce could be when he chose is illustrated by another horse, Fair Rebel, which Stephen recalls (p. 33) as having run on the day he visited Leopardstown with Cranly. He not only recollects the name of the horse, but the precise odds prevailing on June 4, 1902, when Fair Rebel (by Circassian out of Liberty, owned by Mr. W. P. Cullen) won the Curragh Plate of fifty sovereigns. As Fair Rebel never again stood so high in the oddsmakers' favor, this must have been the occasion to which *Ulysses* refers.

in such a matter one can do no more than speculate. But that Joyce intended Nosey Flynn to seem an expert, not a blunderer, is underlined by a curious, half-relevant story he tells *à propos* of Bloom's freemasonry. His tale involves a woman who intruded on a masonic ritual, was discovered, and had to be sworn in a master-mason to prevent her giving away the secrets (p. 175). As usual, Nosey Flynn is perfectly correct in his facts. The lady in question was Elizabeth, only daughter of Arthur (St. Leger) first Viscount Doneraile. She married in 1713 and died in 1773. The incident of her overhearing the masonic ritual took place when she was just seventeen; and several curious portraits of her, in a masonic apron, are said to survive (Cokayne, *Complete Peerage*, IV, 397, under "Doneraile"). The story as such is merely a bit of odd historical flotsam; but Joyce, who never assigned items of this sort at random, can only have intended it to establish the insider's authority of Nosey Flynn. His general exactness renders all the stranger Nosey Flynn's major error in a major recent episode involving the chief interest of his bizarre existence.

## Dooleysprudence: The Vatican Council

There is a cloudy area of facts ill-apprehended, half-recollected, and never understood, where many men, perhaps the majority, spend their intellectual lives. Philosophers of the old school used to deplore the fact; but Joyce found it a cheerful one, and took great comfort in the vision of Mr. Dooley, the "meek philosopher," the "cheerful imbecile," who didn't give a damn for intellectual systems and yet managed "to paddle down the stream of life his personal canoe." In his fiction too, Joyce loved to portray a vague, rambling conversation by fuzzy-minded people who know almost nothing of what they are talking about, but who manage nevertheless, by accumulating small errors, to get pretty close to the main truth. The best example of this chuckleheaded collective woolgathering is the conversation which takes place around Mr. Tom Kernan's bed of pain, in the *Dubliners* story known as "Grace." There are a couple of pious, meaningless roundabouts in the discussion, to begin with; we learn that none of the popes ever preached a word of false doctrine, because they are infallible; and that the Jesuit order never had to be reformed because it never fell away (the fact that it was frequently suppressed is conveniently forgotten). But the bulk of the conversation is taken up with rather specific points. Martin Cunningham and Mr. Fogarty, for example, become embroiled over the motto of Leo XIII. Was it "Lux upon Lux" or "Lux in Tenebris"? Martin Cunningham settles the matter by declaring decisively that it was "Lux upon Lux," by way of distinguishing the papacy of Leo from that of Pio Nono, who had assumed the motto "Crux upon Crux." This sounds suspiciously like a satiric pun, and may, indeed, have been so intended; for in fact the motto of Pio Nono was "Crux de Cruce," while that of Leo XIII was "Lumen in Coelo." Both disputants are wrong on the main point at issue; yet between them they have something roughly like the right idea. The first motto has something to do with crosses, and the second with light. They are wrong, in passing, on a further point, for popes do not "take mottoes." What they are talking about is the so-called "Prophecies of Malachias," in which the Irish saint foretold, in a phrase apiece, the characters of the popes to come.

Martin Cunningham further recalls, in evidence of Leo XIII's colossal mental powers, that he once wrote a Latin poem on the invention of the photograph—as, in fact, he did. The joke of the discussion appears when one looks at the poem itself, for it is no marvel either of Latin versification or of scientific insight.

Ars Photographica (An. MDCCCLXVII)

Expressa solis spiculo
Nitens imago, quam bene
Frontis decus, vim luminum
Refers, et oris gratiam.

O mira virtus ingeni
Novumque monstrum! Imaginem
Naturae Apelles aemulus
Non pulchriorem pingeret.

*Poems of Leo XIII*, ed. H. T. Henry (N.Y., 1902), p. 44.[11]

The highest ambition of a versicle like this is to rise to the dignity of a polished trifle; it scarcely makes one think, inevitably, that "Great wits are sure to madness near allied." Fortunately Mr. Fogarty translates Dryden's line into blundering Dublin grocer's prose—"great minds are very near to madness."

Conversation now turns to the council where the infallibility of the pope was determined, the 20th Ecumenical Council, held at the Vatican from December 8, 1869, to July 18, 1870. Wrong in most of its details, Mr. Cunningham's story about the German theologian who opposed papal infallibility is nonetheless generally right. His name was not Dowling, of course—that's one

11.        THE ART OF PHOTOGRAPHY (A.D. 1867)
        Drawn by the sun's bright pencil,
        How well, O glistening stencil,
        You express the brow's fine grace,
        Eyes' sparkle, and beauty of face.

        O marvelous might of mind,
        New prodigy! A design
        Beyond the contrival
        Of Apelles, Nature's rival.

                (tr. RMA)

sure five; it was Johann Joseph Ignaz von Dollinger (1799-1890); and he was not a cardinal, he was professor of theology at Munich. But he was, for many years before 1870, a leader of the forces opposing the personal infallibility of the pope; and after the decree was promulgated, he did leave the Church, as Martin Cunningham dramatically declares.[12] It is also true that John MacHale opposed the doctrine of papal infallibility, and made two long speeches of opposition in the Vatican Council. But Mr. Fogarty, who thinks dubiously that it was "some Italian or American" who held out to the end, is actually in the right of it. Nearly a hundred of the *non-placets* recorded in test-ballots left Rome before the final vote was taken; and so the final tally of July 18 recorded 533 out of 535 in favor of papal infallibility, though on July 13 the division had been 451 to 150. The two tactless and obstinate *non-placets* on the final ballot were Fitzgerald of Little Rock and Riccio of Cajazzo, near Naples. When the balloting was over, and the decision of the council was evident, they made their submission, not in a voice of thunder, such as Martin Cunningham ascribes to John MacHale, but meekly, by kneeling before the Pope, kissing his hand, and murmuring "Modo credo, sancte Pater"—"Now I believe, holy Father." [13] The usual excuse of those recalcitrants who evaded the final ballot was that the increasing heat of the Roman summer endangered their health. As John MacHale was the senior dig-

12. Incidentally, though for obvious reasons nobody mentions the fact, his book, *Fables and Prophecies of the Middle Ages,* has provided many of the materials for the discussion so far. He discusses at length the prophecies of Malachi, including the two specifically debated by Mr. Cunningham and Mr. Fogarty, and evidently forwarded James Joyce's interest in Joachim and the Joachimites, originally inflamed by an enigmatic reference in Yeats's story "The Tables of the Law" (*Stephen Hero,* p. 176). Dollinger's book, first published in 1863, was translated into English in 1872.
13. Cuthbert Butler, *The Vatican Council* (Longmans, Green, 1930), II, 163-4.

nitary present, it is altogether probable that he availed himself of this convenient escape-hatch. In any event, the drama of Martin Cunningham's story is evidently all his own creation, and so is the absurdity of the pope's pronouncing *ex cathedra* that he is infallible *ex cathedra*.

Mr. Kernan's further recollections of John MacHale contain some inaccuracies, but they are not so clearly deliberate ones, nor so revelatory of a dramatic situation. The event which he recalls is the unveiling of Sir John Gray's statue; it took place on June 24, 1879. The ancient Archbishop was indeed present on this occasion; in fact he was nearly the hero of the day. At the age of eighty-seven he was known reverberantly as "The Lion of the Fold of Judah"; and his presence at a ceremony commemorating a Protestant was looked upon as a fine augury of Ireland's future. To be sure, Edmund Dwyer Gray did not speak at the afternoon unveiling ceremony—in this detail Mr. Kernan's memory betrays him—but he was present. He did speak, in fact he blathered, at the evening meeting in the Antient Concert Rooms; but John of Tuam was not present there (*Freeman's Journal*, June 25, 1879, p. 6). Mr. Kernan is, thus, right and at the same time wrong—fulfilling, thereby, the story's basic image of helpless innocence blundering through a world encrusted with ancient corruption.

## Dates and Numbers

When Bloom leaps over the railings outside #7 Eccles Street, he falls, we are told, "by his body's known weight of eleven stone and four pounds [158 pounds] . . . avoirdupois . . . as certified . . . on the last feast of the Ascension, to wit, the twelfth day of May of the bissextile year one thousand nine hundred and four of the christian era (jewish era five thousand six hun-

dred and sixtyfour, mohammedan era one thousand three hundred and twentytwo), golden number 5, epact 13, solar cycle 9,
dominical letters C B, Roman indication [*sic*] 2, Julian period
6617, MXMIV" (pp. 652-3). Nothing could be more impressively exact than this cumulative account of the precise day when
Bloom weighed himself in a drugstore at 19 Frederick Street,
and some critics have taken it as a revelation of Joyce's passion
for remote perspective. A favorite parallel is with that passage
in the *Portrait* where young Stephen Dedalus is described as
writing his address in a school geography book:

> Stephen Dedalus
> Class of Elements
> Clongowes Wood College
> Sallins
> County Kildare
> Ireland
> Europe
> The World
> The Universe.
>
> (*Portrait*, pp. 11-12)

But the cosmic perspective of *Ulysses* in dating Bloom's adven-
ture with the scales was easily acquired; in fact, the entire passage was copied from *Thom's Directory* for 1904, p. xlix. That
Joyce's perspective could become briefly cosmic is clear; else he
would not have copied this particular passage, in preference to
many others. But it was not all as cosmic as he tried to make his
reader think—or quite as erudite.

Joyce was less concerned with intellectual precision than
with the machinery of precision, with the click and glitter of
accuracy. On one occasion in the novel (p. 663) he goes through
the form of an elaborate mathematical calculation, in order to
discover the relation between Stephen's age and Bloom's. But

arithmetic was never his long suit, and this passage (only half serious, at best) is disfigured by arithmetical errors of primitive simplicity. Having established that when Stephen was 1, Bloom was 17, Joyce tried to project this ratio into the remote future. But the figures trail off into major inaccuracies. In 1952 when Stephen would be 70, if Bloom were 17 times older, he would be 1190, and would consequently have had to be born in 762, not 714 (lines 33-5). This is not a parodic error, Joyce has simply forgotten to count back from 1952, and has worked from 1904 instead. On the other hand, the figures in the last two lines of the calculation should be, instead of 83,300 only 20,230; and instead of 81,396 only 17,158 years. Joyce forgot his basis of comparison, and multiplied Stephen's maximum age of 1190 years by 70 instead of 17.

The mistakes of this calculation are not simply parodic; there is a kind of bumbling logic behind the whole thing. No doubt the whole idea is comic in its intent; on the other hand, this sort of projection can be seen as a deeply considered device of Joycean perspective, and one would not be shocked to find Mr. Hugh Kenner hailing it as a significant Joycean *gnomon*. But if it is a gnomon, the lines of projection are skewed and inaccurate; so it is a warped, fantastic gnomon; and one must decide whether the errors arose from incapacity or intent; and there are very good grounds for determining the matter either way; and neither decision yields us a markedly superior novel. So that in effect Joyce has made more trouble for his reader by being inaccurate than he can ever hope for the passage to redeem. One looks like a fool in charging Joyce with errors of arithmetic. But there are special standards of accuracy for a novel in which some of the effects depend upon the reader's recognizing errors deliberately assigned to the characters and uncorrected within the body of the work. Such a book cannot

very well introduce visible authorial errors without complicat-
ing its own texture and reducing the reader's feelings to those
of a fly stuck in fly-paper.

If the author is to lurk, like God, behind his handiwork, he
must be, like God, infallible—above all in his "errors" and "inconsistencies," which, like miracles, are potent indices to his
intention. If we can dismiss any sizable number of his details
as meaningless or random or misleading, we are bound to feel
less security in the remainder. They may be lucky, as distinguished from unlucky, accidents. And when he insults, through
carelessness or willfulness, our sense of possibility, in a work so
much of which is devoted to giving us a sense of actuality, the
real casualty is our sense of artistic economy. There is no evident
reason why, in discussing Bloom's physical proportions, Joyce
should have assigned him (p. 706) absurd and impossible
dimensions. With a height of 5 feet 9½ inches (p. 712), a
weight of 158 pounds (p. 652), a neck size of 17 inches (p. 695),
well-developed abdominal muscles (p. 665), and a general appearance which nobody considers grotesquely deformed, he has
chest dimensions of less than 30 inches. He might as plausibly
have been assigned a head four inches in diameter—or four feet.
God the Father plays no such malicious and arbitrary tricks in
His creation. Possibly this is another instance of Bloom's hope-
less inaccuracy. Or possibly Joyce, by imputing a physical impossibility to Bloom as a physical organism wished to emphasize
the extent to which he must be seen from within—but this
guess rather smacks of special pleading and there is no real evidence on which to found it.

Faced with such deliberate provocations, the effort to see
*Ulysses* as a consistent tissue of verbal transparencies is bound
to founder. A detail like Bloom's chest size is evidently deliberate and willful; it serves to prevent the reader from losing
himself in the work, and makes him conscious of the arbitrary,

omnipotent author in the foreground of his own work, inventing or suspending as he chooses the laws by which his characters exist. Instead of asking what a detail means in a total structure, we are forced to ask why Joyce violated so casually the structure which he seemed elsewhere at such pains to construct. If the major motive seems to have been a desire to confuse, to unbalance, to fascinate the reader, I think we are bound to think worse of the device, and perhaps of the man who felt impelled to use it.

Perversity and egotism are distressingly available as explanations of Joyce's procedures, and may ultimately have to be invoked; perhaps, however, they may be rendered a bit more seemly by a partial esthetic rationale. Joyce, one would say, is not really interested in pure esthetic form, at all; though he scorns the sort of intrusion upon narrative inflicted by nineteenth-century novelists ("And thus while our hero Walter is trudging off to West Wapping, let us direct our attention to the ever-faithful Prudentia in East Ham. . . ."), he is in his own right a highly intrusive, ever-present author. He intrudes, frequently, as an autobiographical fact which is beyond fictional explanation; he is present as an unexplained animus; he omits, arranges, and juxtaposes elements; and occasionally, to remind us of his power, he appears as an agent of confusion, bafflement, and deliberate frustration.

Like the great novel of Marcel Proust, *Ulysses* describes the formation of the mind supposed to be writing the novel. Its ending (as a narrative, seen from within) coincides with its beginning (as an object, created in time). In addition, the texture of the novel is deliberately roughened and hardened by the juxtaposition of different levels and sorts of meaning or non-meaning. We have seen many of the different levels and varieties of suggested meaning. An elaborate meaning is made to depend on the reader's possession of an outside and relatively esoteric fact. Insignificant trifles are laid before the reader in the same enigmatic, unemphatic way as major concepts. Remote, difficult, and sometimes purely private parallels are casually suggested; and elementary coherence is, on occasion, deliberately violated. In resolving or adjusting these levels of emphasis and intent, the active energies of the reader are elaborately involved. He is invited to take an active intellectual role in the creation of the novel. The whole technique is that, familiar to readers of Eliot's poetry, of juxtaposing incongruities and inviting (or simply allowing) the reader to make a connection between them. One of the ways in which Joyce uses this device is by employing the work of art to fracture its own surface. Whether this is a fulfillment of literary form or an exploitation of it the reader may decide for himself.

Rather different in their effects and in the consequences to be drawn from them are certain minor complexities and inconsistencies in the dating of past events, which create a tangled image of Bloom's personal history. In themselves, chronological inconsistencies and unclarities are of no great moment in our judgment of a novel, unless we are unbearably literal-minded, or the author is. But some oddities of *Ulysses'* time-pattern call for comment. For instance, we learn on p. 651 that early in 1893 the Blooms were living in Lombard Street West; on p. 88, we learn that early in March of the same year they had moved to Raymond Terrace, for that is where Rudy was begotten, and we can date the episode by counting back nine months from his birth (December 29, 1893). Late in the year 1893 and early in 1894, the Blooms lived in the City Arms Hotel at 54 Prussia Street, while (presumably) Rudy was coming into the world and perishing (December 29, 1893; January 9, 1894) (pp. 664, 720, 721). This is an active life but still a conceivable one; and it moves the Blooms out of Lombard Street West some time early in 1893. Bloom's monthly headaches in the hotel (p. 332) do not seem altogether consistent with the circumstance of his wife's being pregnant, or with the tragic story of little Rudy; but there are various ways of adjusting this difficulty. (For one thing, the story of Bloom's headaches depends entirely on the say-so of Pisser Burke, whose imagination may be as active as his tongue.) More troublesome is the fact, indicated on p. 164, that the Blooms were still in Lombard Street West in August 1893, when there was a notable display of sunspots (*Freeman's Journal*, February 28, 1894, p. 4). How in the world, if they were at Lombard Street in August, could they have moved to Raymond Terrace, begotten Rudy there, and had him born in December of the same year? On p. 153 Bloom says he was still in Lombard Street West in 1894; this simply does not jibe with chronology given elsewhere in the novel. The oversight is curious, for the movements of the Blooms are generally carefully charted. When Milly was six (June 16, 1895), they were living in Holles Street; when she was eight (June 16, 1897), they were living in Ontario Terrace in Rathmines. Only the date of their moving to Eccles Street is unknown.[14]

Bloom's employment record is also muddled, and at very much the same period. On p. 153, we learn that he worked for Wisdom Hely six years after his marriage (1888-94); then he lost his job in Hely's, and for a while Molly strummed in the Coffee Palace on Saturdays and sold or rented second-hand clothes (pp. 264, 738). But then, according to one version (p. 153), Bloom got a job in Thom's; according to another version, he was employed by Joseph Cuffe as a clerk in charge of cattle sales (p. 664). Apparently it was Joyce's notion that he worked for Cuffe while living in the City Arms Hotel, which was very

---

14. Did the Blooms ever live in Brighton Square? Joyce suggests (p. 756) that they did; but it is a passing and otherwise unsupported phrase which puts them in the place where Joyce himself was born.

near the cattle market; as an employee at Thom's, he would be more likely to live in the center of town, from where he could get easily to Abbey Street. Bloom's record of known employment is extended on p. 363, where we learn that at some point in his past when he knew Molly well (probably after he was married to her), he worked for David Drimmie's insurance firm. Eight years, from his last years of high school till his marriage with Molly, are largely unaccounted for; perhaps this was the period (p. 517) when he worked in the mail-order line for Kellet's (doubtless D. Kellett's dry goods store in South Great George's Street). None of these problems are in any way solved or alleviated by the never-very-detailed and absurdly mis-transcribed time scheme which Joyce made for the novel.[15]

A notable circumstance about Bloom's past is that the years 1893 and 1894 (which are the years of confusion) are remarkably rich in specifically dated material. These are the years of sunspots (p. 164), water-shortage (p. 655), and of the canal freezing over (p. 738); they are the years of the Glencree banquet (p. 230), of the death of Phil Gilligan (p. 153), of conversations with Mastiansky (p. 651), of Mrs. Riordan's residence in the City Arms Hotel and Bloom's plot to become her heir (p. 664), of the Comerfords's party (p. 738), of the costuming of Big Ben Dollard (p. 264). One or the other of them is also the year of Professor Goodwin's farewell concert and the fiasco of the Hungarian lottery (pp. 154, 732). But the years since 1894 are much less fully represented in the memories of Bloom and Molly. Three events each can be assigned to 1896 and 1897; a couple to 1898; one to 1899, and none at all to the years 1900, 1901, or 1902.

Precise figures do not matter a great deal, here; the general impression will, I think, be confirmed by anyone who examines

15. *U. of Buffalo MSS*, "Finnegans Wake Transcriptions of 'Missing' Notebooks," MS. VI. D. 4.

carefully his notions of the novel. Bloom remembers 1893 and 1894 very well indeed; he remembers 1898 to 1902 hardly at all. It is possible that Joyce's mind dwelt with special fondness on events separated from 1904 by just a decade; there is a prophecy in *Ulysses* that Stephen will write something in just a decade (p. 246), and that is the year of the beginning of *Ulysses*. Perhaps the decades ran backward as well as forward. But it may also be that Joyce, whose memories of 1898 to 1902 were chiefly of university acquaintance and student life, never did bother to fill in the general background of Dublin life. Curiously, the one episode involving Bloom which belongs unmistakably to 1899 is a riot at the granting of a Trinity degree to Joseph Chamberlain. Bloom took part in it, rather against his own character, and in the course of it made the acquaintance of Dixon the medical student; but the episode retains, somehow, the look of transplanted experience. Joyce's imagination would not take him outside the university for this period; his resource was to introduce Bloom within it.

Of actual chronological contradictions there are not, I think, very many. Perhaps the closest thing to one is an oddity of Molly Bloom's history; when she was fifteen years old, it appears (she reached that age on September 8, 1885), she was having her first affair with Harry Mulvey, which went on till "May yes it was May when the infant king of Spain was born" (pp. 744-5); that is, May 1886, when Alfonso XIII of Spain was born. Yet, it seems that she was in Ireland living in Rehoboth Terrace, Dolphin's Barn (p. 756), and acquainted with Bloom when his father committed suicide (June 27, 1886), for she thinks "still his eyes were red when his father died" (p. 726). This is not precisely a contradiction, but it does crowd Molly's personal history remarkably in the spring of 1886.

7

## Autolycus' Bag

Some of the limitations upon Joyce's interest in verisimilitude
are apparent; his willingness to depart from it for specific reasons
—to make a covert point, to muster sympathy for one character
or another, to gratify his own sardonic or Bloom's mousy notion
of humor, to ease a personal anxiety or pay off a personal grudge,
or from sheer sympathy with the muzzy-minded—has been
touched upon. The consistency of his performance in regard to
surface realism must not be overstated, though naturally his
purposeful departures from it stand out in any account. There
are extended passages where he simply transcribed surface reality; there are other passages where his departure from it is so
clearly motivated by fictional convenience that no real problem
of intention exists. At best, then, we have a notably mixed
record. As a result of looking into Joyce's alternating control of
and submission to concrete social reality, we have found ourselves now in *cul de sacs*, now *en plein air*—mildly illuminated

at times, bored no doubt, surprised perhaps, puzzled not infre-
quently. But in all one's thinking about social reality in *Ulysses*,
unless I am badly mistaken, there glimmers before one the hope
that if one digs a little deeper or explores a little further, the
special fact will emerge which draws everything together and
causes all the disparate details, now hanging in suspension, to
fall into sudden order.

Clearly, there is no point, in this or any other investigation,
where such a possibility can be ruled out altogether. And of
course no quantity of negative results constitutes evidence
against the possibility of a positive fact turning up some day. It
is always conceivable that a new way of looking at *Ulysses* will
be found, which at a stroke will reduce to miraculous harmony
all the book's symbols, all its references to external reality.
When that happens, the fellow who has called it impossible
will look very silly indeed. In the meantime, all one can do is
record the fact that close reading of the text with an eye to its
roots in social fact does indeed yield some curious and some
trifling emphases, but none of such a sort that they offer a
"key" to the book as a whole. It is a rough but handy rule, in
reading Joyce this very special way, that the smaller the surface
rock one looks under, the smaller the worm of meaning one
finds. The asperity of this rule has its own cool gratifications.


## Intaglio: Sunken Design


Perhaps the most disconcerting yet characteristic elements in
Joyce's disconcerting novel are those patterns of thought and
feeling which, like the Cheshire Cat or the Snark, are forever
on the verge of disappearing. They may be there or they may
not; if there, they may be significant or they may not; one is
obtuse if one fails to recognize them, but silly and oversubtle

if one makes too much of them. There is not enough assurance that meaning of any sort is intended, or for that matter that equivocation is being performed, for the reader to feel anything but uneasy.

For instance, in several sections of the book, Denis Breen is seen wandering about Dublin, deeply disturbed over a postcard someone has sent him. It contains simply the message "U.P. up," but he is prepared to sue the author, if he can discover him, for criminal libel. Under these circumstances, it presumably makes some difference what the message means, and many guesses have been put forward as to the imputation which has reduced Denis Breen to such a dither. Of course, there is always the possibility that it means nothing whatever; then Denis Breen is projecting his own mental disturbances upon an essential blank. But if the phrase "U.P. up" is a covert way of saying "you urinate," implying "you're no good," or if it implies that he puts his finger U.P. up his anus, he has somewhat more grounds for indignation. If it is a jeer at his sexual incapacity, "you can't get it U.P. up any more," he has still further reason for indignation, and we evidently have grounds for seeing the family life of the Breens as a sort of parallel with that of the Blooms. If it implies that the jig is "U.P. up," the card may be taken as a threat of blackmail; if it means, on the other hand, that it's all "U.P. up" with Mr. Breen, the card announces his approaching death, ties in with his dream of the ace of spades which is a symbol of death (p. 155), and renders him pathetic. In effect, we cannot tell what, if anything, the card is a symbol of, until we know what it is as a surface; and about this Joyce has given us no adequate grounds for deciding. I have given five interpretations of it, and J. J. O'Molloy adds another when he says (p. 315), "it implies that he is not *compos mentis.*" We may find some grounds outside the novel for preferring one of these six meanings to the other five; for instance, on p. 2 of the *Freeman's Journal* for Thursday, November 5, 1903, appeared a report of a suit in which one McKettrick sued a man named Kiernan, for having sent him a libelous postcard. Maybe this has something to do with Denis Breen's behavior, though Kiernan's postcard did not say "U.P. up." On the other hand, the exact expression is used in Arnold Bennett's novel, the *Old Wives' Tale* (Book IV, Chap. 4), under circumstances which give it the last meaning indicated above; a doctor emerges from a sickroom, and announces "U.P. up," meaning evidently that it's all up with the patient. This meaning is given specifically in *The Slang Dictionary* of J. C. Hotten (Chatto & Windus, 1903), which reports that when pronounced U.P., naming the two letters separately, the expression means "settled" or "done." Perhaps this solves the matter for good; I do not think myself it makes as funny a scene or as rich a fictional effect as several of the other interpretations. On the other hand, Joyce evidently did not wish to preclude these other meanings, for in the French translation of *Ulysses*, "U.P. up" is rendered "Fou Tu," a phrase which neatly packages the meanings, "you're nuts," and "you've been screwed," and "it's all up with you." The French of this passage is a good deal more explicit than the English; the original causes a major decision about a secondary character to depend on the possession of specialized outside information.[1]

The dean of studies, Father Butt, whom Joyce mentions on p. 654, is of course the same dean of studies with whom Stephen Dedalus had a celebrated conversation (pre-empted and elaborated from the experiences of J. F. Byrne) in the *Portrait* (pp. 215-22). His original was the Reverend Joseph Darlington. Why

1. In a primitive version of "Cyclops," the Citizen stuck two betting tickets in Bloom's hat and wrote on them "W.C. 13," another enigmatic message with unsavory overtones. But "Jack" (J. J. O'Molloy?) took them off Bloom's hat, and Joyce took them out of the novel, before it reached the stage of proof. *U. of Buffalo MSS,* "Cyclops."

is he "Father Butt" in *Ulysses?* He was carrying butts of candles in the *Portrait*, and he was the butt of young Stephen, who played in relation to him the same role as Charles Stewart Parnell played in relation to Isaac Butt. But to expect a reader to get all this from a single passing mention of the man's name is very likely excessive. In this same passage it may be worth noting that 16 Stephen's Green North is described as the address of the physics theatre of University College. The physics theatre was in the old college building at 86 Stephen's Green South; but 16 Stephen's Green North was, and had been for at least twenty years, the residence of the Archbishop of Dublin (Church of Ireland), His Grace the Most Reverend Joseph F. Peacocke. Joyce could not possibly have altered the address by oversight, any more than a student at Columbia University could confuse Riverside Drive with Morningside Drive. There seems to be, in this confusion of addresses, a latent sneer at Father Darlington because he was an English convert—but, if intended, it lies pretty deeply buried.

Are readings of this sort in the nature of responses or independent creations? However exalted one's respect for Joyce, if one supposes him to have intended an emphasis so complexly concealed to serve as a discernible nuance of his novel, his sense of design must have been sadly awry. Actually, the unity of which Father Butt is a legitimate part is biographical or autobiographical—pertaining to Stephen Dedalus or James Joyce—rather than fictional. If the reference on p. 654 of *Ulysses* were perfectly factual and straightforward, we might take it as one more bit of raw material toward a somewhat chaotic life of S. Dedalus. As it is, the distortions serve chiefly to bring James Joyce and the reader into the foreground—to make his personal motives for distorting, and ours for decoding, the historical record the center of our focus. As he enlarges the outlines of

his work, conceals his attitudes ever more subtly, observes or
mis-observes ever more minutely, and requires his reader to in-
terrelate over greater and greater distances, Joyce gradually
approaches the sort of writing in which success cannot properly
be distinguished from failure, with which formalist criticism
must confess itself powerless to deal. But perhaps this conclusion is premature. In the specific circumstances, it is clear that,
however acute his sensibilities and however determined he is to
find subtleties in the fiction, no reader of Joyce can hope to
appreciate fully the presentation of Father Butt till he has
acquired so much outside information and done so much match-
ing of widely separated texts, that all his responses have become
hopelessly corrupted and self-regarding. Indeed, without the
accident of *Stephen Hero's* partial survival, one would know
the dean of studies' name only after reading 650 pages of a
novel in which he does not appear. If there is an effect to be
gained from this extreme dissociation of details, this extravagant
subtlety of innuendo, it has much more to do with the process
of decoding than with the message decoded. If only because it
distracts the reader from a properly imaginative response to the
novel, and is so easy to impose on any material good or bad, I
suspect the principle is vicious in itself.

When he has Bloom reflect that Corny Kelleher "has Harvey
Duff in his eye" (p. 161), Joyce is counting on the reader's
familiarity with Dion Boucicault's play *The Shaughraun*, in
which Harvey Duff is the contemptible police informer. The
play was popular, the part was very well known, and the point
is confirmed not only in context but by Corny Kelleher's otherwise enigmatic and pointless conversation with Constable 57C
(p. 222). The reference to Harvey Duff does nothing to conceal Joyce's point; the play was thoroughly familiar to the age
and in the milieu of which he was writing. On the other hand,

we never see or are allowed even to guess at the schemes on which Corny Kelleher is informing. He associates, as far as we can see, with underlings of the Castle, not with anyone whom he might, or would want to, betray. Thus his peculiar transaction with Constable 57C, who says to him with bated breath, "I seen that particular party last evening" (p. 222), is a transaction in a specially enigmatic void.

Corny Kelleher is said to work for O'Neill's, and Henry J. O'Neill, the carriage-maker at 164 North Strand Road, did have an undertaking side to his business. Moreover, there was a manager in charge of it, named Simon Kerrigan; but the pursuit of Corny Kelleher's real-life original ends there. It was not an old, established business, nor was Simon Kerrigan a dull and leering hack like Corny Kelleher. The undertaking side of the business had just opened up in 1904, and Simon Kerrigan was a young fellow who had just been put in charge of it. He continued to work at it till his death in 1940. If he did any police work, spying, or secret-service activity, no trace of it remains.

But if Corny as conspirator and Castle agent has no narrative connections, we can salvage some major aspects of him, for his appearance in Nighttown enables him to lay bare certain general qualities of what Joyce considered the moral establishment of Dublin. What he expresses is a degraded "toleration" for youthful wildness, which was peculiarly offensive to Joyce. The Dublin way, Joyce felt, was to accept a certain amount of whoring and drunkenness on the part of young men, to accept it with complacency and even with covert admiration, as a sort of price to be paid for abject conformity in matters of principle and in later life. Corny Kelleher, who trades in corpses when he is not distributing pornography (p. 318), is perfectly at home in a system so well calculated to produce moral corpses. He is an odious, vulgar, knowing man, to whom a certain odor of decay always clings; an ideal fellow to represent, over the prostrate Stephen, the Dublin way of misjudging things. Having these broad and available uses for him, we feel Corny Kelleher less extraneous to the novel, even though the details of his doings are mysterious. There is even a kind of political moral in his being a Castle informer. The sort of appalling degeneracy which smudges his very act of rescuing Stephen evidently exemplifies what Joyce wanted us to think an essential death of the spirit. And it is this death which creates informers.

Thus, by piecing and patching, we put together a view of Corny Kelleher; it involves, as it were, reading the novel backwards, and relating a kind of moral cause which we see on p. 588 to a kind of political consequence which we have seen on p. 222. But on the whole we have some reason to be satisfied with the pattern.

We can feel much less confidence in a pattern hazily suggested by some interrelated passages concerning Mercadante. Bloom has a special fondness for this composer, based largely on his *Seven Last Words of Christ* (p. 81). To be sure, Bloom is not very secure about just what Mercadante composed; on p. 278 he thinks it was the aria "Quis est homo?" which he has imported from Rossini's *Stabat Mater*; and on p. 645 he attributes to Mercadante *The Huguenots*, which was written by Meyerbeer. But this is no more than the customary Bloom bumble-headedness. More curious is Bloom's impression that Mercadante was a Jew; for on p. 336 he tells the Citizen that "Mendelssohn was a jew and Karl Marx and Mercadante and Spinoza. And the Saviour was a jew and his father was a jew." None of the men whose names Bloom cites in his enthusiasm were very good Jews. With the possible exception of Joseph, all of them either apostasized outright (like Bloom himself), or were on very bad terms indeed with the representatives of orthodoxy. But Saverio Mercadante (1795-1870) does not really belong in the list at all, for he was not Jewish by blood or belief.

He was the illegitimate son of Giuseppe Mercadante and a servant girl, Rosa Bia. Apparently the idea that he was Jewish is intended to insinuate another parallel with the Holy Family. As a bastard son of Joseph, Saverio Mercadante would suggest a parallel with the Redeemer, and by flying in the face of biographical fact, Joyce may have wanted to make the correlation categorical—bastard: Jew: redeemer. This would give some point to what otherwise is a printer's error, the phrase on p. 278, *quis est homo: Mercadante*. If "Mercadante" is the answer to the question *Quis est homo?* (as the prolongation of the italic type implies), he has a certain generalized importance which does not accrue to him as the composer to whom a musical piece has been incorrectly attributed. But the first edition, as well as the Odyssey Press, prints "Mercadante" in roman, not italic type.

In some instances, by no means the least successful, Joyce's sunken references are buried so deeply as scarcely to show at all. On p. 249, for instance, we are told that as the Lord Lieutenant passed by, "Poddle river hung out in fealty a tongue of liquid sewage"; and readers have generally felt that "tongue" in this context is a peculiarly effective word. The thought is particularly disgusting, as sewage is made to issue from a mouth; the Poddle is either fawning on the Lord Lieutenant like a slobbering dog (poodle) or sticking out its tongue like an impudent urchin, and on either footing, the word conveys a particularly odious effect. But in fact the Poddle is deeply associated historically with this word. Far up its buried bed, the historians of "Dublin's Little Rivers" report, the Poddle was "joined with the watercourse, the combined streams being divided by the 'Tongue' (a masonry retaining wall), one-third going to the left for the supply of the city, the remainder, generally called the Poddle, flowing by Harold's Cross to St. Patrick's and the Castle, and so into the Liffey" (*Dublin Historical Record* II, 2,

December 1939, p. 62). That Joyce could have counted on his readers to make the connection seems very unlikely; that he knew about the Tongue himself is dubious, for in *Ulysses* he does not seem to have had an antiquarian's eye for Old Dublin.[2] On the other hand, his love was philology, he had a fantastic ear for the connotations of words, and he may have recalled a blurred linkage between "Poddle" and "tongue" of which he made effective use in the novel. But now we are shading off into areas of uncontrolled speculation.

In sending the manuscript of "The Boarding House" to his brother, Joyce mentioned a phrase of five words which he did not in any way identify, but which he left Stanislaus to ferret out because he thought it would amuse him (letter to Stanislaus Joyce, Cornell University Library, July 12, 1905). This I take to be the phrase "like a little perverse madonna," which in the Yale MS of the story appears as "like a little hypocritical madonna." In either version, Polly Mooney is a notably soiled young lady; and the point of the story is the trapping of decent, timid Bob Doran into marriage with a slut. *Ulysses* makes a good deal of the consequences of this petty bourgeois tragedy; we are given to see Bob Doran in Barney Kiernan's, stone drunk and blind to the world, and apparently this is his recurrent condition. The narrator of "Cyclops" recalls, as Bob Doran departs, a story of Paddy Leonard's finding him "up in a shebeen in Bride street after closing time, fornicating with two shawls and a bully on guard, drinking porter out of teacups. And call-

2. Stephen's remark (p. 627) about a "memorable bloody bridge battle and seven minutes' war . . . between Skinner's alley and Ormond market" is about as rich a recall of the pre-nineteenth-century past as Joyce attempts. During the eighteenth century, Bloody Bridge was a scene of warfare between the Liberty Boys, Protestant weavers from Skinner's Alley in the neighborhood of St. Patrick's, and the Catholic butchers of Ormond Market, across the river.

ing himself a Frenchy for the shawls, Joseph Manuo, and talking against the Catholic religion . . ." (p. 308).[3] If Polly is a madonna, Bob Doran will evidently be Joseph the cuckold-carpenter of Nazareth; and "Manuo," if it is to fulfill the anticipations which the rest of the story has aroused, ought to mean something like "Carpenter." But the neat, final connection is just what we cannot make. The French translation offers a hint when it says, "il faisait croire aux deux bougresses qu'il était un Frenchy de Paris, Joseph Manuo." "Joseph" makes the point; but whether "Manuo" reinforces, modifies, or obscures that point—and if so, how—we cannot tell. No person with such a name is discoverable in Paris at the time, and the word does not occur in any of the major European languages, including the Hungarian, or in the Triestine dialect. If something is hidden here, Joyce's joke is very private indeed. But then Joyce is capable of inconceivably private jokes. For example, on p. 60 Bloom sees "whatdoyoucallhim out of," and thinks "his back is like that Norwegian captain's." The story of the hunchbacked Norwegian captain who had an argument with Kerse the Dublin tailor has no points of contact with anything else in *Ulysses*, and indeed is not told in that book at all. To understand the reference, one would have to read *FW*, pp. 311-26, or, more economically, Mr. Ellmann's biography of Joyce. And if these books had never been written, the reference would be perfectly incomprehensible to anyone who had never heard John Joyce's rendition of the story.

Some other learned periphrases and buried allusions are deliberately comic or misleading in effect. The burlesque figure

3. These behind the back conversations—sneering, allusive, and sour of tone—formed a recurrent feature of the "Cyclops" chapter in early versions. There was, for instance, a bitter account of O'Madden Burke, and a similar summary of Stephen Dedalus himself, which culminated in the sentence (always gratifying to Joyce), "He'll never be as good a man as his father, anyhow" (*University of Buffalo MSS*, "Cyclops").

who conducts salvage operations after the Citizen's catastrophic operation with the biscuit box is Sir Hercules Hannibal Habeas Corpus Anderson. Certain inconceivably remote complexities are involved in this improbable sequence of names, of which Mr. Matthew Hodgart will shortly be giving us an exposition. The outrageous, labyrinthine elaborations which he finds in the name are artistically indefensible, but, alas, schematically convincing. In addition to its totemic, military, and mythico-religious aspects, the name may also make allusion to a certain Constable John Anderson, much in the news around 1904. He had been suspended from the Royal Irish Constabulary, charged with criminal assault upon a girl, and then reinstated by the government; hence one connotation of "Habeas Corpus." In any event, this burlesque figure has nineteen titles, of which we are given the initials—K.G., M.B., D.S.O., and the like. Eighteen of the nineteen titles are straightforward and recognized abbreviations. It is funny that one man should have so many titles, but the titles themselves are perfectly conventional, except for the one which follows D.S.O., i.e. S.O.D. This afterthought, added on a late proof, is not in fact an abbreviation at all, but a slang word based on "sodomist," and the French translation of the novel makes this clear by rendering it "Chevalier du Figne." *Figne* is argot for "anus."

Finally, Dr. O'Hare, formerly the tender interest of Nurse Callan, is said (p. 379) to have "died in Mona island through bellycrab three year agone come Childermas." The passage is so full of eftsooneries that "bellycrab" could easily pass as a picturesque antiquarian detail; but an early version of the passage has Dr. O'Hare suffering, more prosaically but realistically, from stomach cancer in Scotland (*U. of Buffalo MSS*, "Oxen of the Sun"); "bellycrab" is of course a fantastic but literal translation of "stomach cancer." It is pleasant to discover an exact meaning behind a merely picturesque surface, but disconcerting to realize how many of Joyce's jokes, without the help of a MS promptory, must remain perfectly impervious.

## The Allusive Trifle

The lines between fact and fancy, between symbol and surface, in *Ulysses* are deliberately crooked; their ins and outs can be traced only by following the details of a particular circumstance through every last meander and curlicue of episode. On p. 328 of the novel, the Citizen reads from the *United Irishman* a skit about a "Zulu chief that's visiting England." In fact, the Alaki of Abeakuta was visiting England during the summer of 1904 and did discuss with King Edward a Bible given him by Queen Victoria (*Irish Independent*, Tuesday, May 31, 1904, p. 6).[4] Arthur Griffith did do a number of skits and sketches in the *United Irishman*, under the pen-name "Shanganagh," and some others appeared there under the initial "P." The style of these skits was generally that of Joyce's parody, on p. 328; but the skit itself is original with Joyce, though the Citizen pretends to read it from the *United Irishman*.

Bloom's former friends (and his only personal acquaintances, so far as we can tell, within the Jewish community), Citron and Mastiansky, lived in St. Kevin's Parade, where Joyce describes them as living, but not at the numbers he mentions. Bloom's tailor was George R. Mesias, with an establishment at 5 Eden Quay, where Poldy first became acquainted with Boylan; and this corresponds to a degree with external reality, for Mesias did have a shop there. But Joyce has obliterated his partner, a man

4. Through the kindness of Mr. and Mrs. Charles Hughes, of the Cornell Anthropology Department, who visited him in early 1961, I am in a position to report that the Alaki still survives, remembers well his London visit of 1904, and is gratified to learn that a record of it is preserved in *Ulysses*.

rejoicing in the name of Haddock. Since the haddock, according to popular superstition, bears the fingermarks of St. Peter, being the fish from whose mouth he took (Matthew xvii:27) the tribute money (Stephen makes enigmatic reference to this myth on p. 548), the conjunction of names offered Joyce a symbolic complex as handy as anyone could want. His decision to erase half of it suggests that he sometimes had to work to keep his symbolism light and allusive. Mesias, comically irrelevant, appears in a parade of false messiahs on p. 487; Haddock would have been too much altogether. Bloom's haberdasher, John Plasto of #1 Great Brunswick Street, also has an odd name, suggestive of Plato and plasticity; not only did he exist in reality, Joyce was devoted to him, and wrote his mother from Paris asking specifically for one of Plasto's hats; no other brand would do (postcard, Cornell Library, April 4, 1903). Clearly the existence of Plasto and Mesias as actual Dublin tradesmen does not forthwith erase them as figures of possible symbolic import. But it does suggest that the connections we make are very much our own—Plato or plasticity, it doesn't make much difference; each concept is relevant to something in the novel, and Joyce did not (in the absence of signs to the contrary) mean one more than the other. As a matter of fact, there is no reason for supposing he meant anything more by Plasto's name than he meant by Mrs. Dwenn's (p. 743) or Mrs. Gus Rublin's (p. 533).

By leaving things open, so that many if not major meanings in the novel depend on nothing more than one's presuppositions, Joyce may have attracted, what he was looking for, his reader's active interest. He also runs the risk of rousing the reader's resentment at being teased. Examples of this teasing process are not very hard to find, and they are not usually much better than cute. On p. 133, in the section titled "Aeolus," Professor MacHugh flicks the loose ties of Stephen and Mr. O'Madden Burke, with the comment,

... You look like communards.

—Like fellows who had blown up the bastille, J. J. O'Molloy said in quiet mockery. Or was it you shot the lord lieutenant of Finland between you? You look as though you had done the deed. General Bobrikoff.

—We were only thinking about it, Stephen said.

Stephen's remark gains whatever point it has from the circumstance that the scene in the newspaper office is supposed to take place at twelve noon. At just eleven o'clock on the morning of June 16, the son of Senator Schaumann fired five shots in the senate-house at Helsinki, fatally wounding General Bobrikoff, the governor-general. The assassin escaped all questioning by immediately committing suicide. Stephen and J. J. O'Molloy are evidently telepathic, though not quite prophetic.

Bloom's mother appears on p. 431, wearing "widow Twankey's blouse," and anyone who is up on popular culture will recognize that Widow Twankey is by tradition Aladdin's mother in the pantomime. A grotesque image of Punch Costello, appearing on p. 495, is described as having an "Ally Sloper nose"; the reference is to a weekly comic book that appeared during the 1890's. Professor Pokorny of Vienna, mentioned by Haines on p. 245 as if he were a Jungian analyst or comparative mythologist, was no doubt Julius P. Pokorny (1887-    ), author of an elementary Gaelic grammar. The "suine scions of the house of Lambert" (p. 554) are evidently neither Sam nor Ned, but monsters; the phrase may refer either to Daniel Lambert the English fat man (1770-1809) or to a family of Lamberts who for several generations were born with bristles all over their bodies (Gould and Pyle, *Anomalies and Curiosities of Medicine*, p. 823, call them the "well-known family of Lambert").

Reading a smutty American magazine on the afternoon of June 16, the boys in Barney Kiernan's snug are impressed (p. 322) with a report of a brutal lynching supposed to have occurred at Omaha, Georgia. Since Omaha (pop. 217) is a respectable little community on the Chattahoochee in Stewart County, it may be worth recording that neither the town clerk nor the oldest inhabitants recall a lynching in the township. Neither does the Tuskegee Institute, which has kept a full file of American lynchings. One such episode did take place in Stewart County before 1933; a Negro named Capt. Lewis was lynched in Lumpkin on May 18, 1897, for alleged arson. Joyce may have copied a distorted account of this episode. This is more probable than that he looked up Omaha, Georgia, on the map. But the oddest reflection is that with a wide-open field of names to choose from, including many with Homeric and Irish overtones, Joyce selected one with no possible import for his novel.

Dublin details provide a more natural, and more accessible, field for Joycean allusion. In the course of his encounter with Stephen in "Eumaeus," the drifter known as Corley mentions having seen Bloom "a few times in the Bleeding Horse in Camden street with Boylan the billsticker" (p. 602). There is nothing unlikely in Bloom's having met with Boylan there, supposing they were the sort of men one could imagine having two words to say to one another. On the other hand, Bloom, as a "prudent member," would not be likely to frequent a pub like the Bleeding Horse; it was far out of his neighborhood, and a good deal lower on the social scale than Barney Kiernan's (which was known, among the lawyers attending the court in Green Street, as "The Court of Appeals"). Finally, Bloom and Boylan have not known one another for long, and the notion of their meeting several times in this pub disturbs an otherwise compact and consecutive chronology in the relation of Boylan and the Blooms. The pub does occupy a position of some importance in LeFanu's novel, *The Cock and Anchor*, where it serves as a center of low scheming. Joyce may have wished to suggest a parallel, but more likely he just liked the fine, *louche* sound of the name. It entered the book at a late stage of the proofs, evidently in connection with Corley's curious submarine view of Dublin lowlife. The Bleeding Horse still stands in Camden Street.

Dublin slang is of course freely peppered through *Ulysses*; no artist with Joyce's interest in words could possibly overlook so rich a field. On p. 146 the newspaper editor makes passing, unexplained, and basically gratuitous reference to "the waxies' Dargle," a picturesque expression which only direct or indirect acquaintance with Dublin lingo will gloss as "the annual picnic, formerly held near Ringsend, of the Dublin shoemakers." Sometimes Joyce's Dublin expressions are so exotic as completely to muddle even the most devoted of proofreaders. On p. 178 Bloom, we are told, "passed the reverend Thomas Connellan's bookstore. *Why I left the church of Rome? Bird's Nest.* Women run him." The expression "bird's nest" is Dublinese for a Protestant proselytizing center;[5] the passage would make much more sense if the book-title did not have a question-mark after it, and if "Bird's Nest" were not italicized, as part of the title. The phrase would then be Bloom's derisive comment on the character of the establishment. There is no authority for the change in any of the editions, but the Rosenbach MS contains just the changes hypothesized. Of course a sensitive ear will notice that "Women run him" is a rough and abrupt sentence; so that perhaps, by eliminating a period, "Bird's Nest" might be made an adjectival phrase modifying "women." This final guess finds confirmation in the *Little Review* which printed the passage, "Birds nest women run him."

Fresh or peculiar manners of speech always appealed to Joyce; and in many details of the novel he simply recorded

5. There was in fact a literal Bird's Nest Institution at 19 and 20 York Street, Kingstown, run by a Protestant missionary society.

what any Dubliner of 1904 would have heard for himself—for
example, the Dublin United Tramway Company's timekeeper
at the opening of "Aeolus" bawling off the tramcars at Nelson's
Pillar. "I suppose," says a contributor to the *Dublin Historical
Record* (XII, #4, November 1951, p. 101), "the Despatchers
at the Pillar are still generally remembered—Captain Delayney
until 1912, and Mr. Peter Mahon after that date—with their
characteristic way of addressing the tram by its route name
rather than the driver in person."

Epithets are often used to convey more or less covert allusions, either historical or personal. When the editor appears in
"Aeolus," Professor MacHugh announces grandly, "And here
comes the sham squire himself" (p. 125). The epithet refers
to Francis Higgins, known as the sham squire, a Dublin journalist and political informer of some notoriety in the days of
Lord Edward Fitzgerald; it gains its point from the fact that
Higgins too was once editor of the *Freeman's Journal*. A good
many of the specific references in the novel are to events which
were common knowledge at the period and in the milieu which
the book depicts; and here, it seems clear, Joyce gains an effect
he could not get in any other way, at the cost of a very slight
confusion for the reader. "Come along with me to the sub-
sheriff's office," says Ben Dollard, on p. 241; "I want to show
you the new beauty Rock has for a bailiff. He's a cross between
Lobengula and Lynchehaun." Neither Ben Dollard nor James
A. Joyce seems to have had much reason to like bailiffs, so
the animus is unconcealed. But is Lobengula a herbaceous plant
or a species of man-eating tiger, and what is a Lynchehaun? As
a matter of fact, Joyce has collocated news items which are a
decade apart and widely disparate in their connotations. Lobengula, the more considerable of the pair, was an African chieftain,
who was reported (in the *Freeman's Journal* of January 20,
1894, p. 5) to be on the Zambesi recruiting Matabele to march

on Buluwayo; he died in this campaign. Lynchehaun was one of the aliases of an Irish murderer named James Walshe, who fled to America and claimed to be a political martyr. His misdeeds and misrepresentations were discussed in the *United Irishman* for September 26, 1903, p. 5. Joyce has brought the two names together as types of criminal ferocity; the surface of his novel is rendered a little richer if we know what is being juxtaposed, but the names have a sort of exotic and ferocious impact even if we do not.

By way of defining the characters of actors in his novel, Joyce often settled first on certain words which would be used about or by them—distinctive words, that is, by which they would be strongly identified. In the little notebook which he used to record these details, he set down for Gogarty two telling words, which the reader need not be reminded how he used—"stately, plump." In addition, of the distinctive words which he put into Buck Mulligan's mouth, a surprising number can be identified as the special words of Oliver St. John Gogarty. A letter from James to Stanislaus Joyce, dated between January 6 and 15, 1907, reports the fact that Gogarty's mother is dead, using within quotes the exact words which Mulligan is accused (p. 10) of having used of Mrs. Dedalus (letter in the Cornell University Library). Stanislaus himself recorded in his diary of September, 1904, certain verbal habits of Gogarty:

Gogarty uses two words well, the Dublinized Jesus = "Jaysus," and the word box. A "Jaysus" is a guy. Then there's an "awful Jaysus," and "hairy Jaysus" and you can act or "do moody Jaysus" or "gloomy Jaysus." A "box" is any kind of a public establishment or a hall where any society hold meetings for some purpose. The rooms of the Hermetic Society are a "ghost-box," a church is a "God-box," a brothel "a cunt-box." He has a good name for priests, too, a strange name in keeping with their ridiculous appearance and manner in the street, the name of certain Chinese priests—the "Bondses" [Bonzes].

Joyce appropriated the word "box" for Stephen to use in thinking of the Hermetic Society's "Yogibogeybox in Dawson chambers" (p. 189). "Jaysus" appears on p. 213, in the mouth of
Mulligan, but not quite in the broad sense noted by Stanislaus—
"then you go and slate her drivel to Jaysus." "Gloomy" and
"moody" both appear in Mulligan's mouth, though not in connection with "Jaysus" (pp. 11 and 18). "Hairy" is generally
reserved for low speech by vulgar characters (Nosey Flynn,
the Citizen, anonymous Nighttowners), but "bonzes" turn up
in Mulligan's mouth, on p. 395. The songs of "Medical Dick
and Medical Davy" and the "Ballad of Joking Jesus" are of
course both Gogarty's; and, though neither was ever printed,
both survive among Joyce's papers, in the forms in which he
used them, one on a postcard from Gogarty, the other in a
version transcribed by Vincent Cosgrave from Gogarty's original. "Staboo, stabella" and "Rosalie the coalquay whore" are
also from Gogarty's bawdry; and a note about Gogarty's behavior, in the Cornell Library (Bd. MS 35), preserves notice
of the fact that "he addresses lifeless objects and hits them
smartly with his cane." A postcard from Gogarty to Joyce, dated
February 13, 1904, makes reference to "Jehovah who collects
foreskins"; Joyce adapted the phrase slightly, and caused Mulligan to use it on p. 15 of *Ulysses*. Similarly, a communiqué
from Gogarty to Joyce, dated May 3, 1904, is headed "The
Bard Gogarty to the Wandering Aengus." Joyce retained "Wandering Aengus" as Mulligan's epithet for Stephen (p. 212) but
also adopted the "bard" for his hero as a way of diminishing
Mulligan's threat to Stephen's poetical character. "Wandering
Aengus" offers some interesting complexities. Joyce clearly uses
it with symbolic import; it recurs, particularly, when Stephen
Dedalus is about to take divinatory readings from some birds.
The fact that Buck Mulligan uses it in the novel mirrors the
fact that it was, in real life, a phrase of Gogarty's; but the sym-

bolic import of the name is rather specifically tied down by
the appearance of the birds, as well as by its traditional significance in Celtic mythology.

Even ordinary words, making perfectly good literal sense,
sometimes have covert private meanings. "Don't mope over it
all day," Mulligan says to Stephen, on p. 11. "I'm inconsequent.
Give up the moody brooding." In the *Letters of James Joyce*,
p. 54, one finds a letter from Joyce to Gogarty, dated June 3,
1904, addressing the recipient under the title "Inconsequent."
Even if we were aware of the Joyce family's habit of inventing
epithets for all their acquaintance, we should not get the full
force of this word, unless we had read a particular surviving
letter. The one word here has a separate, private meaning for
Gogarty alone—not a very important meaning, to be sure, but
on such highly polished surfaces the very slightest ripple may
indicate a buried emphasis, a hidden point. Sometimes the
point is there with no ripple at all to indicate its presence. Yet
some part of the stinging quality of Joyce's style may be due
to this quality of mind, the habit of dispatching words against
people like darts, to pin them to the wall.

Sexual and excretory references have provided a particularly
unhappy ground for diggers after buried significance in Joyce's
writing, and there seems no doubt that, owing to the peculiar
delusions on which he was nourished and which he cultivated,
these topics are unusually prominent in his fiction. Precisely
because he is so frequent and full on the matter, however, it
seems idle to burden him with the results of adventitious speculation. For instance, in the *Portrait* (p. 44), that knowing
young man Athy says that various boys are to be expelled or
whipped for "smugging" in the "square" with Simon Moonan
and Tusker Boylan; and some point has been made of this
mysterious sin, supposed to be analogous with HCE's dark
misdeed in the Fiendish Park. But the "square" is simply the

school urinal; and one has to be pretty obtuse not to guess what "smugging" means, above all when it is indicated that Simon Moonan and Tusker Boylan are effeminate boys. In fact, Wright's *English Dialect Dictionary* lists as the second meaning of this verb, " to toy amorously in secret." Joyce had a conviction, notably expressed in his essay on Oscar Wilde (*Critical Writings*, p. 204), that homosexuality was "the logical and inescapable product of the Anglo-Saxon college and university system, with its secrecy and restrictions." As a generalization this may or may not be true, but I do not believe there is anything particularly mysterious about Joyce's conviction, or about the incident in the "square" at Clongowes.

As Stephen wanders across Sandymount strand, in the section called "Proteus," he sees water flowing "in long lassoes from the Cock lake," and this has seemed to some eager readers a physiological reference (p. 50). But the passage is by no means a simple one. First, Cock Lake is an actual pool in Sandymount; cockles are found there and liberally eaten throughout the Sandymount district, hence the name of the pool has been corrupted to Cockle Lake. But this is indeed a corruption, for the lake is named from cocks or cockboats (whence the analogous word, "coxswain") which used to paddle about there (D.A. Chart, *The Story of Dublin*, London, 1932, pp. 307-8). Second, the French translation of the novel, though assiduous in rendering other double entendres, makes no effort to do so here; it simply gives the English name in its original form, "Du lac de Cock." On the other hand, the nearby sentence "Better get this job over quick" does indeed suggest that Stephen is urinating. One cannot imagine what other job he could be up to, in those particular circumstances, which would leave no trace of itself in the prose. Joyce may even be adumbrating a certain deprecatory parallel between Stephen's mind or body and sewage-laden Dublin Bay. He tended to think of body fluids like blood, urine, and menstrual flow as inner oceans, and the flow of words through Stephen's mind merely extends the basic parallel. But these reflections are more suited to the fleshly Bloom than to the intellectual Stephen; the parallel, if it exists at all, is carefully muted, and the physical act of urination remains far in the background—where we had better leave it. The novel is already well stocked with bathroom noises, and in this passage at least, there is better music to listen to.[6]

## Special Names

Certain sorts of names evidently had a special attraction for Joyce, and one need not look beyond their general character-

6. While we are getting rid of messy symbolism, let us dispose of the notion that *Chamber Music* is a collection of poems concerned with micturition. This extraordinary view rests primarily on a reading of poem XXVI, "Thou leanest to the shell of night," with some minor assistance from XXV. But in a letter to his wife, dated August 21, 1909, and presently in the Cornell Library, Joyce described the imaginary woman for whom he wrote the poems which he was sending to Nora as a special personal gift. He said that, as he imagined her, she was a girl with a cultured and aristocratic background, and that it was for her specifically that he had written poems such as "Gentle lady" and "Thou leanest to the shell of night." Yoking these two poems together as equivalents is more telling evidence of their fundamental idealism than either the imaginary lady to whom they were addressed or the real woman to whom they were presented. To be sure, the fact that the poems were "seriously" written is no token that Joyce always regarded them seriously. Particularly in matters involving the sexes he alternated between lofty idealism and crude vulgarity; in company with Gogarty, or Jenny, he was likely to make a jest of what his inmost mind held sacred. But this should have no effect on a reading of the poems themselves; what an artist thinks of his work after it is done will no doubt vary widely from what he thought while it was doing. The "shell of night" was not a chamberpot, but the arch of Heaven, as in the Lady's song in *Comus*. It is all very well to say it should be both, but to impose this kind of litter on the fragile structures of *Chamber Music* is obviously to smother them.

istics to understand their appearance in his fiction. For example, he was fascinated by names which might belong to either sex or which suggested the wrong sex. Bloom's middle name is Paula (p. 707), while his wife's name, Marion, is epicene. This preoccupation seems to be responsible for the appearance (on p. 527) of a man named Charles Alberta Marsh, who has no other visible function. It may also have had a subordinate influence on the appearance of Mary Cecil Hay(e) (p. 226) and Denis Florence McCarthy (p. 693), whom Joyce despised on good and sufficient literary grounds, but whose names may have been introduced, in part, to satisfy this peculiar interest. Aside from their general badness, one of Miss Hay's novels may have intrigued Joyce by virtue of its title: *Nora's Love-Test*. But, though Nora's love-test was the discovery of her father, Miss Hay's novel contributed nothing tangible to *Ulysses*.

Among Bloom's supposed schoolmates at the Erasmus Smith High School in Harcourt Street, five are named, in positions of varying emphasis. Only one of these names appears in the early records of the high school, in or about the period described as "Bloom's ultimate year, 1880" (p. 687). That is Abraham Chatterton, nephew of Hedges Eyre Chatterton, described in the novel as a granduncle or great-granduncle of Ned Lambert (p. 123). Abraham Chatterton was not only an alumnus of the Erasmus Smith School; in 1904 he was registrar and bursar. As he was born in 1862, he was eighteen years old in 1880 and had already matriculated at Trinity College, Dublin, when Bloom was graduating from the high school; thus he would not very likely have been an intimate of the fourteen-year-old Bloom. His name may have appealed to Joyce by combining a Jewish with a Protestant-sounding name. (The Erasmus Smith School was originally a Protestant foundation, to which a Jewish boy would normally have gone, and to which Jewish boys still go.) Similarly with Owen Goldberg, another

of Bloom's supposed high-school chums. Various Goldbergs
inhabited Dublin, but there is no way of laying hands on Owen.
Nor, indeed, need we do so, if we sense that his name is the
most important thing about him. Councillor Abraham Lyon,
of Clontarf West Ward, accompanied by Alderman Cowley
(who is imaginary), appears on the steps of City Hall (p. 242),
probably for the same reason.

Jack Meredith (p. 535) may or may not be John W. of 97
Haddington Road; and a Donald Turnbull (also p. 535) is
found at 53 Harcourt Street (both in *Thom's Directory*, 1904).
Both addresses are close to the Harcourt Street address of the
high school. Finally, the most prominent and most baffling of
Bloom's high-school chums is Percy Apjohn. He is described
as a playmate and confidant of Bloom's, who attended the
Erasmus Smith School with him (p. 535); with Bloom he discussed problems of philosophy (p. 651); he took a photograph
of Bloom in the position of "the childman weary, the manchild
in the womb" (p. 722); and he was killed in action at the battle
of Modder River (November 1899) (p. 689). Relatively speaking, Percy Apjohn bulks very large in *Ulysses*. One would not
be at all distressed to find him a perfectly imaginary character.
Bloom's background needs filling out with acquaintances, and
Joyce would have been perfectly within his rights in inventing
acquaintances with whom to fill it out. But Percy Apjohn has
just enough reality to be distracting. There was a Thomas
Barnes Apjohn, who lived at Rutland House, Crumlin, near
where Bloom is supposed to have talked with Percy. Thomas
Barnes Apjohn kept this address till 1908, and then moved to
the house of his sister, Mrs. Barnes, at 40 Brighton Square,
Rathgar, where he died, aged seventy-two, on August 4, 1911,
of cardiac failure. The address is right next door to the house
(at #41) where James Joyce was born. But there is no mention of Percy Apjohn, either in the family plot at Mount

Jerome, or at the Erasmus Smith High School, or in British
Army records. His name, being Welsh, fulfills no particular
pattern in the novel. As Mrs. Stoer and Mrs. McDowell are
Sandymount names, Apjohn is a Crumlin and Rathgar one.
But it is a striking name in itself, and Percy Apjohn is a rather
prominent individual to be acting merely as a bit of background.
All Bloom's schoolfriends who can be traced seem to fit somewhere on the south side of Dublin (the Jewish district is in
and about Clanbrassil Street), so that it is a bit surprising to
find them congregated (p. 160) on Goose-green Avenue, in
Drumcondra. But evidently it was the name, not the geography
that appealed to Joyce. Besides, Bloom is so hungry at this
point that he even imagines a squad of Irish constables are
goose-stepping.

When Bloom goes out in the morning to get his breakfast
kidney, he has two butcher shops to choose between; he may
get a mutton-kidney at Buckley's or a pork-kidney from
Dlugasz. The distinction between two different sorts of butcher
shops is of course a social commonplace in Dublin; but Joyce
adds a special ironic, not to say grotesque, touch by making
the pork butcher a Jew, while the Christian (to whom pork
is not unclean) sells mutton. Geographically, the shop to
which Bloom walks is just about on the spot occupied by
J. Kenny, pork butcher, at #12 Dorset Street lower; but the
name Dlugasz seems to be adapted from that of a Polish historian, Jan Dlugosz (1415-80), who latinized it as *Longinus*.
Buckley's would have been the establishment of John Buckley,
victualler, at #48 Dorset Street upper.

The people with whom Bloom associates at the newspaper
office, like those with whom Stephen associates at the library,
may be pretty securely identified; may Joyce have intended to
imply something about the literalism of both milieus? Red
Murray, as Mr. Ellmann has pointed out, is Joyce's Uncle John

under his everyday nickname (p. 115; Ellmann, *JJ*, p. 18);
Ruttledge (p. 115) was the advertising manager; Brayden was
the publisher (pp. 115, 116); and Pat Mead contributed the
character of the editor, with a touch from John Wyse Power
(Ellmann, *JJ*, pp. 297-8). Mr. O'Madden Burke, who speaks so
euphoniously and has such an indistinct connection with the
enterprise, is pretty surely Mr. O'Leary Curtis, who is described
as having a pompous, full-mouthed manner of speech and no
settled journalistic position. Professor MacHugh is "Professor"
Hugh MacNeill (Ellmann, *JJ*, p. 298). Chris Callinan, who
never appears on stage, though he is several times mentioned,
and included in the list of Molly's "lovers" (pp. 136, 231, 478,
571, and 716), was a Dublin journalist famous for his gaffes,
bloopers, and Irish bulls. Jakes McCarthy, whose name is used
to picturesque advantage by the editor (p. 134), was also an
actual pressman of the *Freeman's Journal* (*Dublin Historical
Record*, XIII, 1, p. 9). Paddy Hooper was the paper's last
editor; and Jack Hall, who is described as having a drink with
him at the Oval (p. 128) is J. B. Hall, whose book, *Random
Notes of a Reporter* (London and Dublin, 1929, pp. 84-5),
contains an anecdote about Dick Adams "the besthearted
bloody Corkman the Lord ever put the breath of life in"
(p. 135). Davy Stephens, who appears on pp. 115 and 460, was
a rather conscious Dublin "character," self-styled "the prince
of newsvendors," who boasted often of the number of novels
in which he had been represented. Joyce apparently felt honor-
bound to add *Ulysses* to the number.[7]

In dealing with the whole area of the newspaper office, it is
clear, Joyce made few attempts to disguise his basic materials
or to tantalize his reader. He reproduced a milieu which those
familiar with it immediately recognized in its details; and it is

7. An illustrated account of Davy Stephens appeared in the *Weekly Freeman* of December 15, 1906, p. 15.

not only a public landscape, it is tonally consistent. From the aspect of the uninvolved reader, the latter consideration is the more important. Penrose, that "priesty-looking chap" who roomed with the Citrons, who was attracted to Molly, and who provided an occasion for Bloom to exercise his defective mnemo-technic (pp. 153, 179), has a name the provenance of which was almost completely private to Joyce. Evidently Penrose was an employee of the Volta Theatre when Joyce was responsible for its operation in 1909 (as he made first eleven, then fifteen shillings a week, it is no wonder if he was meager and "priesty-looking"). But though he is a dark figure in the fiction, and in his relation to a real-life original, Penrose is by no means a fictional problem. We cannot see him very well in *Ulysses*, but we do not expect to see him very well. Because he is little more than a name to Bloom, he need be little more than a name to the reader. On the other hand, a man named "Wetherup" is twice quoted (pp. 125, 644) on points of proverbial philosophy, as if he were an aphorist on the order of La Rochefoucauld. Evidently he was W. Weatherup of 37 Gloucester Street upper, who served for a while in the office of the Collector-General of Rates with John S. Joyce. But we learn this poignant truth only by dragging a fine-meshed net through the backwaters of Joyce's biography. It is the contrast between his challenging posture and our meager resources for identifying him—it is a deliberate structural inconsistency—that causes us to sense Wetherup as an enigma. Indeed, it is not clear how extensive an enigma he is. Perhaps aiming to explain one darkness by another deeper darkness, Stuart Gilbert has said that Wetherup is Mackintosh (Ellmann, *JJ*, p. 530). Though in a sense it consolidates the confusion, I cannot feel that this maneuver diminishes it. The chief point about Mackintosh is that he is the thirteenth mourner at the funeral (p. 108), and so a vaguely mysterious and threatening figure. Though nobody knows him, he is prominent enough, for that very reason, to be an object of curiosity. The accident which christens him "Mackintosh" serves of itself to rouse the reader's curiosity about his real name. Joyce has only to play with this unfulfilled curiosity, and to refrain from satisfying it. But if Mackintosh is really only Wetherup and Wetherup only an ancient friend of Joyce's father, we may be excused for feeling that the fewer answers we have for the novel's riddles, the better off we are. As with Stephen's shaggy-dog riddle at the school, the puzzle is less puzzling than the answer.

The three society women who accuse Bloom of molesting them, and whose horsy proclivities direct them to fitting revenge (pp. 457-60), do not have any proper characters in the novel; they are simply domineering femininity personified. But their names come from interesting places scattered up and down the past. Mrs. Mervyn Talboys (Hannah) bears the name of an extinct sixteenth-century peerage (in early versions of the novel she had the name Mrs. Paget Butler); Mrs. Yelverton Barry's name inverts that of Barry Yelverton, the distinguished eighteenth-century Dublin solicitor who helped to found the Dublin Historical Association and was raised to the peerage as Viscount Avonmore (she was originally Mrs. Brereton Barry). Though Sir Daniel Bellingham was first Lord Mayor of Dublin in 1665, Mrs. Bellingham's name was probably suggested by the circumstance that on June 11, 1904, Charlotte Elizabeth, daughter of Alfred Payne and widow of Frederick Gough, was married to Sir Edward Henry Charles Patrick Bellingham, fifth Baronet, second creation, former Lieutenant-Colonel in the Royal Dublin Fusiliers.

As has already been remarked, the visit of the Lord Lieutenant to the Mirus Bazaar took place on May 31, not June 16; but Joyce altered more than the date. The people who are described, in *Ulysses*, as escorting the Lord Lieutenant are a queer mixture, some of them real, some imaginary, some imported from diverse occasions. In reality, His Excellency's entourage consisted of Lady Evelyn Ward and the Hon. Mrs. Ward; Mr. Walter Callan, Additional Private Secretary; Mr. Victor Cockran, Comptroller; and Lt. the Hon. Cyril Ward, R.N., A.D.C. (*Irish Independent,* June 1, 1904, pp. 4-5). Joyce, in adapting the episode to a novel, deleted altogether the Hon. Mrs. and the Hon. Cyril Ward (because they raised on extraneous question of possible family relationship), Mr. Walter Callan (perhaps because he might get mixed up with Nurse Callan, or Callan of Callan, Coleman), and Mr. Victor Cockran, Comptroller (because, perhaps, his title seemed too businesslike for this festive occasion). He introduced the Hon. Gerald Ward, A.D.C., and Lt.-Col. H. G. Heseltine, conceivably from *Thom's Directory,* but more probably from the *Irish Independent* of June 17, 1904, p. 5. For on the 16th of June, accompanied by the Lady Evelyn Ward, Mr. Fetherstonhaugh, and Mr. Callan, private secretary, they accompanied the Lord Lieutenant on a visit to the County Clare. On this trip, it is worth noting, His Excellency stopped briefly at the Queens Hotel, Ennis, where Rudolph Virag had committed suicide (according to the novel), long before.

To replace some of the people whom he had excised, Joyce brought into the Lord Lieutenant's entourage at the Mirus Bazaar two ladies for whom there is no warrant in any of the records. Mrs. Paget and Miss de Courcy (p. 248) appear in none of the contemporary descriptions of the Mirus Bazaar [8] or the Lord Lieutenant's company. But we need not be at a total loss for their identities; the names are not common in Dublin, and *Thom's Directory* for 1904 lists a Mrs. Paget at

8. The most elaborate of these descriptions appeared in *The Figaro and Irish Gentlewoman* for June 11, 1904, pp. 425-31; it listed all the exhibits, exhibitors, and participants, in paralyzing detail.

2 Ranelagh Road and a Mr. Wheeler de Courcy, barrister, at
Willfield, Sandymount Avenue. Whether Joyce intended some
sardonic point by including them in the list,[9] or whether he
intended only to pay a passing compliment to casual acquaintances, cannot now be determined.

Sometimes Joyce is portentous and specific on a matter of
fact which seems to, but does not in fact, have a discoverable
significance, either private or public. Miss Douce, one of the
barmaids at the Ormond Bar, does not have either a first name
or an address, because her name is derived from Joyce's Parisian
friend, Joseph Douce; but Miss Kennedy has both. Her first
name is Mina, and she lives at #4 Lismore Terrace, Drumcondra. The address is a real one, but between 1883 and 1913,
a period of thirty years, nobody is listed as living there who had
any ascertainable connection with Joyce, or whose name resem-
bled "Kennedy." It is possible that the Joyce family themselves
lived there too briefly to have left their name in *Thom's Directory*, though they are unlikely to have disturbed the eleven-
year tenancy of Alexander Kirkland (1891-1902) or the three-
year tenancy of Patrick Bradley (1905-8). (Thomas M. Darcy
was there in 1903 and William Molony in 1904; but during
these years the disintegrating Joyce family is securely established
at St. Peter's Terrace, Cabra.) #4 Lismore Terrace may have
had some special connotation for Joyce, no doubt from the
days when he and his family lived at Millbourne Avenue nearby,
but not even intimate local knowledge of the neighborhood,
unless eked out by accident, would enable one to understand it.
As a conceivable effect in the fiction, it has about the same

9. Their names suggest at least indirectly an echo from the heroic Irish
past. Sir John de Courcy was a Norman hero of the age of Strongbow;
among possible Pagets, whom Mrs. Paget might bring to mind, is the Earl
of Anglesey, Lord Lieutenant of Ireland in the mid-nineteenth century.
The presence of the ladies in the Lieutenant's cortège stretches it out
in time as well as space.

quality as any other random Dublin address—6 Benburb Terrace, or 11 Dargle Road, for example.

There are plenty of these little knots of private specificity
in the book. We are given half-a-dozen fixes on the identity
of Ned Lambert—his brother Sam, his employment in a seed
and grain store in Mary's Abbey (no doubt that of George
John Alexander & Co.), his kinship with Hedges Eyre Chatterton. But none of these hints and suggestions fit together in
the way which makes it so simple a matter to discover the
originals of Tom Kernan, O'Madden Burke, and Long John
Fanning. Details which lead us elsewhere to a root in biographical reality or to a perception of clear artistic intent, scatter
here and diffuse themselves into a tangle of unrelated particulars. Paddy Lee, who forms an integral part of Stephen's
mother's reproach (p. 566), would remain similarly unknowable if it were not for a random query accidentally preserved
in a letter from James to Stanislaus Joyce (3 December, 1904;
in the Cornell Library). When we know that Paddy Lee was
real enough to be an acquaintance of Stanislaus Joyce, we know
at least that we do not need to know any more about him in
order to read *Ulysses*.

The death of Phil Gilligan, twice mentioned in the novel
as a crucial event for Bloom (pp. 153, 689), is supposed to
have taken place in 1894, the year of the great fire in Arnott's
department store. We are told that he died of phthisis in the
Jervis Street Hospital; but we do not know his age, his address,
his occupation, his character, his appearance, his domestic circumstances, or how he became acquainted with Bloom, who
recalls his death and nothing else. He cannot be traced under
the name of "Gilligan" in Dublin mortuary records; perhaps
the best clue toward his existence is the fact that in 1901 there
lived at #9 Royal Terrace, Clontarf, a Mr. John Gilligan,
whose next-door neighbor (at #8) was John Joyce. If he is

merely a boyhood neighbor, dredged out of Joyce's memories but otherwise functionless, Phil Gilligan has not much place in *Ulysses*. Yet his name appears in the U. of Buffalo time scheme of the novel, which Joyce drew up, evidently for his own guidance (see above p. 188). In other words, his death is one of 25 or 30 skeletal events in Joyce's plan of the book. I do not think it unlikely that, in Joyce's private consciousness, or among the twelve kilos of materials which he had left over after completing his novel, reminiscences of Phil Gilligan were substantial. What remains in the book as we have it is a mere stump of character. This effect is functional as it enables us to sense the depths of Bloom's memory, within which whole acquaintances lie almost completely silted over; but it is inartistic as it allows Gilligan to occupy a disproportionate position in the novel, compared, for example, with the modest space allotted to Gardiner, Cranly, the sisters and brothers of Stephen Dedalus, and other characters who stand in direct relationship to the protagonists. So also with Molly's memories, which include the recent death of Nancy Blake (p. 743), and unexplained acquaintances named Miss Gillespie (p. 743), Mrs. Dwenn (p. 743), Mrs. Galbraith (p. 736), Georgina Simpson (p. 727), and Conny Connolly (p. 752). One or two of these names are adequately explained by context, one or two are mentioned elsewhere in the novel, two or three point toward identifiable originals, but mostly they are unexplained, unconnected names out of the past. Because no special emphasis is laid on these names, we tend to treat them like ordinary fictional names, the biographical or symbolic significance of which never comes into question.

Thus we see that Joyce's handling of proper names represents a mixed and inconsistent practice. Whatever public meaning he attached to the isolated names which he scattered through the novel is muted by the many names which have only a private meaning, or none at all. Mrs. Paget and Miss de Courcy stand out in slightly higher relief when we know they were not copied with everyone else from a list in the *Irish Independent* or the *Freeman's Journal*, but the best guess we can make at their significance (if, indeed, they have a significance at all) is only a guess. The fact that Wetherup is only an old friend of John Joyce's, and Paddy Lee a perfectly commonplace boyhood chum of James and Stanislaus, suggests that some at least of the problems are not worth solving. The book, in other words, shades off here and there into a world of indistinct personal associations and arbitrary details, where the difference between understanding and not understanding an allusion is very slight.

Conscious equivocation plays some part in Joyce's handling of proper names. For instance, Molly remembers a Dr. Collins whom she once consulted (p. 755), and describes his manner in such detail that his original is generally recognized as Dr. Joseph Collins, an American physician whom Joyce met in Paris (Ellmann, *JJ*, p. 530). But she also gives his address as "Pembroke Road," and there, at number 65, is found Dr. J. R. Collins, M.B., B.S. Dub. Neat little patterns of interlaced identity and imagination, like this one involving the two Dr. Collinses, or that other one involving Gabriel, Constantine, and Bernard Conroy (see above, p. 62), suggest a kind of deliberate ingenuity being exercised on an extremely private problem. Art is evidently at work here, though it is an art of very acute angles playing upon materials far removed from the ordinary texture of prose fiction.[10]

On the other hand, when one of Joyce's standing preoccupa-

---

10. A muzzy but deliberate name-puzzle set by Stephen on p. 607 can be worked out fairly easily. Cicero as a name comes from Latin *cicera*, chickpea, and might well be something like Podmore in English; Napoleon = Buonaparte = Goodbody; and Jesus = Christ = Anointed = oiled = Doyle.

tions is involved, subtlety goes by the board. Almost as intrusive as Joyce's concern with random urination is his preoccupation with the literary solecisms of his contemporaries, which
results in a spate of names, titles, and quotations from the worst
that has been known and thought in the world's literature.
Lady novelists of the nineteenth century are particularly frequent in *Ulysses*. Joyce's itch to blast and confound this species
leads him to muster up not only Mary Cecil Hay, Maria
Susanna Cummins, Miss Rhoda Broughton, Mrs. Margaret (?)
or Nora (?) Hungerford, Mrs. Henry Wood, and the authoress
of *Henry Dunbar*, Mary Elizabeth Braddon; it leads also to
that extended, perhaps overextended, parody of the sentimental
style in "Nausicaa." [11] On the same principle, ancient private
enemies of James Joyce are revived and quoted to, presumably,
devastating effect. On p. 189 we have a misquoted snatch of
the worst poem by Louis H. Victory, once one of Joyce's
Clontarf neighbors, and on pp. 357-8 another snatch, unfortunately not misquoted, from Joyce's favorite literary butt, Louis
J. Walsh of Magherafelt. He had already been pilloried in
*Stephen Hero* (p. 83); the reference in *Ulysses* has an extra
specificity ("of Magherafelt"), as if to emphasize provincial
origins and tastes. The poem by Albert William Quill, describing the loss of the lifeboat crew during the shipwreck of the
*Palme* on Booterstown Strand (p. 622), appeared in the *Irish
Times* for January 16, 1896 under the heading "An Antispastic
Dithyramb," and was just as terrible as one would suppose from
Joyce's description: "a fine piece of original verse of distinctive
merit." These names form no artistic pattern, and serve no

---

11. The travesty of *Paradise Lost* which Stephen apparently once contemplated (p. 182) borrows its title from that of a novel by Marie Corelli, *The
Sorrows of Satan*, which Joyce had read (letter to Stanislaus Joyce, in the
Cornell Library, February 28, 1905), and which he could have seen in
dramatic form.

visible artistic function beyond their obvious one of expressing Joyce's scorn for an illiterate age and community.

It is only to be expected that Joyce's use of real and imaginary names should show varying levels, measures, and directions of intent. Composed as it was over a period of years, involving thousands of details, and blown upon by the winds of innumerable ideas, resentments, fixations, interests, and accidents, the novel could not conceivably show complete consistency of design in all its secondary and tertiary patterns. It has been said that "Joyce's entire literary canon is a controlled composition" (Marvin Magalaner, *Time of Apprenticeship*, p. 117); but the adjective "controlled" as used here calls for a good deal of definition and some justification. Surely the "control" was very general that could produce a harmony unflawed by the loss of four fifths of *Stephen Hero* and all of *A Brilliant Career*. It certainly does not extend into such details as the handling of proper names within even a single fiction.

And yet the tendency to seek large structural symbols precisely in these small verbal correspondences has flourished mightily in Joyce criticism. It has been solemnly argued, for instance, and in a learned journal too, that because Betty Byrne, who sold lemon platt on the road the moocow was coming down (*Portrait*, p. 1), has the same last name as the original of "Cranly" who is John the Baptist to Stephen's Jesus, she must be Elizabeth the wife of Zachary, and the Precursor's mother. Then the moocow can be Mary Jane Joyce and the Virgin Mary as well. Since Joyce was reproducing, in the story of Baby Tuckoo and the moocow, a story told by his father in the distant past,[12] it seems particularly gratuitous to saddle the fable with an esoteric meaning. But let us suppose

12. See the letter from John Stanislaus to James Joyce, dated January 31, 1931, presently in the University of Buffalo Library. It is partially reproduced by Patricia Hutchins, *James Joyce's World* (London, 1957), p. 151.

it has one, this very meaning which has been proposed. The principle is then established that Joyce expects us to read "Byrne," wherever used, as implying a relation to "Cranly"; and we must come to terms, somehow, with Davy Byrne the publican, Mr. and Mrs. Leggett Byrne the dancing instructors, Mollie Byrne, the soprano, and sundry other Dublin Byrnes. Moreover, if we are entitled to read a real-life name in place of a character's fictional name wherever it seems possible to make some sort of symbolic connection, Martin Cunningham will be "Cain," John Wyse Nolan will be "Power," and Bloom will be a "Hunter." Under such urging, the fiction will quickly degenerate into an uncontrollable tangle of allegorical equivalents, having neither outline nor impact.

## Newspapers and Guidebooks

The Dublin newspapers supplied Joyce with material for his novel which he culled, clipped, copied, and adapted at his pleasure. Even on matters remote from the immediate Dublin scene, they served to enrich his prose, to flesh out his cosmos, and sometimes to supplement his scholarship. Occasionally, his copying amounts to a considerable batch of material, above all when Joyce did not feel secure of his command over technical details. Thus the whole latter half of the description of the Dublin waterworks, on p. 655, comes from a letter to the *Irish Independent* written by Ignatius J. Rice, and published in the issue of June 15, 1904. The description on p. 233 of three lawsuits listened to by the elderly female in the Four Courts is taken word-for-word (at the occasional expense of intelligibility) from the legal calendar on p. 2 of the *Irish Independent's* issue of June 16, 1904.

Topics supposed to be under current discussion on Bloomsday were naturally taken from contemporary newspapers. The Citizen makes a great point of flogging practices in the British navy as a blot on civilization (p. 323); Mr. Swift MacNeill, M.P., was the chief mover of this agitation, which finally succeeded in having flogging abolished in 1906. In the meantime, it produced much elegant copy for journalists, for example, a column on p. 4 of the *Freeman's Journal* for July 13, 1904. The reforestation of Ireland, bruited on p. 321 of *Ulysses*, was a recurrent theme of the nationalist press; a characteristic effusion on the topic will be found in the *United Irishman* of March 19, 1904, p. 1. (Needless to say, the Irish National Foresters had nothing to do with the project of reforesting Ireland; they were chiefly notable for the fancy Robert Emmett costumes in which they decked themselves on ceremonial occasions, for instance, the Lord Mayor's inauguration, reported in the *Telegraph* of March 17, 1904, p. 4. John Wyse Power was not an Irish National Forester, and the parody-wedding with the trees is a piece of Joycean tomfoolery with no point beyond the incongruity of like-sounding names.)

Mr. Philip Beaufoy of the Playgoer's Club, London (p. 68, etc.), was a real person, who contributed to *Tit-Bits* two or three stories a year, and made thereby six to ten guineas per annum. The stories he wrote were neither better nor worse than the average prize Tit-Bit—that is, they were terrible. Beaufoy was one of a stable of *Tit-Bit* producers, whose names crop up again and again through the 1890 files of this wretched little magazine. The high point of his invention was a gentlemanly thief, who frequently staggered his plebeian colleagues and made off with imperial fortunes by means of ruses which in real life would not have deceived a suckling babe. Presumably, Joyce was amused by Mr. Beaufoy's gentlemanly name and address, contrasted with his meager literary output and low standards. As for the magazine itself, Joyce liked it, one would guess, because it made a fetish of minute accuracy (for a while, there was a guinea prize for any reader who pointed out a typographical error), and because it devoted a whole section to odd bits of useless, esoteric information.

The story of the English hangman vacationing in Ireland and earning his vacation money by practicing his trade may have reached Joyce through Alf Bergan's recollection of the event itself; but a story on p. 9 of the *Weekly Freeman* for January 14, 1899 may also have served to jog his memory:

The English hangman has been busy in Ireland this week. On Saturday he hanged a man named Patrick Holmes at Kilkenny. On Tuesday he killed another murderer at Armagh jail; while still another victim awaited his hands in the same building on Friday. Many years have passed since so many executions took place within a few days in this country. We trust that when he leaves our shores, Billington will not be summoned back again for the rest of his life.

In the novel, Billington is replaced as the executioner by H. Rumbold, in order to satisfy Joyce's grudge against the British Minister to Bern; but Rumbold, in giving his credentials, is made to say that he "was assistant when Billington executed the awful murderer Toad Smith."

In the course of the "Aeolus" and "Cyclops" chapters, mention is made of a "Canada swindle case" (pp. 126, 316); the accused was a man named Saphrio, Saphiro, or Wought, who had swindled (among others) a man named Zaretsky or Zireski by offering to procure him transportation to Canada for twenty shillings. (Low as transatlantic emigration rates were at this period, they never got quite as low as a single pound.) Joyce drew his details of the trial from the Dublin papers, all of which carried reports; but he altered several details, for the sake primarily of neatness. The case was not tried by Sir Frederick Falkiner, rather, Mr. Swifte, K.C., was the magistrate; the

remanding, moreover, did not happen till Friday, and final
sentence was not delivered till mid-July, when Saphrio got
twelve months at hard labor (*Freeman's Journal*, July 12,
1904, p. 2).

When Bello sits down on Bloom, lights a cigar, and starts
to read the evening paper (p. 522), he is evidently reading
from the *Evening Herald* of June 16, 1904, where, on p. 3, the
two items which he particularly mentions are found in close
proximity. For the sake of euphony, however, he has altered
both of them. Keating Clay was elected Vice-Chairman of the
Richmond Asylum (Richard Jones was elected Chairman);
and Guinness Preference shares continued dull at 16 11/16.
Joyce seems to have cancelled Mr. Jones because of his commonplace name and rounded off the price of the stock to 16¾ for the
sake of euphony. Craig and Gardner who unavailingly advised
Bello to buy a certain lot of stock are Craig, Gardner & Co.,
chartered accountants, with offices at 40 and 41 Dame Street.
Even in the details of horseracing, Bello knows where he stands.
He has *Throwaway's* price right, and plans to race Bloom in
the Eclipse stakes, not only because he is being eclipsed, but
because it is a specially tough race, with high entry fees and
a rich prize.

The schooner *Rosevean* arriving from Bridgwater with bricks,
and carrying W. B. Murphy back toward the arms of his family
has "crosstrees," as we know from Frank Budgen (*James Joyce
and the Making of Ulysses*, London, 1937, p. 57), in spite of
the fact that these spars are usually called "yards," because
Joyce wanted to do something with the idea of crucifixion; and
indeed Stephen as he looks at the laundry blowing on the
line at Ringsend, sees two crucified shirts (p. 42), and later,
as he parodies the Creed, makes explicit the religious meaning of "crosstree" (p. 195). But the schooner's name, which
has seemed to enthusiasts to be compounded of Rose, Eve,

and Ann, was copied from the Shipping Intelligence report on p. 3 of the *Irish Independent* for June 16, 1904. She was the only sailing ship which arrived on that day; and she is, in the novel, as she was on the pages of the *Independent*, the schooner *Rosevean*, Bridgwater, bricks. Making her specifically a three-master instead of a generic schooner points another tremulous finger at the crucifixion, and the religious overtones surely illustrate a quality of Stephen's vision. But the symbolic weight of the schooner's name and cargo is probably slight.

On p. 136, J. J. O'Molloy and Professor MacHugh combine to tell a story about some postcard-vendors being called up before the recorder for selling pictures of Joe Brady and the Invincibles in Phoenix Park. The incident was doubtless suggested by a report on p. 2 of the *Freeman's Journal* for June 9, 1904. In actual fact, the vendors appeared before Mr. Mahony, not the recorder (we have seen that Joyce generally conflates all the Dublin judges into the figure of the recorder); and Lady Dudley did not enter into the story. The prosecution took particular objection to the custom of selling the postcards to tourists; and there may be a sarcastic identification here. But in fact the viceregal lodge was in the immediate vicinity, and there is nothing improbable in the notion of the vicereine patronizing a postcard-seller. Joyce probably intended the story to be taken seriously, and any glancing hits at the vicereine as a tourist, which one derives from knowing the original circumstances, would therefore be peripheral. His introduction of Lady Dudley aimed simply at improving a story taken in its main outlines from the public press.

The cabby, reading random items from the *Evening Telegraph* on p. 643, has a number of things thoroughly but not quite gratuitously muddled. The meeting of the Cabdriver's Benevolent Association, in London, at which the former Viceroy, Earl Cadogan, presided, did not take place till the night

of Monday, June 27. As for the note about Sir Antony Mac-
Donnell having left Euston yesterday for the under-secretary's
lodge in Phoenix Park, it seems to have been copied from the
London *Times* of Friday, June 17, p. 6; it did not appear in
the *Telegraph* or any of the other Dublin papers. Joyce is apparently having private fun with the idea of a woozy cabdriver
reading all the newspapers, even those not yet printed, in the
sorry pages of the scrubby Dublin *Telegraph*. Like all manifestations of Mr. Dooley, the cabdriver sees more than his eyes see,
and is wiser than his mind knows. When W. B. Murphy picks
up the paper, an immediate difference is apparent. *He* can find
only real things to read about—Iremonger's exploits on the
cricket field (he did in fact make 128 not out for Nottingham
versus Kent)—and the finding of the drowned man. Joyce's
game of reality and illusion is so subtle as to be almost impenetrably private.

When he made Molly Bloom a native of Gibraltar and
undertook to have her last reverie include a picture of her girl-
hood, Joyce of course ventured (as in *Ulysses* he rarely did)
outside the realm of his own personal experience. Never in
Gibraltar himself, or for that matter in Spain, he had to rely
for his image of the Rock on his imagination and on what he
could learn from books. Fortunately, he had the advantage of
a directory for Gibraltar, very much like that published by
Alexander Thom for Dublin; thither he resorted, and from this
directory took most of the specific material, proper names, and
social details out of which he composed his picture of Molly's
memory of Gibraltar in 1885. Being a good deal smaller than
Dublin, Gibraltar was a great deal easier to cross-index, and
Joyce suffered from no shortage of materials. The *Gibraltar
Directory and Guide Book*, issued annually after 1873, not only
describes the major geographical features of the Rock, and lists
all the streets and walks by their English and Spanish names;

it provides a census of the inhabitants, by name and address. It was from this directory, obviously enough, that Joyce learned about stores like Benady Bros. and Abrines (pp. 746 and 764); they both appear in the issue of 1884. Joyce need not have gone beyond the same source to learn about such geographical features of the Rock as Crutchett's Ramp, Paradise Ramp, Rodger's Ramp, Willis Road, Ince's Farm, O'Hara's Tower, St. Michael's Cave, the Devil's Gap Stairs, and picturesquely titled Calle las Siete Revueltas, which is known in lean, unlovely English as City Mill Lane (Calle Real on p. 744 comes off better as Waterport Street). De la Paz and De la Gracia are frequently Gibraltar names; so are Rosales y O'Reilly, Pisimbo, and even Opisso— all of which families, I am assured by the present editor of the *Directory*, still have representatives on the Rock. Father Vial plana, whom Molly recalls, is evidently Father Vilaplana as Joyce had him, correctly, in MS; an oddity of his appearance in Molly's memory is that he did not arrive at Gibraltar till 1910. Similarly, Larbi Sharon, the egg and poultry dealer whose shop Molly remembers (p. 767), also advertised in the *Directory* for the first time in 1912. Hence it would seem that Joyce used several numbers, if not a whole run of *Gibraltar Directories*. He certainly used them thoroughly, since this publication seems to supply a hint even for "old Luigi near a hundred they said came from Genoa" (p. 750); we are told in the Historical Notes that Catalan Bay is inhabited chiefly by descendants of Genoese fishermen, and that they catch chiefly bream and sardines—as Molly very accurately recalls. The woodcocks and pigeons which she remembers startling into flight (p. 746) are, in the same way, survivors of a note on Gibraltar plant, fish, and bird life which Joyce copied from the *Directory* and which survives, along with Molly's popping of the paperbag, in a tangled note of words and properties to be used in "Penelope" (*U. of Buffalo MSS*, "Notes for the Episodes," Penelope).

The time of Molly's sojourn on Gibraltar presented Joyce with some special problems in chronology. The short stay on the Rock of the Dublin Fusiliers was a particular inconvenience; arriving in January 1884, they were relieved in February 1885.[13] Literally speaking, this circumstance would never have given Molly time to be caressed by Harry Mulvey under the Moorish wall on her fifteenth birthday (September 8, 1885). Things are already crowded to the point of confusion in this period (see above, p. 189); so Joyce's best solution was to extend Molly's stay on Gibraltar indefinitely before 1884. But this move produced problems of its own. Molly is made to recall (p. 742) a visit of Ulysses S. Grant to Gibraltar which took place, historically, in 1877, when she was just seven years old and when her father was supposed, somehow, to be fighting in the battle of Plevna. Clearly, Joyce is stretching historical circumstance here, in order to bring Molly into contact with a man named Ulysses. Another mark of intent is that Molly is made to remember Grant as getting off a boat, when in fact he arrived by train from Madrid. As historical inaccuracies, these are the merest trifles; but they do provide evidence of a deliberate parallelism. Most of Joyce's Gibraltar details, on the other hand, are stage properties widely familiar and readily to hand. Features like the Barbary apes, the wind known as the *levanter*, and the phrase "rock scorpion" for a Spaniard born in Gibraltar, were conveniently available from a dozen different sources, and Joyce appropriated them from no loftier motive, it would seem, than a desire to enrich his social background.

13. This was the 2d Bn., Royal Dublin Fusiliers, formerly the 103rd Regt. of Foot (Royal Bombay Fusiliers). The 1st Bn., while it was still the 102nd Regt. of Foot (Royal Madras Fusiliers), served on Gibraltar from April 1876 to January 1879.

## Loose Ends, Namesakes, and Failures

Rooting around among the proper names in *Ulysses*, one gets a broad impression that most are generally available, some are redeemable by a ludicrous sort of old-matchbox-and-broken-bottletop research in Irish social debris, and still others represent intimate personal associations of James Joyce. Even if they can be placed at an address or in a social milieu, these latter generally claim a place in the story by virtue of qualities which only Joyce knew about. Perhaps an esthetic rationale can be found for them by declaring that they reproduce the untidiness of everyday life, through which we make our way, surrounded by thousands of names, familiar and unfamiliar, meaningful and meaningless, mythic and actual, fanciful and literal. Thus the surface of the novel is seen to be deliberately cluttered, even booby-trapped; in many particulars, it is a series of riddles with illogical answers or none at all.

Esthetically, one objection to such a procedure is that it destroys all semblance of *consonantia, claritas,* and probably *integritas* as well, within the novel. The darkness in most works which use secrecy as a literary device is carefully focused. We do not know what the actual relations are between lover and lady in the typical Renaissance sonnet-sequence; the work of art encircles this central darkness and invites us to project guesses into it. Joyce's puzzles occupy unimportant places in the novel and tantalize by sometimes offering, sometimes withholding the reward. They distract more often than they focus our attention. They frequently nag.

As readers, we can respond to these procedures in a whole gamut of ways, depending on nothing more ultimate than temperament. As critics, I suppose we have to impose a limit on the

amount of insoluble confusion any work of art can admit, and
so far as any element in the novel provides more distraction
than harmony, judge its inclusion a fault of artistic economy.
What, for instance, is old Dr. Murren doing in the book?
Thinking of euphemisms for cemeteries, Bloom remembers him
(p. 112), and also associates him with a pregnancy of Molly's
(p. 159). He enters the book nowhere else, has no character
where he does enter, and does not perform, even in Bloom's
memory, any distinct action. The "Hades" passage on p. 112,
which is Bloom's inner monologue, reads:

Entered into rest the protestants put it. Old Dr. Murren's. The
great physician called him home. Well it's God's acre for them.

Does the fragment "Old Dr. Murren's" mean that "entered into
rest" was old Dr. Murren's expression? Or did old Dr. Murren
himself die? In that case the pronoun "him" in "The great
physician called him home" would refer specifically to Dr.
Murren. "Them" in the last sentence definitely refers to Protestants; was Dr. Murren, then, a Protestant? Does his name make
reference to "murrain," plague, derived through Old French
from Latin *morior*, to die? Or is it the name of a real person,
and so presumably free from deliberate symbolic import? In the
*Little Review* and the MSS, Dr. "Murren" was Dr. "Brady."
Why did Joyce change the name in "Hades" and "Lestrygonians," but not in "Circe" or "Penelope"? The "Lestrygonians"
reference to Dr. Murren is also dark. Bloom is thinking of old
Mrs. Thornton the midwife, a very real person, of 19A Denzille
Street, who delivered Margaret, Charles, Eileen, and Florence
Joyce (Ellmann, *JJ*, p. 760). She had her hand crushed by old
Tom Wall's son—a reference, no doubt, to Thomas J. Wall,
K.C., chief divisional magistrate of the City of Dublin police
district.

Got her hand crushed by old Tom Wall's son. His first bow to the public. Head like a prize pumpkin. Snuffy Dr Murren. People knocking them up at all hours. For God'sake doctor. Wife in her throes. Then keep them waiting months for their fee.

The fact that in Bloom's mind Mrs. Thornton associates with Dr. Murren may or may not imply that Bloom knew him as a gynecologist. If so, the conjunction of funeral and childbirth connotations suggests Rudy, and it is perfectly conceivable that snuffy old Dr. Murren, attending Molly and her child at that time, used about Rudy the expression "entered into rest." On the other hand, there is no assurance that Joyce intended us to think anything like this, and neither Bloom nor any other character in the book ever thinks of Dr. Murren again. So that even if we are correct in our guess as to who he is, no dramatic effects follow from it. No Dr. Murren practiced in Ireland between 1890 and 1910. As a figure in a fiction, I propose that Dr. Murren isn't worth the trouble he involves.

Similar loose narrative ends abound in the novel. Bloom recalls (p. 368) the "cigary gloves Long John had on his desk the other" day; presumably he has had business with the sub-sheriff, and the circumstance invites to speculation but with no chance of reaching a firm conclusion. Bloom tells himself (p. 85) the sad story of Jack Fleming who embezzled money to gamble and then ran away to America where he now keeps a hotel. It is an instructive fable, suggested by Bantam Lyons's interest in the horses, but bears no discernible relation to anything else in the book, and we never know whether, or how, Jack is related to any of the other Flemings. In fact, the passage was an afterthought, first inserted on a late proof. We can of course easily resign ourselves to a little vagueness in the novel, simply because it covers so much ground and wishes to seem so deeply rooted in the past. Bloom is bound to have had experiences and known people to whom Joyce's method precludes our ever getting a formal introduction. Dublin is a city rich in social flotsam and jetsam; without derelicts like O'Callaghan the boot-lace seller, scroungers like McCoy, and messy memories like that of Jack Fleming, it would scarcely be Dublin at all. On the other hand, many of these figures seem rather special to serve as mere background. And sometimes, as with Father Con-mee and Lady Maxwell (above, p. 17), the complex of con-tacts and relationships among these background figures becomes so choked and enigmatic as to leave the reader hanging in a curious void between hint and shrug. Bloom, for instance, re-calls (p. 169) that Tom Kernan knows how to dress a salad, and asks himself (p. 363), "Did I forget to write address on that letter like the postcard I sent to Flynn?" Tom Kernan is never seen elsewhere in any proximity to a salad, and the in-formation is utterly pointless in context. The Flynn in question is no doubt Nosey Flynn, the only man of the name whom we have encountered in the novel. But why would Bloom be writ-ing him a postcard? Nothing in the novel suggests that Bloom and Flynn are anything more than nodding acquaintances, and, aside from a couple of passing appearances in the fan-tasies of Nighttown, Flynn never appears again in the thoughts of Bloom. Nothing in their conversation at Davy Byrne's sug-gests that they have ever communicated or attempted to com-municate on any subject beyond the day's gossip. It is probably more economical of the reader's energies to suppose that Bloom was writing to another fellow named Flynn than to invent cir-cumstances under which he would be writing to Nosey Flynn. Indeed, Joyce has included a great many namesakes in the novel, and his practice of explaining nothing has caused a good many readers to run aground on these hidden reefs.

Everyone knows that Marcus J. Bloom the dentist, before

whose offices at #2 Clare Street the blind stripling was brushed against by Cashel Boyle O'Connor FitzMaurice Tisdale Farrell, was merely a namesake and not a relation of Poldy. Martin Cunningham says so on p. 331. But J. C. Doyle, the man who is going to sing with Molly and Blazes in Belfast, is not Jimmy Doyle, the chief figure of "After the Race," as Richard M. Kain thought; as already indicated, he was a well-known singer about Dublin, whose name appears in many of the musical announcements of the early century. There is no basis for connecting either J. C. or Jimmy Doyle with Luke and Carolyn Doyle, who had charades at their house in Dolphin's Barn and gave the Blooms a dwarf tree for a wedding present (p. 692). None of these people is connected with Madame Doyle, court dress milliner (p. 247).[14]

Bernard Corrigan, the brother-in-law of Paddy Dignam, is not Father Bernard Corrigan who confessed Molly Bloom and perhaps slept with her—as Mr. Kain also supposed. Neither one of them has any identity which can be traced outside the book; but the newspaper account of Dignam's funeral (pp. 631-2) could not possibly have failed to mention the fact of the brother-in-law's being a priest, and the chances are that Master Patrick Aloysius Dignam would not think of him as Uncle Barney, if he were in orders.

Dixon the interne who dressed Bloom's bee-sting is J. F. Dixon, junior, formerly of the Mater Misericordiae, transferred to the National Maternity Hospital in Holles Street to meet the needs of Joyce's story. He lived at 12 Conyngham Street. Mr. Kain thought he was Dixon the smiler, who appeared in the *Portrait*, but for no evident reason; the registers of University College, Dublin, list a James Ed. Dixon among the class

14. The passage in *FW* where everyone is called Doyle (pp. 574-6) probably plays with the Doyle-Christ conversion worked out above, p. 223, fn. 10, from p. 607 of *Ulysses*.

entering in 1896, and this may be the original of either or both of our men.

O'Callaghan the bootlace seller, who used to be a solicitor with offices in the same building as Molly's namesake (p. 92), is a figure whose roots in reality can be traced a little way; for Henry R. Tweedy, crown solicitor for County Waterford, had offices in Hume Street after 1898; but though he sometimes shared the space with as many as thirteen other solicitors, none of them was ever named O'Callaghan. Various guesses may be made in the direction of identifying several of them with O'Callaghan the bootlace seller, but no definite evidence appears. Thus Joyce's rather elaborate leads for identifying O'Callaghan all fade away. In any event, this O'Callaghan has nothing discernible to do with O'Callaghan "the half-crazy faddist, respectably connected though of inadequate means" who is described on p. 630. Whether either of them is connected with a medical student named O'Callaghan who sheltered James Joyce one turbulent evening in the spring of 1904 (*Diary of Stanislaus Joyce*, pp. 114-15) does not appear.

Kitty O'Shea in Grantham Street (p. 736) is only the namesake of Parnell's lady; living at #3, with Mrs. McAllister (who has nothing to do with the earnest student in the *Portrait*) and Miss Lynch (no relative of Vincent), according to *Thom's Directory* for 1882, was Miss O'Shea. Here the danger of confusion is very great but nothing is said to avert it.

Kathleen Kearney, whom Molly despises as a "sparrowfart" (p. 747) and whose parents are described in "A Mother," is no relation to the Kearney who acted as Bloom's guarantor in the Capel Street Library (p. 64); this latter is much more likely to have been Joseph Kearney, book and music seller, at #14 Capel Street.

Kerwan the builder (p. 162) looks like a misprint for Derwan the builder (pp. 442, 475); but in fact there were in Dublin two men with names like this, both builders. Michael Kirwan seems to have built chiefly for the Dublin Artisans' Dwellings Company, for two of the streets lined with their dwellings bear his name. The other man was James Derwin, Alderman in 1904 for Drumcondra Ward.

Hester Stanhope, Molly's friend at Gibraltar (p. 740), is a namesake of Lady Hester Stanhope, the great Victorian eccentric who retired to a monastery in the Middle East. There is no apparent reason within the novel why she should have been given this rather distinctive name.

Alderman Robert O'Reilly, who made such a hog of himself at the Glencree banquet, is a real person, by trade a tailor, who can be traced, rather discreditably, through the political registers of the 1890's and 1900's; but there is no reason to suppose him related to the man known as "Maggot" O'Reilly, known to the Blooms as a family friend, and listed among Molly's lovers. Old Mrs. Keogh, the cook in the whorehouse (p. 527), may or may not be related to Myler Keogh the fighter, to Katy Keogh of the birthday poem, or to the chap in Keogh's who gave Ben Dollard and Father Cowley the Blooms' address. Ignatius Gallaher, the ingenious journalist, on the other hand, *is* related to Ger. Gallaher, one of Father Conmee's three little boys (p. 217), and to Mrs. Joe Gallaher, who was in real life a daughter of Major Powell (pp. 441, 753, etc.). Nurse Quigley of pp. 385 and 510 may or may not be related to Mrs. Quigley of p. 247. McCann, to whom Stephen owes a guinea (p. 31), is probably, but not surely, identical with MacCann, the campus politician of the *Portrait*, who is modeled on Sheehy-Skeffington—to whom Joyce, historically, owed money in the summer of 1904. Lewis Werner the jeweler (p. 246) is to be distinguished from Herr Louis Werner the musical conductor (p. 92). James Stephens the poet and novelist (p. 190) is of course unrelated to James Stephens the Fenian (p. 161); and the Rev. T. Maher,

S.J. (p. 312), is not Father Maher (p. 649), though one might easily be distracted into looking for a connection.

On the other hand, Cecil Turnbull (p. 651), supposed to be a boyhood friend of Bloom along with Owen Goldberg, may very well be the same person as, or a brother of, Donald Turnbull (p. 535), who plays exactly the same role as his namesake. Miss Dunn on p. 525 is supposed to be the same person as Miss Dunne on p. 226. M. Moisel and O. Mastiansky of p. 532 are probably supposed to be Philip Moisel of p. 689 and Julius Mastiansky of pp. 651 and 716. George Robert Mesias, on p. 275, is the same as George S. Mesias (p. 487). Levenston's dancing academy (p. 179) is the same as Levinstone's (p. 560); Mrs. Fleming (pp. 86, 88, 92, 659, 749) is no doubt the same as Mrs. Flemming (p. 753); whether or not she is related to Jack Fleming (p. 85) cannot be told. Mr. Coghlan (p. 62) is evidently the same as Mr. Coghlin (p. 65). Georges Fottrell (p. 453), irresistible offspring of a French compositor, is the same as George Fottrell (p. 338); Old Dr. Brady (p. 571), Dr. Francis Brady (p. 716), and Doctor Brady (p. 739) are evidently all the same fellow, and no relation to either Joe Brady the Invincible or Brady of Brady's cottages. Tom Wall (p. 159) is the same as old Wall (p. 599). "Ned and J.G.," who are paralyzed with the laughing (p. 337), are of course Ned Lambert and J. J. O'Molloy; and "great Marie Kendall," the charming soubrette who is placarded throughout Dublin, though the mother of the late, great Kay Kendall, is no relation to Mr. and Mrs. Kendal, whom Molly saw at the Gaiety (p. 754). Captain Grove (pp. 740, 741) is the same as Captain Groves (pp. 742, 767); Tunny's (p. 553) is the same as Tunney's elsewhere in the book; Prescott's (pp. 82, 760) is the same as Presscott's (pp. 177, 365); St. Fursa (p. 291) is St. Fursey (p. 333). Sidney Parade (p. 292) and Sir Philip Sidney (p. 209) are the same as Sydney Parade (pp. 680, 695) and Sir Philip Sydney (p. 202). Methusalah

(p. 663) is the same as Methusalem (p. 330) and Mohammed (p. 76) is Muhammad (p. 292). These are doubtless picayune points such as any competent proofreader could uncover; they derive naturally from the circumstance that the manuscript never underwent a careful, professional styling; and they contribute generously to the rough and grainy texture of the novel.

# 8

## Conclusion

Casting a cursory eye back over the record, without trying to summarize it in detail, I think we can see some of the motives controlling Joyce's selection and adaptation of materials in his novel. In the figure of Mr. Hugh C. Love he paid off an old family score; in imagining the erotic adventures of Molly Bloom, he scratched the open sore of a jealous wound within his own mind. Frequently he copied down the details of store fronts and street addresses, number by number from the pages of *Thom's Directory*; once in a while, as in the case of Reddy and Daughter's, he varied from reality with significant thematic intent. In selecting incidents, accidents, and details from the story of Tom Rochford, he created a symbolic pattern which is clear, consistent—and grotesque. In adapting the funeral of Matthew Kane to that of Paddy Dignam, he altered freely the circumstances and personalities of the case, but without any apparent symbolic intention—unless the pretty clearly marked temperance moral be thought a symbolic significance. On the other hand, he invented the drowned man, and underlined his fate as the victim of sirens by having him perish off Maiden's Rock, which though not an imaginary geographical feature is obscure enough physically to invite significant symbolic reinforcement. Though he altered the name of one principal in the prizefight to satisfy a private grudge, he preserved that of the other principal, and retained the main outlines of the contest —perhaps as a tribute to reality, certainly from indifference to any and all motives impelling him to change them. Feeling himself specially attracted to vocal music, he remembered several outstanding performances which he had heard and reproduced them recognizably in the novel. His tendency to convert all Dublin's judges into the single figure of Sir Frederick Falkiner is perhaps an act of fictional economy, perhaps a symbolic identification of the agents of the law with Hawkeye; the reduction of all pantomimes to *Sinbad the Sailor* is an inner economy, no less striking. Names which he found picturesque, silly, or otherwise peculiar, he preserved, often with a scrupulous indifference to the feelings of their owners. He concealed major ironic intentions in the apparently imaginary names of Father Conmee's three little boys, as well as in the deliberate errors of Mr. Deasy and Myles Crawford; he played private jokes with Bloom's interest in house valuations, the timing of General Bobrikoff's assassination, the misdating of the Phoenix Park murders, and the wrong address of Father Butt's physics theatre. We cannot be sure what, if anything, he meant by altering St. Amant from a colt to a filly or by the representation of Tom Rochford's dyspepsia.

Many of the changes that Joyce imposed on the raw materials of his book and some of the selections that he made among them are designed to confuse or blur, rather than to create or emphasize patterns. The relations between Dedalus and Mulligan are a good deal less clear on the essential point of finances than those between Joyce and Gogarty. Wetherup, Lynchehaun, Jakes McCarthy, and the crookbacked Norwegian captain are partially or altogether private references. The total range of detail invoked by Joyce is so great that a sizable percentage of it is sure to remain inaccessible to each reader. Dr. Murren, hairy Iopas, and Lanty MacHale's goat are not essential to a broad understanding of the book, and I don't suppose it takes great force of character to live in ignorance of what these particular names mean, since they are so easily detachable. On the other hand, it seems harder to accept the intrusion of random or obscurely related figures into lists which seem to be all of one sort. Why is the unknowable "Hayes" listed among Irish heroes? Why are Mesdames Gerald and Stanislaus Moran, of Rocbuck, in the hue and cry pursuing Bloom? If Joyce had to have someone from Roebuck pursuing Bloom in order to invert the traditional chase-order, why did he pick these real ladies? Of course anyone can invert the question and ask, Why not? But the idea is simply that pointed particulars are sometimes significant in this novel, sometimes not; and the only way to find out, in any particular instance, is to investigate. Joyce's lists, his learning, his logic, the very physical dimensions of his characters trail off toward the unstructured impossibility, the vaguely unverifiable, as often as they hold to a clear and satisfying logical or symbolic relation.

The close reading of *Ulysses* thus reveals that the meaningless is deeply interwoven with the meaningful in the texture of the novel. Two conclusions follow. The man who has read the book in depth, in its appalling detail, will have greater faith in the few patterns of thought and feeling which seem to be unequivocally asserted. He has tested them against the details of the text; they work out. But, after all, he will reflect, *Ulysses* is a novel, not a cryptogram. Whatever he said about a lifelong

reader, Joyce intended, and had to intend, that *Ulysses* be read
as a novel. In fact, the book loses as much as it gains by being
read closely. The reader who confronts this novel like a rational
novel reader and not like a compulsive idiot must necessarily
sense only in passing the little details of verbal by-play, the
little patterns of fact and fiction, the buried allusions and errors.
As a novel reader, he is in pursuit of more significant game; as
the reader of a novel constructed on epic lines, he has all sorts
of parallels, counterparts, balanced ironies, and lines of development to keep his appreciative faculties occupied. He cannot
run down each tiny irony, each buried error, and sort out the
significant from the insignificant. As a result of general unwill-
ingness to do this, Joyce has been carelessly printed and even
more carelessly read. A good deal of accidental, adventitious
nonsense has been accepted unquestioningly, simply because
readers found it too hard to question everything they did not
understand—witness, for example, the "bird's nest" title and
the "past" of Ephraim.

There is a fine story that when Joyce was dictating a bit of
*Finnegans Wake* to Samuel Beckett, someone knocked at the
door, Joyce said "Come in," and Beckett wrote it down in the
MS. He offered to erase the phrase, but Joyce preferred to let
it stand, and there, somewhere in the middle of things, it still
is (Ellmann, *JJ*, p. 662). I do not want to deplore or defend
this fictional technique, but to propose that something like it
took place in *Ulysses*. Certainly an event of this sort would
account very happily for the occurrence in Bloom's thoughts
of Stephen's phrase about Shakespeare walking in Gerard's rosery
of Fetter Lane, greyedauburn (p. 276). The theory of Joyce's
surpassing readiness to accept accidents is tidier than any notions which present themselves of Stephen's thoughts passing
into Bloom's mind or of Bloom identifying with Stephen.

However we account for its presence (and that presence is

generally less awkward and obtrusive than in this instance), it is plain that a great deal of social flotsam and jetsam entered the book. Though Joyce's actual motives are unknowable, there is no trouble at all in constructing a number of hypothetical functions for this material, based upon its evident presence. Sometimes it appears for its own sake, sometimes as a result of motives private to Joyce, sometimes for specific and clearly defined artistic reasons, sometimes with the aim of puzzling the reader, and for a great variety of other reasons which would be tiresome to recapitulate. I have tried to illustrate, not to exhaust, the range of possibilities. But if anything like this range of possible reasons applies, it is folly to read the book closely and analyze it elaborately in pursuit of a subtly insinuated intellectual or artistic direction. One might as well try to distinguish and appreciate the exact aroma of a jigger of Scotch drowned in a glassful of ginger ale. When Joyce wrote to his Aunt Josephine asking about the Powell family, he defined very precisely the sort of material he wanted—"any God damn drivel you may remember" (*Letters,* p. 174)—and the more deeply we explore the book's substructure, the more we find it to incorporate, not only in its details but in some of its larger architectural components, Dublin debris of this sort.

Joyce's use of unstructured and unmodified materials drawn straight from life was by no means an idiosyncratic venture. The idea was startlingly present in the artistic atmosphere of Europe during the first quarter of the twentieth century. Just about the time of *Ulysses'* appearance, the arts of collage, *trompe-l'oeil,* and *objet-trouvé* experienced a second or first birth at the hands of the plastic artists. Bits of rope, match, or newspaper began to be attached to paintings, holes were cut in their surfaces, toilet bowls and sparkplugs appeared unadorned on pedestals as works of original sculpture; while in the symphony halls, vacuum cleaners and airplane motors were orchestrated into

scores alongside the conventional instruments. Harsh cacoph-
onies, broken textures, and deliberate incongruities, were consciously, even willfully cultivated. Artist and audience stood in
a new, unmediated relation to an object which might be cate-
gorized as either "life" or "art." Partly, the rationale for this
new mode of vision was its shock value; partly also it derived
from a sense that the "esthetic" experience, at its purest, was an
act of direct vision. Disdaining all formal structure, all nudges
and helps from the artist, along with all the lesser attractions
and distractions of "moral meaning," "narrative interest," and
"representational accuracy," the found object mutely challenged
one's ability to *see* it. Whether structured or unstructured, the
artistic work was simply something to see, or, at best, to see
into. To the artist, this mode of work offered unlimited resources of uncommitted reserve; to the viewer, an exhilaration
of challenge, almost creative in its rigor.

Seeing the book against this background, the resentful reader
of *Ulysses*—unless he wants to reject a great swatch of modern
art along with it—has no reason to conclude that the book is
a hoax, or that its use of puzzles and privacy is merely perverse.
After all, the broad structure of the book is very little affected
by the patterns of this sort which one finds, or fails to find, in
its interstices. Their existence, their authenticity, their effective-
ness have little to do with the proper novelistic qualities of
*Ulysses*. All this study has tried to do, in effect, is to read the
bits of newspaper out of which Joyce's collage was made. When
we have cleared away the various confusions and digested the
various insights rising out of this very special view, we still have
the picture; we are still left with the moving and complex confrontation of Bloom, Stephen, Molly, and the icy void. Readers
who think there is a complicated, coherent symbolic message
stitched into the crevices and laced through the casual references of the novel are certainly in trouble; the reading I have

undertaken produces no evidence to support this view and many things to complicate it. But readers who have sensed a mingled affection and contempt in the author's view of Bloom, a mingled admiration and irony in his view of Stephen, and a kind of sacramental vulgarity in Molly—who have sensed the novel's scope, relished its humor, and recognized a joyous brutal vitality behind the artifice—have not missed very much. Different temperaments will always see different colorings of feeling in major works of art. Some readers, I daresay, will always feel that *Ulysses* is essentially joyous with overtones of bitterness and ironic scorn, while others reverse or modify the proportions. There is evidence to support many different views of the book —more evidence for some views than for others—and it is the business of criticism to talk its way as far as it can toward consensus. Quite conceivably some of the details investigated in this book may find applications in this discussion, but unless I am much mistaken, they will not advance it decisively in any particular direction. More likely, by showing the variety of Joyce's practices upon his materials and the diversity of his objectives, this study may foster a measure of healthy skepticism about the extent to which any single view of his novel can be deduced from or imposed upon its details.

For the plain truth is that *Ulysses* is not simply a formal construct, and does not have the quality, so gratifying to formalist criticism, of a single self-consistent abstract design. It is not the product of a "pure" esthetic impulse—or, if so, its purity is so inclusive as to call for a special definition of the work of art. One key to this definition would be the presence of the artist within the work of art, not simply as an overt and dramatic character (Stephen Dedalus), but as the *terminus ad quem*, the retrospective arranger, the manipulator of the characters, and perhaps even the secretive and willful manipulator of the manipulator. Whether as a merely esthetic rationale these notions can be made to work for the novel as we have it, is the last of our questions.

The mind of Joyce-over-the-novel is, evidently, that toward which Stephen's mind is developing—by some process, clearly enough, of approximation to the mind of Bloom. The act of Stephen in willfully, even rudely, remaining aloof from the mind of Bloom contrasts tacitly with Joyce's extended sojourn there. What the young man rejects with contempt the older man finds worthy of careful exploration. Critics have sometimes wondered why Joyce, having brought Telemachus and Odysseus into conjunction, did not have them demonstrate more rapport. An idle request—for nothing has happened to Stephen on June 16, 1904 which could properly cause him to comprehend Bloom—while Bloom's very position in *Ulysses* renders it obvious that he has been comprehended by Joyce. The relation between the mind of Stephen and the mind of Joyce involves both disparity and analogy. Whatever lines we draw in defining Stephen's character, if projected eighteen years into the future, must be understood to yield the author of *Ulysses*; contrariwise, what we are allowed to know about Stephen is understood to be only what serves the purposes of the author of *Ulysses*. Two of the main differences between them are Bloom and Bloom's experience of Molly; but these eighteen years cannot and should not be represented in full. Things must be understood to have happened of which we have no evidence, many other things to have happened at random, without relevance to Stephen's transformation into Joyce. These intermediate events (1904-22) darken the atmosphere of Joyce's perspective, and lend opacity as well as finality to the figure of Joyce the novelist. He, at least for the purposes of this book, is ultimate.

In his capacity as ultimate, Joyce appears explicitly and pervasively within his own novel as the creator of that pattern of episodes, parallels, and parodies which has been so widely criti-

cized as artificial. Artificial it doubtless is, but its artifice calls
attention to the artificer, and I venture to think deliberately.
The ordinary novel establishes early a firm scale of representational conventions, and by maintaining them throughout the
book supports our tacit readiness not to criticize them. Even a
novelist as mannered as Meredith, who gives us a narrowly
angled view of nature and society, does not encourage us to
transcend or circumvent his chosen angle of vision. Joyce, by
writing from eighteen angles, shocks us into awareness of the
act of authorial choice, seventeen times more than the average
novel. The eighteen sections of the novel are occasionally themselves remarkably divided in tonality—for example, "Cyclops"
mingles the low, realistic argot of the anonymous speaker with
passages of mock-heroic parody, and "Nausicaa" falls into two
distinct parts, stylistically. These tonal shifts, whatever their
exact number, are numerous enough to have a clear effect on
the novel; they suggest an author, behind them all, identified
with none, an author standing as remote from his styles as from
his characters, manipulating them.

Thus though we talk about Joyce-over-the-novel as a *terminus ad quem*, we cannot really see or define his position. He is
somewhere beyond his book, manipulating it so that now we
suspend our disbelief in it as a world, now we are made in-
tensely aware of it as a created object. The reader's attention
thus alternates between those two intricately related entities,
the developing mind of Stephen Dedalus and the more complexly fractured, more subtly manipulative mind which one
senses behind the book itself. Joyce's novel includes as one of
its effects the interplay of double confronting mirrors. Even
when Stephen is off stage, the problem of Stephen remains
before us in Joyce's attitude toward Bloom. How can that lean
and predatory mind, which is common to Stephen and Joyce,
come to terms with the blurred six-inch margins of Bloom's

brain? The answer appears in an act of vision, an act performed in "Penelope" by the Joyce whom Stephen Dedalus has climactically become.[1] The persona of Joyce outside the novel carries almost as much dramatic weight as the persona of Stephen within it; and the complex interrogatories, exchanged across the frame of the fiction, contribute richly to its anxious, self-exploratory, and "modern" character.

"But I suspect, Stephen interrupted, that Ireland must be important because it belongs to me" (p. 629). In a spirit not very different from this, Mallarmé is said to have remarked that "Tout existe pour aboutir à un livre." Whether as Faust, who balloons himself to envelop the world, or as Berkeley, who shrinks the world to fit under his shovel hat, this is the modern ego at work. Threatened alternately with implosion and explosion, it is haunted by a question of dimension; only the book will give it so much as a provisional proportion. In Joyce's favorite metaphor, he as author is mother, containing the book as baby, which after it is born will contain, discover—one might almost say, create—him. "The book describes its own creation"; we have heard this so often about literary works, and it has so often implied the abrogation of all outside references, the reduction of the literary creator to a spider spinning words out of his own bowels, that the phrase has a somewhat depressing ring. As a formula, it is both trite and trivial. But *Ulysses* takes us a wider circuit than most books, and in the course of describing its own begetting does something to convince us that the process was worthwhile. Its glancing, zigzag perspectives upon itself do much to prevent the whole demonstration from becoming mechanical.

Finally, there is an appetite for self-destruction in Joyce and

---

1. A brief observation on the British Museum note-sheets for "Circe" confirms Joyce's awareness of this direction in his book: "Go away from language to learn. (SD + LB = idem.)"

in his fiction which is very reminiscent of Swift. He breaks the
texture of the book which he has taken such pains to establish,
for no other evident reason than that he has got the reader to
trust in it. He is contemptuous of smooth surfaces and easy
responses; he fractures them to display power over his world,
himself, his reader. The book which he produced is a great and
intricate work of mind; it is also a violent and ingenious machine for the extinction of mind. Loaded with ambivalences
of arrogance and loathing, it is an intricate, unstable balance of
creative and destructive instincts. It is a book and an anti-book,
a work of art particularly receptive to accident. It builds to
acute and poignant states of consciousness, yet its larger ambition seems to be to put aside consciousness as a painful burden.
It is designed to fascinate the reader's thoughts by involving
them in the labyrinth of the book's structure and references;
but then to entangle and frustrate them, to answer one puzzle
with another, to conceal and withdraw, so that all the mind's
sterile ingenuities may be swept away in the final blind vitality
of an assertion from the loins.[2]

So far as they contribute to our awareness that Stephen
Dedalus, that glittering and opaque young man, will become
the author of a novel which is also glittering and opaque,
Joyce's buried meanings and deliberate impenetrabilities may
be called dramatic and so functional. So far as we sense that
the catastrophe which Stephen Dedalus left his father's house

2. Mr. Stanley Poss, in a calisthenic but perceptive article, "*Ulysses* and
the Comedy of the Immobilized Act," in *ELH*, March 1956, pp. 65-83,
describes the simultaneously static and kinetic quality of the novel under
the image of a moving picture. But though action or potential action is
constantly immobilized in *Ulysses*, and this has interesting effects on our
judgment of the novel's "meaning," the stasis is not swallowed up in the
kinesis, as in the cinema—rather the contrary. The structure of the book,
in these terms, is more similar to an extended equivocation; its feeling is neither of mobility nor repose, but of varied and inconclusive strain, till the
final vision either transcends or undermines it.

to find is the book we have been reading, the experience of reading it becomes a self-contained cycle. As a pattern, this arrangement is unexceptionable, assuming as it does the perfect coincidence of autobiographical with artistic unity. In esthetic practice, in *Ulysses*, it seems to have produced an arrangement where accumulation of insignificant or incomprehensible details often dulls the perception of comprehensible ones, where artistic tensions are frequently allowed to fall slack.

Ulysses has its *longueurs*, its esthetic lapses, its ingenious sterilities; what epic does not? But it has also the quality of the very greatest epics in that one feels, beneath the massive structural balances required by the form, the movement and passion of an intricate individual vision. Its author had to be a shaman as well as an architect. This indeed is the peculiar challenge of the epic. Though it requires them, it cannot be written by a man who possesses only the virtues of an industrious bricklayer. The man who cast twenty years of his working life into the composition of *Finnegans Wake* clearly saw his writing as a sacramental act, requiring of him something more than a genteel adjustment to the esthetic assumptions of his readers. And if his book has become, like a handful of others, a magic book for modern times, one reason may be that it forces us to examine ourselves as closely as we examine it. One thing is sure. *Ulysses* is a novel by a man who insisted that his public, like his friends and associates, take him All or Not at All. It is more, or at least other, than an esthetic document; it simply does not trim its sails or dispose of its forces in the prudential esthetic way. The novel is, in part at least, a gambler's act of throwing his whole personality—his accidents, his skills, his weaknesses, his luck—against the world. It does not make a neat allegorical pattern. It does not make a self-contained construct. It never will. When we have read it as subtly, as complexly, as richly, as sympathetically as we can, there will remain in *Ulysses* (besides those qualities so widely appreciated that it would be idle to rehearse them here) an appreciable element of the perverse, the non-prudential, the anti-systematic and, even, the frankly destructive. That is one way it forces us to see what is only to be indicated as—not itself.

This is nothing to be afraid of. All is not lost when we cast off the formalist presumptions about *Ulysses*, which have tempted so many critics into the pursuit of thin-spun patterns based on wiredrawn evidence—and which, more importantly, have promised, so delusively, to so many readers, the revelation of an all-inclusive symbolic pattern, a "hidden meaning" in the book. All is not lost; we surrender a type of patterning, often illusory and confusing, only to assert more strongly an energy which every reader must have sensed. Great and wonderful as the novel is, one of the preconditions of its greatness is precisely its readiness to fracture and escape all closed and formal patterns. I have spoken of *Ulysses* in the act of composition as a headlong plunge into the pit of self, an unraveling of private association-patterns which were only gradually and partially sorted out to form a fictional structure; what kind of plunge would it be which produced only a tidy package of allegorical messages for the edification of Ph.D. candidates? The *clou* of the book is that turn by which the perversely "rational" mind in "Ithaca," forever pouring out mechanical answers of the most paralyzing irrelevance, suddenly gives way to the dark rhapsody of "Penelope." It is the wonder of this tremendous imaginative achievement that it builds, out of the commonest trash, and in perfect indifference to the reader, a movement which envelops and absorbs him. The sensitive reader does not experience this chapter as an ingenious fulfillment of intricate pattern, set apart from him by a cool esthetic distance and seen by him, judicially unmoved, as a whole. Molly's mind, spinning in planetary majesty on its self-centered axis, calmly accepts him within itself, enveloping him in her indifference to everything which has made and kept him a reader, as the book literally becomes the world. Flaubert's famous dictum is tame by comparison with the amazed reader's sudden discovery—*Madame Bloom, c'est moi!* I don't mean that we feel personal sympathy for Molly, so much as that we consent to her unfolding comprehension of us in the climactic symbol of the book. She has become the motion of life itself, self-befouling, self-purifying, an enormous imago in which to be drowned and devoured, born and reborn, cherished, corrupted, deceived, and blessed.

A book so rich in magnetic fields cannot be complimented as a very fine piece of writing, however exalted the critical vocabulary in which one dresses this excellent literary judgment. *Ulysses* is literature but it is not just literature; it is a visionary book, like those of Blake, intricate in many of its strategies but surpassingly direct in its impact. Few books, of our time or any other, respond more generously to the formulas of criticism, or encourage one more persistently to transcend them.

## Samples from the Manuscripts

1. "Proteus," paragraph 1, *U. of Buffalo MSS*
(Slocum & Cahoon 5,b,ii).

<pre>
Sorrel nag                    ~~transmagnificandjewbangdanciality~~
   lurch                                 seasedge
     brew              III        Crosshaven strand, was I there?
       beseeching hand
</pre>

Ineluctable modality of the visible: it must be that at least if no

more. My eyes ~~do not see it, they~~ think it rather than see. ~~These~~

spawn
signs around of all things I am read: ~~and render: furrows~~ of sea-

wrack, the tide coming in, that rusty boot. Bottlegreen, bluesilver, rust.

solid
Yes, coloured signs, limits of the diaphane. But he adds: in bodies.

solid
Then he has become aware of them before of them coloured.

sconce                    Sure
How? By knocking his head against them    Go easy. Yes, he was bald

and a multimillionaire, <u>maestro di color che sanno</u>. Wait now: limit of the diaphane in. Why in? Diaphane, adiaphane. If you can put your five fingers through it is a gate, if you cannot it is a door. Shut your eyes and see:                    COMPARE p. 38.

2. "Oxen of the Sun," sentence 1, *U. of Buffalo MSS* (Slocum & Cahoon 5,b,vii).

By no pomp of pride or mark of mightiness is the wellbeing of
the witness of
a people more surely proven than by ~~its~~ solicitude for its own continuance ~~nor can we ever possibly with justice esteem a nation which sets small store by~~ and where this quality either is lacking or is set small store by we cannot with justice esteem a nation so little
be          realm
provident however wide her ~~dominion~~ be she ruled never so wisely.

                                        COMPARE p. 377.

3. Note-sheet fragment for "Penelope," among "Notes for the Episodes," *U. of Buffalo MSS* (Slocum & Cahoon 5,b,i). (Slocum & Cahoon do not indicate that some of these notes refer to "Penelope.")

|            | men have laboursavers, women no |            |
|------------|---------------------------------|------------|
|            | sat next her in a cab, turn over page |      |
| heel?      | with glove he–ll, you can imagine, |         |
|            | work ruind figure, give an, BB priest, |    |
| living?    | lining bellows, made up bill, women |       |
|            | get baff. from sucking men, vexatious, | vexations? |
|            | go mass, confession besides it was him, |  |
|            | not me, asks re BB who is that cad? |       |
| country?   | Tweedy counter, then Harolds +  |            |
|            | Rd, have they no shame in them  |            |
|            | plate L Bloom, former by land, sorrow— |    |

going by water, wealthy marriage,
fair W. some person's thoughts, loss
in business affairs, death watch,
red token in candle letter, shoes
towards bed, sweep, spider's
web is suitor, a great one for
cridon?                 man in the middle sneeze it's                squeeze?
not true, short little finger =
keep smell off my drawers. dances
poorly, a great scolding, without
date of year, Prussia street,

4. Note-sheet fragment for "Circe,"
*British Museum Additional MSS #49975.**

ibis sparrowhawk Heather white cow dungbeetle equine face jackals
at Bourse fanfare Bantam Lyons wobbly legs forelocks shaking on
horse sidling prances Adam, was tem   pho you're a credit to yr
country, sir, Noah's ark exposure lechery with dissolute grandam,
gave example of excessive sensuality, LB insited medically, women
pour scented roselcaves from top window, victor, Bloom parade,
LB explains plans, I believe in him, David's house, Emmanuel,
postexilic hegemony, white bull of Apocalypse, Belial, Messiah the
tailor, hid under Jahveh's seat, pseudo-Messiah, ben Joseph or ben
David, Abulafia Asher menanaus s of Judas Abram, Laemlcin of
Istria, LB pissed against, his prick preserved, fife & drum band
triumphal arch, escaped from Eustace's private asyl. for lunatic
gentlemen, 3 x 3, LB carries sheep on back, he stinks fetor judaicus
hollow I believe in him, I Bloom, tell you L Bravo ! magnesium
photo taken, LB speaks Hebrew (official translation) pregnant can
you believe a word he says throw him out world's greatest Cead
Mile Failte destiny on the Well ordeal of witch Music Sculpture
Justice Industry Commerce Palmistry Chemistry Publicity boo voice
alleluja chorus boo unbridled lust just like old times

* Underlined words are doubtful readings, blanks are completely illegible.

*Appendix B*

VARIANT READINGS IN THE TELEMACHIAD AS BETWEEN
*Little Review* AND THE FINAL TEXT

(In alternate readings, *Little Review* texts precede those from
Odyssey Press edition; underlinings represent materials added after
*Little Review*.)

MOD. LIB.
PAGING

p. 5.  on the mild morning air.                                    (LR)
       by                                                          (T)

       Two strong shrill whistles answered through the calm.

p. 6.  Give us a loan of your noserag to wipe my razor.           (LR)
       Lend                                                        (T)

p. 7.  what Algy calls it: a great sweet mother?                  (LR)
                           grey                                    (T)

       I must teach you. You must read them in the original. *Thalatta!*
         *Thalatta!*

       and on the mailboat clearing the harbour mouth of Kingstown.

       He turned abruptly his quick searching eyes               (LR)
                           great                                  (T)

p. 8.  That fellow I was with in the Ship with last night,       (LR)
       That fellow I was with in the Ship last night,            (T)

       This dogsbody to rid of vermin.

       as I fear that of his. The cold steelpen.

MOD. LIB.
PAGING

| | | |
|---|---|---|
| p. 9. | The cracked lookingglass of a servant. | (LR) |
| | Cracked lookingglass of a servant. | (T) |
| | Stephen freed his arm quickly. | (LR) |
| | quietly. | (T) |
| p. 11. | A clod began to cover the sun slowly, wholly, shadowing | (LR) |
| | A cloud began to cover the sun slowly, shadowing | (T) |
| | It lay beneath him, | (LR) |
| | behind | (T) |
| p. 13. | Warm sunshine merry over the sea | (LR) |
| | merrying | (T) |
| | Stephen hauled his upended valise | (LR) |
| | haled | (T) |
| | Bless us, O Lord, and these they gifts. | (LR) |
| | thy | (T) |
| p. 14. | I told her to come before nine. | (LR) |
| | after eight. | (T) |
| | The blessings of God on you, Buck Mulligan said, | (LR) |
| | cried, | (T) |

Printed by the weird sisters in the year of the big wind.

| | | |
|---|---|---|
| | or is it in the Upanishade? | (LR) |
| | Upanishads? | (T) |
| p. 15. | She praised the goodness of her milk, | (LR) |
| | the | (T) |
| | A wandering queen, lowly form of an immortal | (LR) |
| | crone | (T) |

her conqueror and her gay betrayer, their common cuckquean,
a messenger from the secret morning.

p. 16.　but her woman's unclean loins, <u>of man's flesh made not in God's</u>
<u>likeness,</u> the serpent's prey.

Irish, Buck Mulligan said. <u>Is there Gaelic on you?</u>

Are you from the west, sir?　　　　　　　　　　(LR)
Are you from west, sir?　　　　　　　　　　　(T)

Sure we ought too, the old woman said　　　　(LR)
　　　　　　to,　　　　　　　　　　　　　　　(T)

<u>Wonderful entirely.</u>

Stephen filled again the three cups.　　　　(LR & ML)
Stephen filled the three cups.　　　　　　　(T)

p. 17.　The <u>unclean</u> bard makes a point

<u>They wash and tub and scrub.</u> Agenbite of inwit. Conscience. Yet
<u>here's a spot.</u>

p. 18.　while he called for a clean handkerchief. <u>Agenbite of inwit.</u>

Are you coming, young fellows?　　　　　　　(ML)
　　　　　you　　　　　　　　　　　　　　(LR & T)

<u>Resigned he passed out with grave words and gait,</u> saying, wellnigh
<u>with sorrow:</u>
　　　　—<u>And going forth he met Butterly.</u>

p. 19.　with his heavy bathtowel upreared ferns or grasses.　(LR)
　　　　　　　　　　　　　the leader shoots of ferns.　　(T)

<u>Japhet in search of a father!</u>

I'm always tired in the morning,　　　　　(LR)
We're　　　　　　　　　　　　　　　　　(T)

p. 20.　*That beetles O'er his Base into the sea,*　　　　(LR)
　　　　*That beetles o'er his base into the sea,*　　　(T)

He gazed southward over the bay. Eyes, pale as the sea
the wind had freshened, paler, firm and prudent. The
seas' ruler, he gazed over the bay, empty save for a sail
tacking by the Muglins.　　　　　　　　　　　(LR)

p. 20.  Eyes, pale as the sea the wind had freshened, paler, firm
        and prudent. The seas' ruler, he gazed southward over
        the bay, empty save for the smokeplume of the mail-
        boat, vague on the bright skyline, and a sail tacking by
        the Muglins.                                                  (T)

p. 21.  Now I eat his food.                                          (LR)
                salt bread.                                           (T)

p. 22.  was not at all unkind.                                      (LR)
                all unkind.                                           (T)

        et in unam sanctam catholicam                               (LR)
        et unam sanctam catholicam                                   (T)

        the slow growth and change of rite and dogma like his own rare
            thoughts, a chemistry of stars.

        and Arius, waring his life long                             (LR)
                warring                                              (T)

p. 23.  I got a card form Bannon.                                   (LR)
                from                                                 (T)

        The father is rotton with money.                           (LR)
                rotto                                               (T)

p. 24.  Dressing, undressing.

        as Stephen walked up the path and smiling at wild Irish.

        Horn of a bull, hoof of a horse, smile of a Saxon.

        Liliata rutilantium. Turma circumdet. The priest's grey
            nimbus in a niche where he dressed discreetly. Jubilan-
            tium te virginum.                                        (LR)

        Liliata rutilantium.
        Turma circumdet.
        Iubilantium te virginum.
        The priest's grey nimbus in a niche where he dressed
            discreetly.                                              (T)

        A sleek brown head, a seal's, far out on the water, round.

MOD. LIB.                              II
PAGING
p. 25.   —Asculum, Stephen said, glancing at the name and year   (LR)
                                                         date   (T)

         A thing out in the water.                              (LR)
                               waves.                           (T)


p. 26.   Their likes: their breats, too,                        (LR)
                          breaths,                              (T)

         And the story, sir?                                    (LR)
               history,                                         (T)

         under glowlamps, impaled, with faintly beating feelers:


p. 27.   A riddle? Ask me, sir.                                 (LR)
         A riddle, sir? Ask me, sir.                            (T)


p. 28.   showing an open sopybook.                              (LR)
                       copybook.                                (T)

         His thick hair and scraggy neck gave witness of        (LR)
               tangled                                          (T)

         Ugly and futile: lean neck and thick hair              (LR)
                             tangled                            (T)

         His mother's prostrate body the fiery Columbanus in holy zeal
               bestrode.


p. 29.   In long shaky strokes                                  (LR)
                  shady                                         (T)

         With her weak blood and wheysour milk she had fed him

         Too far for me to lay a hand of comfort there, one or lightly.   (LR)
                          to lay a hand there once or lightly.  (T)


p. 30.   their many forms closed round him, the garish sunshine
               bleaching

         a pocketbook bound by a rubber thong.                  (LR)
                                   leather                      (T)

MOD. LIB.
PAGING
p. 31.  —No thanks at all, Mr. Deasy said. You have earned it.

His hand, free again, went back to the hollow shells.   (LR)
Stephen's hand, free again,                             (T)

*Put money in thy purse.*                               (LR)
*Put but money in thy purse.*                           (T)

A poet, yes, but an Englishman too.                     (LR)
A poet but an Englishman too.                           (T)

it seems history is to blame:                           (LR)
history is to blame:                                    (T)

Mulligan, nine pounds, three pairs of socks, one pair brogues,
ties.

p. 32.  Mr Deasy stared sternly for some moments over the
        mantelpiece.                                    (LR)
        Mr Deasy laughed with rich delight, putting back his
        savingsbox.                                     (T)

I remember the famine in '46.                           (LR)
I remember the famine.                                  (T)

Glorious, pious and immortal memory. The lodge of Diamond in
Armagh the splendid behung with corpses of papishes. Hoarse,
masked and armed, the planters' covenant. The black north and
true blue bible. Croppies lie down.

But I am descended from sir John Blackwood

who voted against the union.                            (LR)
          for                                           (T)

He voted against it                                     (LR)
          for                                           (T)

Two topboots jog jangling on to Dublin.                 (LR)
              dangling                                  (T)

p. 33.   Excuse me, he said over the shoulder,                    (LR)
                          his                                      (T)

         He saw their speeds, <u>backing king's colours,</u>

         But prompt ventilation of this all important question ...   (LR)
                              important question ...                  (T)

         amid the bawls of bookies <u>on their pitches</u>


p. 34.   by ... intrigues, by ... <u>backstairs influence, by ...</u>


p. 35.   Gabble of geese.                                         (LR)
         Gabbles                                                  (T)

         Their eyes knew their years of wandering                (LR)
                          the                                     (T)

         <u>What if that nightmare gave you a back kick?</u>

         A faithless wife first brought the strangers to our shore
         here, O'Rourke's wife, Prince of Breffni.                (LR)
         A faithless wife first brought the strangers to our shore
         here, MacMurrough's wife and her leman O'Rourke,
         prince of Breffni.                                       (T)


p. 36.   —That will do Mr Deasy said. There is no time to lose.
         to the Mr Field M.P. There is a meeting of the cattle
         trade association                                        (LR)
         —That will do, Mr Deasy said briskly. I wrote last night
         to Mr Field, M.P. There is a meeting of the cattle-
         traders' association                                     (T)

         Stephen said again, bowing again to his bent back.       (LR)
                          bowing to his bent back.                (T)


p. 37.   —Yes sir, Stephen said, turning back and swallowing his
         breath.                                                  (LR)
         —Yes, sir, Stephen said, turning back at the gate.
         Mr Deasy halted, breathing hard and swallowing his
         breath.                                                  (T)

MOD. LIB.                        III
PAGING
p. 38.   *maestro di color ceh sanno.*                   (LR)
                     *che*                               (T)

         My two feet in his boots are at the end of my two legs,   (LR)
                                         his  legs,              (T)

         and am for ever in the black adiaphana.        (LR)
                             adiaphane.                  (T)

         the other a gamp poking in the beach.          (LR)
         the other's gamp poked in the beach.           (T)


p. 39.   Belly without belmish,                         (LR)
                     blemish,                            (T)

         did the couple's will.                         (LR)
                 coupler's will.                         (T)

         When is Arius to answer?                       (LR)
         Where is poor dear Arius to try conclusions?   (T)

         the steeds of Mananaan.

         Sure re's not down in Strasburg terrace        (LR)
                 he's                                    (T)

         Couldn't he strike a bit higher than that, eh?  (LR)
                     fly                                 (T)

         And and and and tell us Stephen,


p. 40.   In his broad bed uncle Richie,                 (LR)
                         nuncle Richie,                  (T)

         Master Goff and Master Shapland Tandy,

         Wilde's *lequiescat.*                          (LR)
                 *Requiescat.*                           (T)

         Papa's little lump of love.                    (LR)
         Papa's little bedpal. Lump of love.            (T)

         Damn your lithia water. It lowers.

MOD. LIB.
PAGING

| | | |
|---|---|---|
| p. 40. | None of your damn lawdeedaw airs here; | (LR) |
| | air here; | (T) |

the rich of a rasher fried with a herring?

| | | |
|---|---|---|
| finely shaded, with rushes of air, | (LR) |
| of the air, | (T) |

| | | |
|---|---|---|
| p. 41. | *Descende, calve, ut ne amplius decalveris.* | (LR) |
| | *nimium* | (T) |

| | |
|---|---|
| see him now clambering down | (LR) |
| me | (T) |

| | |
|---|---|
| clutching a monstrance, basliskeyed. | (LR) |
| basiliskeyed. | (T) |

| | |
|---|---|
| fat with the fat of the kidneys of wheat. | (LR) |
| of kidneys of wheat. | (T) |

Dan Occam thought of that,

the imp hypostasis tickled his brain.

| | |
|---|---|
| Brining his host down | (LR) |
| Bringing | (T) |

| | |
|---|---|
| that the buxom widow in front | (LR) |
| fubsy | (T) |

| | |
|---|---|
| On the top of the Hewth tram | (LR) |
| Howth | (T) |

| | |
|---|---|
| crying to the rain: *naked women! naked women!* | (LR) |
| *naked women!* | (T) |

| | |
|---|---|
| after a few thousand years, a mahamanyantara. | (LR) |
| mahamanvantara. | (T) |

| | | |
|---|---|---|
| p. 42. | A porterbottle stood up, pitted to its waist, | (LR) |
| | stogged | (T) |

| | |
|---|---|
| He hopes to win in the *groslets.* | (LR) |
| *gros lots.* | (T) |

MOD. LIB.
PAGING

p. 42.  *La Vie de Jésus* by Mr. Léo Taxil.            (LR)
                     M.                                      (T)

        *Paut pas le dire à mon père.*                  (LR)
        *Faut*                                          (T)

        when I was in Paris, boul' Mich', I used to.

        barrier of the post office shut                 (LR)
        banging door of the post office slammed         (T)


p. 43.  Fiacre and Scotus on their creepystools in heaven spilt from their
        pintpots, loudlatinlaughing: *Euge! Euge!*

        *Le Tutu,* five tattered numbers

        a saucer of acetic acid in her hand.            (LR)
                                   hands.               (T)

        newmake there tumbled beauties,                 (LR)
                 their                                   (T)

        their wellpleased pelasers, curled conquistadores.   (LR)
                 pleasers,                               (T)
        *Il est irlandais. Hollandais? Non fromage. Deux irlandais, nous,
        Irlande, vous savez? Ah oui!* She thought you wanted a cheese
        hollandais.


p. 44.  You're your father's son. I know the voice.

        Mr. Drumont, famous journalist,                 (LR)
        M.                                              (T)

        Maud Gonne, beautiful woman,

        Mr. Millevoye, Félix Faure,                     (LR)
        M.                                              (T)

        The froeken who rubbed his nakedness            (LR)
        The froeken, *bonne à tout faire,* who rubs male nakedness   (T)

        Not this *Monsieur,* I said.

        a flame and acrid smoke lights our corner.      (LR)
                                    light               (T)

MOD. LIB.
PAGING

p. 44.   How the head centre got away, true version.          (LR)
                                       authentic version.     (T)

the lair in Butte Montmartre he sleeps short night in,       (LR)
the Montmartre lair he sleeps short night in,                (T)

frisky as a young thing!                                     (LR)
                  thing's.                                    (T)

Tell Pat you saw me, won't you? I wanted to get poor Pat a job
one time.


p. 45.   Take all, keep all.

resting his ashplant by him.                                 (LR)
                  in a grike.                                 (T)

And these, the stoneheaps                                    (LR)
        there,                                                (T)

de bloodz odz an Iridzman.                                   (LR)
        oldz                                                  (T)


p. 46.   They have tucked it safe mong                       (LR)
                           among                             (T)

tores of tomahawks aglitter                                  (LR)
torcs                                                        (T)

The dog's bark ran toward him,                               (LR)
                  towards                                     (T)

York's false scion, in breechers of silk                     (LR)
                  breeches                                    (T)

Lambert Simnel, with a tail of nans and sutlers,

They were waiting for him now.                               (LR)
        are                                                  (T)

Can't see! Who's behind me?

sheeting the beds of sands quickly,                          (LR)
        lows                                                 (T)

p. 47.  He turned, hounded back,                              (LR)
                  bounded back,                               (T)

barked at the wavenoise, herds of seamorse.

They wade a little way in the water                           (LR)
          waded                                               (T)

and then set off at a calf's gallop.                          (LR)
          loped                                               (T)

sniffling rapidly like a dog all over the dead dog's bedraggled fell.
  Dogskull, dogsniff, eyes on the ground,

Here lies poor dogsbody's body.

Along by the edge of the mole he dawdled, smelt a rock
  and, from under a edge of the mole he dawdled, smelt
  a rock. Something he buried there, his grandmother.
  He rooted in the sand,                                      (LR)

Along by the edge of the mole he lolloped, dawdled,
  smelt a rock and from under a cocked hindleg pissed
  against it. He trotted forward and, lifting his hindleg,
  pissed quick short at an unsmelt rock. The simple pleas-
  ures of the poor. His hindpaws then scattered sand:
  then his forepaws dabbled and delved. Something he
  buried there, his grandmother. He rooted in the sand,      (T)

Haroun al Raschid.

p. 48.  they passed.                                          (LR)
                  trudged, the red Egyptians.                 (T)

dull red muffler                                              (LR)
          brick muffler                                       (T)

trudging to Romeville.                                        (LR)
bing awast, to Romeville.                                     (T)

under her rancid rage.                                        (LR)
                  rags.                                       (T)

Unfallen Adam rode and not rutted.

trekking to evening lands.

MOD. LIB.
PAGING

p. 48.   Ides, myriadislanded,                                    (LR)
           Tides,                                                 (T)

         My tablet.                                               (LR)
           tablets.                                               (T)

         fleshless lips of air: mouth to her moomb.               (LR)
                                   womb.                          (T)


p. 49.   roar of oataractic planets,                             (LR)
              cataractic                                          (T)

         manshape ineluctable, call it back.

         The virgin at Hodges Riggis' window                     (LR)
                          Figgis'                                 (T)

         She lives in Leeson park, with a grief and kickshaws,

         Talk that to someone else, Stevie:                      (LR)
                         some                                     (T)

         Talk about apple dumplings,


p. 50.   for his nap, sabbath sleep. *Et vidit Deus. Et erant valde bona.*

         Hlo!                                                     (LR)
         Alo!                                                     (T)

         welcome as the flowers in May.

         As I am. As I am. All or not at all.

         a naked woman shining in her court,                     (LR)
                                 courts,                          (T)

         At one he said. Found drowned. High water at Dublin bar.

         a pace a pace a porpoise.

         Hook it quick. Pull. We have him.                       (LR)
         Hook it quick. Sunk though he be beneath the watery
            floor. We have him.                                   (T)

MOD. LIB.
PAGING
p. 51.   brown eyes saltblue.

Old Father Ocean.

I thirst

Allbright he falls, proud lightning of the intellect, *Lucifer, dico,
   qui nescit occasum.*

Monsieur Drumont, gentleman journalis.                     (LR)
                                 journalist.                (T)

That one is going to.                                       (LR)
                   too.                                     (T)

That one. This. Toothless Kinch, the superman.             (LR)
That one. Toothless Kinch, the superman.                   (T)

homing, upstream, silently moving, a silent ship.

## Appendix C

## THE ROSENBACH MS, THE *Little Review*, AND THE TEXT

Generally speaking, the Rosenbach MS of *Ulysses*, purchased by Dr. Rosenbach from John Quinn to Joyce's outspoken dismay, represents a more primitive state of the book than the version published in the *Little Review*. Within "Telemachus" alone, it varies from both *Little Review* and the "final" Odyssey text in more than 25 significant passages, standing alone many times against the more corrected versions, and in matters of import with generally inferior readings. Moreover, where the *Little Review* differs from the volume text (see above, Appendix B), the Rosenbach MS usually follows *Little Review*. Most of the minor exceptions to this rule can be accounted for by the circumstance that the printer of *Little Review* was an ignorant, slapdash fellow, with the further professional handicap of moral sensitivity. Thus he introduced on his own a goodly number of errors, misspellings, and patches of bitched type, to be found neither in the MSS nor in the final text. But there are several passages (for example, in Appendix B above, p. 45, item 1, and p. 47, item 5) where the MS agrees with the text in a substantial correction of *Little Review*. The oddity here is that a (presumably) early MS agrees with a final form of the text against what looks like an intermediate form—*Little Review*. One possible theory for explaining these rather involved facts is that Joyce kept the early chapters of *Ulysses* in a number of MSS, on which he entered corrections and improvements, as opportunity offered, without systematic collation. The MS now in the Rosenbach Foundation was copied from one or several of these early documents; *Little Review* and the final text resulted from a separate editorial operation. Everything about the Rosenbach MS indicates that the first sections of it, particularly, were copied out mechanically (not without boredom) from pre-existing MSS, perhaps with the specific notion that it could be sold to a collector, perhaps for use by a typist, but certainly at a decided remove from the ardors of creative synthesis.

# Index